BREXIT AND LIBERAL DEMOCRACY

This book analyses Brexit in the larger context of the crisis in liberal democracies and the continuing rise of 'nationalism'. With electoral verdicts favouring right-wing populists across the world, the volume argues that Brexit has become a key event in understanding global political currents, as well as emerging as a watershed moment in the current political climate. The author focuses on the underlying currents that shaped the Brexit vote and delineates the various strands of arguments that inform the current political climate. The volume also locates the deepening divide within the discourse and understanding of democracy, as well as the abysmally low level of rhetoric informing the debates around it. Further, it links this up with other 'nationalist' waves across the world, including South Asia.

A nuanced reading of a key event, this book will be of great interest to scholars and researchers of politics, especially political theory, political sociology and history.

Amir Ali teaches at the Centre for Political Studies, Jawaharlal Nehru University, New Delhi. Previously, he taught at the Department of Political Science, Jamia Millia Islamia, New Delhi, and was Agatha Harrison Memorial Visiting Fellow at St. Antony's College, University of Oxford. He has written a book on *South Asian Islam and British Multiculturalism* (Routledge, 2016).

BREXIT AND LIBERAL DEMOCRACY

Populism, Sovereignty, and the Nation-State

Amir Ali

LONDON AND NEW YORK

First published 2022
by Routledge
2 Park Square, Milton Park, Abingdon, Oxon OX14 4RN

and by Routledge
605 Third Avenue, New York, NY 10158

Routledge is an imprint of the Taylor & Francis Group, an informa business

© 2022 Amir Ali

The right of Amir Ali to be identified as author of this work has been
asserted by him in accordance with sections 77 and 78 of the Copyright,
Designs and Patents Act 1988.

All rights reserved. No part of this book may be reprinted or reproduced or
utilised in any form or by any electronic, mechanical, or other means, now
known or hereafter invented, including photocopying and recording, or in
any information storage or retrieval system, without permission in writing
from the publishers.

Trademark notice: Product or corporate names may be trademarks or
registered trademarks, and are used only for identification and explanation
without intent to infringe.

British Library Cataloguing-in-Publication Data
A catalogue record for this book is available from the British Library

Library of Congress Cataloging-in-Publication Data
A catalog record for this book has been requested

ISBN: 978-0-367-40524-3 (hbk)
ISBN: 978-0-367-40525-0 (pbk)
ISBN: 978-0-429-35650-6 (ebk)

Typeset in Bembo
by Apex CoVantage, LLC

CONTENTS

Preface		*vi*
1	Brexit: beginning to write about a never-ending process	1
2	The Thatcherite prelude to Brexit	27
3	Brexit, the 2007 financial crisis and austerity	53
4	'Let's take back control': Brexit and the assertion of sovereignty	74
5	Brexit and the worsening climate of democracy	93
6	Brexit, and the sum of all fears: racism, Islamophobia and anti-Semitism	117
	Conclusion: Brexit: conclusively inconclusive?	139
Index		*145*

PREFACE

The 2005 movie *V for Vendetta* is set in the dystopian future of 2020, the very year when Britain declared its independence from the European Union (EU), was then ravaged by the effects of the Coronavirus pandemic and, by all available indicators throughout the year 2020, was on course to crash out of the EU without a deal on the last day of the year. It was perhaps the Biden victory in the November elections that prevented this, and a deal was struck a day before Christmas Eve. It quickly became another excuse for Prime Minister Boris Johnson to engage in yet another round of superficial grandstanding before the inevitable devil in the detail of the document caught up with him. Some years earlier, his predecessor Theresa May had suggested, in a speech in January 2017, that 'no deal was better than a bad deal'.[1] The deal arrived at by Johnson was clearly a case of any deal being better than no deal. *V for Vendetta* is a bleak depiction of a Britain that has fallen into the hands of an autocrat and is challenged by an anarchist who decides to blow up Parliament, like the 5 November 1605 Gunpowder plot. Boris Johnson's tenure as Prime Minister has significantly undermined parliamentary democracy. His particular manner of excoriating parliament can be said to have parallels with the dystopian setting of the movie as Johnson continues to create a bleak Brexit landscape, all the while suggesting to his people that things are going to be just fine.

This book arose out of a sense of disquiet from the results of the 23 June 2016 referendum, in which a narrow majority in the UK voted to leave the EU. That sense of disquiet only kept growing over the last four years as the realization dawned that the UK was intent on, or at least the narrow elite leading the UK, was intent on leading the country out of the EU through the hardest of Brexits. As the years have rolled by, this book argues that the climate of democracy has significantly worsened. The shock aftereffects of Brexit were reinforced with the victory of Donald Trump in the November 2016 US Presidential elections. Elections across the world seemed to be returning far-right populists to power in ever-larger numbers. And then in the year 2020, the Coronavirus pandemic hit the world. Even in the face of an unprecedented pandemic of this magnitude, it seemed that the task of Brexit could not be postponed, and the simple message was that Brexit had to be done, come what may.

One of the primary concerns of this book is the question of liberal-democracy and whether the theory and practice of this kind of polity can be sustained in the UK and across the world. The victory of Joe Biden in the US Presidential elections was met with relief in many quarters, as there emerged a feeling that democracy may have just been saved by the skin of its teeth. Chapter 5 deals very centrally with the idea of Brexit and liberal democracy. This also explains the main title of this book. In terms of the three other concepts contained in the sub-title after the colon, 'sovereignty', 'populism' and 'nation-state', sovereignty receives separate treatment with one full chapter (Chapter 4) devoted to it. The other two concepts are to be found, explained and aiding in the explanation in all the other chapters. The idea of the nation-state is to be found mentioned in many chapters, but it is in the last chapter (Chapter 6, 'Brexit and the sum of all fears') that the nation-state serves as the central conceptual rubric to understand the phenomena of anti-Semitism and Islamophobia. Similarly, when it comes to the concept of populism, references to it are to be found in Chapter 1 of the book and in Chapter 2 on the 'Thatcherite prelude to Brexit' and also in Chapter 3 on 'Brexit, the 2007 financial crisis and Austerity'. However, the concept of populism can be said to resolve itself completely in Chapter 4 on sovereignty.

In terms of disquiet, the researching and writing of this book have proceeded along with the possibility of a no-deal Brexit moving from the far-flung fringes of extreme right-wing daydreaming to almost being presented as fait accompli during Boris Johnson's prime ministerial tenure. Brexit has drawn widespread attention from across the world on account of the political spectacle that it has become, a spectacle accentuated by the robotic monotony of former British Prime Minister Theresa May and aggravated by the buffoonery of her successor Boris Johnson. The continuing interest in Brexit has seemed to belie, at least for the time being, the sense that Britain does not really matter anymore, with the inevitability of British decline from the heights of imperial domination to the agonies of deindustrialization often cited as the reason. A group of ardent, hard-line Brexiteers has attempted to revive interest in the countries of the former British Empire as a post-Brexit trade strategy, almost preposterously suggesting that the Commonwealth could replace the EU.

When two referendums took place in the French-speaking province of Quebec in 1980 and 1995 to decide independence from Canada, people were tired of the regular happening of such political exercises. The exercise would derisively be referred to as the 'never-endum referendum'.[2] Supporters of Brexit have been largely successful in preventing a second referendum and thereby ruling out the possibility of a 'never-endum referendum'. The Brexit process has, however, led to the exiting of the UK from the EU becoming a never-ending future, a veritable Brexiternity.[3]

viii Preface

The writing of a large part of this book happened under the curious circumstances of the Coronavirus pandemic lockdown. As a result, possibilities of travelling and applying for research funding were ruled out. An enterprise such as writing a book results in the accumulation of many debts of gratitude. The most immediate ones go to my wife Asfa and our daughters Asma and Madiha. We remained ensconced in our house on the JNU campus during the days of the lockdown. Asfa has ensured that I was able to proceed with the writing of the book, even as I inflicted upon everyone in the household some of the more boring details of the Brexit process. My elder daughter, Asma, has often listened patiently and good naturedly to things I would have to say. Madiha, the younger one, thinks Brexit is boring and has advised me that I should write more stories, especially funny ones, and that illustrations in my book might just help. It is this advice that I need to think about more seriously. My parents have always asked me about the progress of the writing on the daily basis that we chat on video calls, almost as if they were asking me if I had done my homework. My parents-in-law stayed with us for a while as I made revisions to the book and the presence of grandparents made my daughters perhaps pester me just a little bit less, and this would have most certainly helped in advancing the cause of the book.

I would like to thank all of my colleagues at the Centre for Political Studies, JNU, and in particular the office staff, as it was always such a relief to see them during the lockdown days every time I went to my office to pick up books and papers. Sometimes, I think that it was a miracle that we could continue with some semblance of academic activities as we held online meetings and taught remotely to students sitting in far-flung corners of the country. In particular, I must mention Asha Sarangi, who, as Chairperson in the tumultuous times that we have been through, has stuck to the job with a tenacity that is admirable, to say the least. Gurpreet Mahajan has never allowed any of my ideas to escape the critical scrutiny of her gaze. Rajarshi Dasgupta has always had something insightful to say whenever he read some of the popular pieces in the media that I wrote on Brexit. To my students at JNU, whose absence for many months from the campus gave it such a deserted and forlorn look during the days of the lockdown, I can only say that it has been a sheer delight to watch them return to the campus and to welcome them back with the renewed hope that the cause of meaningful academia that JNU has always stood for shall never be abandoned. It has reminded of those wonderful lines from the great Urdu poet Faiz Ahmad Faiz: *Gulon mein rang bhare baad-e-nau-bahar chaley/Chaley bhi aao ki gulshan ka kaarobaar chaley* (The flowers must be filled with colours and the balmy winds of yet another spring must begin to blow again/Come hasten here now as the garden's tasks await your arrival to begin all over again). Aakash Chakrabarty at Routledge has, over the years, become a dear friend as he has, with his gentle smile, encouraged and watched another vague idea grow into a manuscript and then a book.

Amir Ali
New Delhi

Notes

1 'FactCheck: did Nigel Farage coin the phrase "no deal is better than a bad deal"'? *thejournal.ie*, 14 May 2019. www.thejournal.ie/nigel-farage-no-deal-bbc-fact-check-4632847-May2019/. Accessed 23 January 2021.
2 Nick Bryant, 'Neverendum referendum: voting on independence Quebec-style', *BBC News*, 7 September 2014. www.bbc.com/news/magazine-29077213. Accessed 9 February 2021.
3 Denis Macshane, *Brexiternity: The Uncertain Fate of Britain*, I.B. Tauris, London, 2019.

1

BREXIT

Beginning to write about a never-ending process

The writing of this book was begun three years after the 23 June 2016 referendum, in which, shockingly for many, a majority of 52 per cent of the electorate decided in favour of leaving the EU. The Brexit referendum has sent tremors right across the world. While the complex technicalities of the Brexit process tend to bore people, there has been a remarkable level of interest in the spectacle that Brexit has become. The British have just not seemed to be able to make up their minds about the terms on which they wanted to or could leave the EU. The coverage of Brexit in a country like China exceeded interest in the Trump presidential victory, the same year as the Brexit referendum.[1] This was just one measure of the kind of interest that was generated globally, despite the UK's continuously shrinking influence, of which Brexit itself seemed to be one more confirmation.

Part of the Brexit spectacle was the manner in which former Prime Minister Theresa May's deal with the EU to decide the terms of withdrawal was defeated three times by the British Parliament. The generally anodyne proceedings of the House of Commons, the lower popular chamber of the Parliament, acquired a riveting quality for television viewers. In those early days of the Brexit saga, no deal was not the frighteningly real prospect that it was to become with the assumption of the Prime Ministerial office by Boris Johnson. Theresa May, for as long as she occupied 10 Downing Street, came across as an uninspiring and robotic Prime Minister. Her political rhetoric was repetitive and suggested the malfunctioning monotony of a machine whose wiring had gone haywire and whose batteries were dying. This was an impression that was most effectively created by *The Guardian's* parliamentary sketch-writer, John Crace.

However much hostility may have prevailed between her and other EU leaders, there were kind words that were said about her by the EU Commissioner Jean Claude Juncker, when he called her 'a woman of courage'. His words suggested that there was a certain tenacity with which May pursued the deal that she was

2 Brexit

hammering out with the EU.[2] Juncker's words sounded like a political obituary for the end of a political career that had been capped by a short Prime Ministerial stint. At the very end of that short Prime Ministerial stint, May's actions in Downing Street, especially with regard to her Brexit deal, were similar to the actions of those merely going through the ritualistically mechanical motions prior to an imminent and impending political death. Her tenacity with regard to pursuing a deal presented a study in contrast to her successor Boris Johnson, who hardly showed any signs of seriousness.

For many observers of the Brexit phenomenon across the world and viewing it from the outside, Brexit has been an unbelievable phenomenon of a country not just at war with itself, but almost determined to cause self-harm. In the second week of August 2019, data from the Office for National Statistics revealed that the gross domestic product (GDP) fell by 0.1 per cent.[3] With the previously parlous state of the economy that went into a double-dip recession back in 2012–2013, the onset of the Coronavirus pandemic in early 2020 has made the state of the UK economy truly precarious. One would have thought that this worldwide crisis and its associated uncertainties that have hit the UK especially hard would make Prime Minister Boris Johnson and his brave band of Brexiteers wary of pushing ahead. There were no signs of any such lowering of the rhetoric on Brexit.

The dismal economic figures in August 2019 could be seen as a response to the rather shocking declarations on the part of Boris Johnson, just before becoming Prime Minister, that the UK would leave the EU on 31 October 2019, come what may. Johnson, in his own words, suggested that Britain would exit the EU 'do or die'.[4] The callous indifference from Johnson with regard to the consequences of a no-deal Brexit is disturbing, to say the least. What explains the urgency and enthusiasm to take a step like no-deal when the implications of this are unknown, and all available indicators suggest that the results could very well be chaotic? The bleakness of a no-deal situation was laid out by the government's six-page document Operation Yellowhammer, which warned, among many things, of huge disruptions to food-supply chains, a rise in food prices and a rise in public disorder.[5] The brazen indifference with regard to no-deal Brexit has often been attributed to Johnson's rather chaotic personality and his style of functioning in politics, where it has often been suggested that he has been embarrassingly underprepared for cabinet meetings.

Johnson's style of functioning is akin to the high-risk gambler, who wagers on almost impossibly high stakes, hoping to rake in huge political benefits. This is most certainly an unhinged sort of politics, reckless to say the least, and tending to militate against even the slightest hint of warning and caution. Lurking in the shadows of Johnson's No. 10 was the dark genius of Dominic Cummings, who seemed to be meticulously planning every single move to ensure that Britain left the EU without a deal. The intriguing question really is whose interest does this kind of an extreme no-deal move serve? The people who voted for Brexit did not factor in a no-deal Brexit. They were never told about one in the manner that Dominic Cummings's genius invented the figure of £350 million a week that could be saved by leaving the EU and that could be channelized into the beleaguered National Health Service (NHS).[6] The only self-serving interest fulfilled seems to be the small cabal that runs Johnson's horrendously right-wing cabinet. Here, the pursuit of a no-deal Brexit seemed to have almost become the belief of a mystic cult, preparing for an apocalyptic end to Britain's association with the EU, to be followed by the new golden dawn of British independence. Mr Johnson's strategy has seemed to be an irresponsible and adventurist one of maximum risk and maximum disruption, true to his personality, and perhaps one should add his hairstyle as well.

Taking the most extreme and audacious steps could well have become the new style of doing politics, which contrasts with earlier, more ponderous and deliberative ways of trying to evolve some semblance of consensus. That seems to be the bygone style of more cautious politicians. There seems to be a premium on taking the more audacious and risky political moves, outwitting the opponent in the process and leaving many gobsmacked. The Indian Prime Minister, Mr Narendra Modi, seems to have perfected such political tactics. His sudden and shocking decision to demonetize 86 per cent of India's currency supply on 8 November 2016, incidentally the very day of Donald Trump's presidential victory in the US, would be an instance of this blitzkrieg style of politics, where the opposition remains shell-shocked by the sheer audacity of the move.[7] This was again seen in Mr Modi's decision in August 2019 to abrogate Article 370 of the Indian Constitution, which was an instance of a familiar asymmetrical federalism that gave special status and autonomy to the state of Jammu and Kashmir. This special status was an acknowledgement of the specific historical circumstances leading to the accession of Jammu and Kashmir to the Indian Union in 1947. Here was another instance of a complete throwing of all constitutional caution to the wind in a move that has been seen by some as the political equivalent of the earlier demonetization decision.

A new Blitzkrieg style of politics

The unfolding Brexit saga, and the kind of politician that it has positioned as Prime Minister in Boris Johnson, represents the inauguration of a new kind of blitzkrieg politics, intended to shock and awe. The unthinkable, in this case no-deal Brexit, moves from the realms of remote possibility to perhaps the only possibility. The aspect of throwing all constitutional caution to the wind, which accompanies this kind of politics, was especially evident when Boris Johnson initially suggested that he could prorogue Parliament to prevent it from interfering with his much-desired Brexit on 31 October 2019. To the disbelief and outrage of many, that is precisely what he did towards the end of August 2019. In a remarkable judgement, the UK Supreme Court ruled that Johnson's decision to suspend Parliament for five weeks was unlawful.[8]

There also emerged, just a few weeks into the Johnson premiership, the likelihood of calling a snap general election, just before or immediately after the Brexit deadline. This desire to call an election was to go on to become something of an obsession with Johnson and his supporters, as Parliament kept blocking him and frustrating him in early September 2019 by preventing an early election and blocking the possibility of a no-deal Brexit.[9] Indeed, the successive defeats that he was humiliatingly subjected to showed the manner in which Parliament was able to run rings around him. The crass populism that Johnson then took recourse to was to cry out for the voice of the people. The enthusiasm for an election that Johnson has displayed can only be interpreted in terms of the high-stakes politics that forms the framework of analysis here. In other words, the transformation of politics that we have witnessed in the last few years of the second decade of the twenty-first century is a movement away from subtle-manoeuvring and back-channel parleys to high-octane rhetoric and the taking of the most reckless course of political action. Johnson's call for an election was his only way out of the unbelievable political course of action that he had embarked upon. He boxed himself into a corner with Parliament surrounding him, and his only way out was by proroguing Parliament and then the subsequent dissolving of this very same Parliament through the call for an election, in the hope that it would yield a more pliant one. With his success in the December 2019 Parliamentary election, the worst instincts of democracy seem to have come to his rescue.

As if all of this was not edge-of-the-seat thriller politics enough, the loss of Mr Johnson's parliamentary majority by the decision of the Conservative MP Philip Lee to cross the floor of the house to join the Liberal-Democrats only added to the drama. This dramatic crossing of the floor was timed just as Johnson was giving a statement in the House of Commons.[10] Johnson's predictably populist strategy has been to cast Parliament as the impediment and obstacle in the way of the people's will. The playing off of Parliament against the people was not only a cynically populist ploy, but also seemed to represent desperation on the part of Johnson. The only way forward from the high-stakes gambling politics that it has been suggested he is prone to doing is to go to the people in a general election in the hope that people would be so revolted by Labour leader Jeremy Corbyn that they would deliver in his lap a popular mandate that his Premiership so clearly lacked. That is exactly what happened.

This audacious, high-stakes gambling politics that has emerged not just in the UK but in many liberal-democracies across the world is symptomatic of a deepening crisis of liberal-democracy. The possibility of liberal-democracies resolving this kind of turbulent politics is bleak, and this could culminate in the very termination or death of liberal-democracy itself.[11] Perhaps a little apocalyptically, it is suggested that the Brexit phenomenon is not merely representative of a worsening crisis of liberal-democracy, but more ominously holds out the very real possibility of reaching to the brink of the death of the liberal-democratic order across the world.[12]

Over-zealous commitment to the electoral component of democracy

The blitzkrieg style of audacious, high-stakes politics is further combined with an exaggerated and over-zealous commitment on the part of politicians to the electoral component of democracy. It has felt a little strange when politicians have revealed such zeal to honour the Brexit referendum result. This is done despite the referendum being an advisory one and significant evidence that the referendum result was skewed to the Leave side by the workings of Cambridge Analytica, which harvested Facebook data of millions of voters who were then sent targeted messages so that they could just be pushed over to vote leave. There was a degree of psychological manipulation involved and the deployment of what can only be called extreme propaganda tools.[13] Remarkably, the more patriotic flag-waving elements have been behind some of the most frenzied support for Brexit. Those who have most vociferously demanded the taking back of control and thereby the assertion of a more muscular sovereignty seem to be the ones least perturbed by allegations that the Brexit referendum could very well have been influenced by Russian hackers, far away from the UK, in places such as St. Petersburg, where the Internet Research Agency (IRA) is located.[14] The same over-zealousness to the referendum could be seen in Theresa May, earlier a Remainer, who then switched to emphatically keep making the point that the UK was leaving the EU, thereby putting to rest the idea of any second referendum on the issue. There has been an inexplicable element of exaggerated deference to the referendum verdict as a manifestation of the will of the people. It reflects a particularly populist appeal to the people, and this book seeks to understand some of the dangers inherent in this kind of appeal.

The question remains as to why a slim majority of 51.8 per cent of the UK citizenry was so eager about leaving the EU. The eagerness does not seem to abate even in the face of the very real prospects of economic hardships and numerous inconveniences. The general sense of modern liberal democracies has been that they facilitate the advancement of individual rational self-interest and that all of these little rational choices then add up to making the economy stronger and more prosperous, spreading the benefits all around. The British seem to have lost their famed pragmatism and their level-headed common sense as they make demands of the kind that have fuelled Brexit.

This becomes especially tragic when one considers the fact that the roots and genesis of Brexit lie in a genuine discontent and grievance against the EU, especially in working-class areas and more so in the de-industrialized North. It becomes more tragic when one notices that the very genuine grievance becomes transformed into ever-higher levels of hatred against immigrants. In doing so, at least two key issues go missing. First, the fact that the EU and the kind of globalized world order that it represented led to many being left behind, stranded by a tidal wave of globalization that has lifted the lives of some, but then desolated the lives of so many others. Globalization created a set of left-behind losers, who cannot be faulted for the fate that they suffered. Second, the misery of many lives, especially working-class ones, has been compounded by the malicious and grinding austerity policies initiated by the Cameron-led Conservative coalition government when it was voted into office in 2010, in the shadow and aftermath of the 2007 financial crisis.

Brexit bravado refuses, in its St. George's spirit, to slay this dragon of austerity and instead empowers the very figures that have emerged from the very belly of the beast that created the financial crisis that in turn led to the cruel and crushing austerity measures that then led to the Brexit insurrection against the EU. Boris Johnson's cabinet is almost like a rogue's gallery of the most extreme and hard right-wing political opinion Britain has been able to muster since the Second World War. There is the anachronism that is Jacob Rees-Mogg, suited and booted more to the eighteenth century than the twenty-first.[15] Rees-Mogg would represent the more unadulterated English elements in the cabinet. Mr Johnson has the slightest hint of a taint, and a Muslim one at that, coming from, of all places, Turkey. Johnson's great grandfather, Ali Kemal, was an official of the Ottoman Empire. Perhaps Mr Johnson washes away that taint with liberal doses of Islamophobia when he suggests that Muslim women wearing burqas look like 'letterboxes' or 'bank robbers'. Far from jeopardizing his political prospects, Mr Johnson's Islamophobia seems to have helped him along in his rise to the very top of British politics. Contrast this with someone like the Labour Leader Jeremy Corbyn, who, in the eyes of many in Britain, is as divisive and toxic as Johnson but against whom accusations of anti-Semitism stalled any possibility of being elevated to Prime Ministership.

Then comes the example of individuals such as Sajid Javid, Priti Patel and Rishi Sunak, whose names hint at connections with other, further and more distant parts of the world. Each one of them seems to have the most hard-line point of view on Brexit that perhaps acted like an entry card into the Johnson cabinet. Javid is an interesting example of an individual with a Muslim name, and a second-generation migrant with roots in Pakistan whose rise up the greasy pole of British politics is remarkable. He was appointed the Chancellor of the Exchequer, the number two in Boris Johnson's cabinet, only to resign when he fell out with Dominic Cummings.[16] Javid's rise to this summit of political power was achieved through his admiration and belief in Thatcherism, a gospel of go-it-your-own-individualism, where there is no such thing as any society that needs to be left behind. Javid is not part of the typical British Establishment. He is the son of a Pakistani immigrant who was a bus driver in Bristol. He did not go to Oxford but did well to go to the University of Exeter. He had a high-flying career in investment banking with Deutsche Bank, selling suspect financial products such as Collateralised Debt Obligations (CDOs) that were instrumental in bringing about the 2007 financial crisis. In May 2018, Javid became the British Home Secretary, after which he infamously took that cruel stand against Shamima Begum to deprive her of British citizenship. Shamima Begum was 15 years old when she left the UK to join the Islamic State. After a few pregnancies, she realized the futility of her teenage adventurism and wanted to return to the UK, which Javid's Home Office promptly blocked by stripping her of her British citizenship.[17]

Javid's rise to Home Secretary was presciently portrayed in the British Pakistani novelist Kamila Shamsie's work *Home Fire*. The Home Secretary in the novel, Karamat Lone, is of Pakistani origin and not looked upon favourably by his fellow Pakistanis because of the manner of his rise. He is referred to by another character in the novel as 'Mr Striding away from Muslimness'. He takes an intransigent position on the return of 19-year-old Parwaiz, who has joined the ISIS and, upon seeing the horrors, wants to return.[18]

Priti Patel as Home Secretary, and earlier as International Development Secretary, has been controversial, to say the least. Previously, in Theresa May's government, Patel had to resign as International Development Secretary after it emerged that she had a series of meetings with Israeli officials and lobbyists without informing the Foreign Office, when she was holidaying in Israel.[19] In Johnson's cabinet, there has been a series of accusations against her of bullying, leading to the resignation in February 2020 of Philip Rutnam, a senior civil servant in the Home office, who subsequently initiated legal action against Patel.[20] In contrast to Home Secretary Priti Patel, Chancellor of the Exchequer, Rishi Sunak, comes across as a far more emollient personality, and he received praise for his furlough scheme that was initiated in the early days of the pandemic to cover up to 80 per cent of the wages of individuals as a result of the stalling of economic activity. Given his lack of experience, his stellar rise seems to be explained by an unswerving and unquestioning loyalty to Johnson. The overall story of the Johnson cabinet is one of a lack of political heavyweights who could threaten to overshadow Johnson himself.

The criterion for entry into Johnson's cabinet seems to be all about an unflinching and unquestioning commitment to a hard, no-deal Brexit. In the cacophonous circus that Brexit itself has become, the two genuine issues outlined earlier, namely the genuineness of the grievance underlying Brexit and the accentuation of this grievance by austerity measures, have been thoroughly lost. The attention span of the ring master of the circus, Boris Johnson, is perhaps even shorter than that of a 5-year-old. Worse, his ambitions are legion, and in his relentless self-aggrandizement, he seems to be one of those politicians who can rip apart constitutional principles without the faintest bit of remorse. He has been compared to Mr Trump across the Atlantic, or the pond as it is referred to by those Brits who like to believe that the distance across the Atlantic is even less than the English Channel separating them from Europe.

The Brexit raft

In the novel *The Stone Raft*, by the Portuguese writer Jose Saramago, there is the imaginative idea of the Iberian peninsula, consisting of Spain and Portugal, breaking off from the rest of Europe from the Pyrennees and floating off into the Atlantic.[21] A British novelist could think of writing about the UK rafting away from Europe and heading off in the direction of the US, perhaps to dock at Cape Cod in Massachusetts, where the Mayflower landed, carrying the first English Pilgrims in 1620. The prospects of a no-deal Brexit in the treacherous waters of the Atlantic are bleak. For one, the Brexit raft is likely to break apart in the form of Scotland and Northern Ireland at the very outset of the voyage, even before it can get beyond the choppy waters of the Irish Sea. It is only the insanity of English nationalism that could contemplate rowing whatever is left of the raft away from Europe and towards America. The survivors of the Brexit raft would have doubtless looked forward to the warm embrace of Donald Trump upon reaching the shores of the US, a prospect they would have been disabused of owing to his electoral loss. While large sections of world opinion were horrified by the prospects of a Trump re-election, the fact that Brexiteers were rooting for Trump in the White House says a lot about the Brexit project, which is about creating a regulation-free and reckless capitalism that undermines workers' rights and environmental safeguards. Upon reaching the shores of America, Brexiteers could warm up to the prospect of being fed chlorinated chicken. The last part about chlorinated chicken is a reference to the new trade deal that the UK would have liked to strike up with a Trump administration and which would include the import of chlorine-washed chicken from the US that would undermine existing stringent EU food, health and safety standards.[22]

The problem of Brexit as just wanting to go back and then get on

The problem of Brexit is that both sides, the Remain and Leave, have wanted to go back to a desired order. Brexit can be read as a much larger process of discontent against globalization and thereby signals a need to perhaps move forward. Let us take the generally more reasonable and less tempestuous Remain side. While the Remain side generally represents a point of view that is more accommodative on immigration and the mutual coexistence of people from different parts of the world living in Britain, its great flaw is the desire to merely revert and thereby go back to Britain's earlier membership of the EU. The Liberal Democratic party and the sudden revival in fortunes that it fleetingly experienced as the Brexit crisis unfolded are a good example of what is termed here as the Remain tendency, wanting to merely revert to the status quo ante. The revival in fortunes of the Lib-Dems is significant, as in the 2015 elections they did extremely badly, and this was seen as resulting from their being a part of the coalition government led by David Cameron with Lib-Dem leader Nick Clegg as Deputy Prime Minister. They were much criticized for failing to act on the question of rising university tuition fees. Despite the fleeting revival of fortunes the Liberal-Democrats experienced, they performed very badly in the December 2019 elections, with the leader Jo Swinson losing her seat.[23]

There is an element of the vacuous in the Liberal-Democratic Party, as a result of which it cannot seem to be able to factor in the reasons for Brexit. Also, the vacuity at the heart of the Liberal Democratic position fails to sufficiently engage with the inherent problems with the EU as an institution. The Lib-Dem position teeters on the edge of a supercilious and condescending contempt of all those in favour of Leave, especially the section of Leave supporters belonging to the deprived and working class. One of the most powerfully disturbing books to read on the poverty that has been allowed to fester in a society like the UK is Darren McGarvey's *Poverty Safari: Understanding The Anger of Britain's Underclass*. The following passage from McGarvey's book effectively sums up how the middle class, university-educated and the *Guardian*-reading just don't seem to 'get it' about how Brexit happened:

> Brexit Britain, in all its dysfunction, disorder and vulgarity, is perhaps a glimpse of what happens when people start becoming aware of the fact they haven't been cut into the action but have no real mechanism to enfranchise themselves beyond voting. Brexit Britain is a snapshot of how things sound when people who are rarely heard decide to grab the microphone and start telling everybody how it is. When people vote against their own interests because they don't think it's going to matter either way. People who are then called 'arseholes' and scum by middle class liberals for expressing genuine shock that their vote actually did bring about change – for the first time in their lives. Luckily, the 'liberal intelligentsia' and the 'metropolitan elite' possess enough influence, cultural capital and personal agency to construct their own vast parallel reality in the event that coarse, under class concerns do start bleeding into the conversation. A parallel reality where 'twibbons', safety-pins, free-hugs, Huffington Post think-pieces, Tumblr blogs and gender-neutral gingerbread products are all that's needed to resolve a crisis. When the full wrath of working class anger is brought to bear on the domain of politics, sending ripples through our culture, it's treated like a national disaster. Following these political earthquakes, a deluge of condescending, patronising and emotionally hysterical social-media posts, blogs and online campaigns are launched, ruminating about the extinction level event – which is what is declared whenever this specialist class, on the left or right, get a vague sense that they are no longer calling the shots. That they have been defied. That culture is no longer being curated with them in mind. For these people, not getting their way feels like abuse.[24]

The attitude of the Lib-Dems on Brexit can be captured in two stands that its former leader Jo Swinson promptly took. The first was the almost instinctive refusal of even countenancing the possibility of Jeremy Corbyn as the leader of a national unity government that could be formed to tide over the Brexit crisis and especially the biggest wave of the crisis, which was the possibility of a no-deal exit.[25] This stand was taken by Swinson in mid-August 2019. The second came in early September 2019 during the Parliamentary session that was so rudely prorogued by Prime Minister Johnson. The Lib-Dem leader started making the case for a revocation of Article 50 to underline her party's unequivocal Brexit policy. This is again reflective of the Lib-Dems prominently holding up the Remain desire of merely wanting to go back to the situation that prevailed before the 23 June 2016 referendum. Prominent Conservatives on the Left and some Labour members on the right of the party, such as Chuka Umunna, moved over to the Lib-Dems.[26]

In contrast, the one aspect of Labour's immobility on the Brexit issue is that it at least does seem to understand the roots of working-class anger that has manifested itself in Brexit and which the quote from McGarvey's book so evocatively captures.

10 Brexit

It is another matter that this realization locked Labour into a kind of political stasis in late 2019 where it did not know what to do next: call for a second referendum or readily accept the prospect of a general election that Boris Johnson was getting so eager and excited about.

Different sections of the party thus represent a massive churning within Labour on the issue of Europe. Former Labour leader Jeremy Corbyn stridently holds on to his lifelong left-wing Euroscepticism, while the current Labour leader and former shadow Brexit secretary Keir Starmer has a more open stance towards Europe. This kind of massive tug of war within the Labour party on Europe has meant that the party seems to be supremely unable to capitalize as an opposition party. It has taken advantage neither of the ineptness of May's Conservative government nor of Johnson's antics. As a result, serious questions were raised about Jeremy Corbyn's ability to win an election and the inevitable contrasts have always been drawn with Tony Blair's supposed wizardry at the hustings.

Brexit: Labour torn apart, Lib-Dems hugging the centre ground and the Conservatives' 'great moving right show'[27]

The Brexit crisis and the effect that it has had on the three mainstream parties of the UK can be captured by the sub-heading to this section. The crisis seems to have least affected the Lib-Dems in terms of the political ground that they have occupied. If politics was about the Butskellite Consensus of the 1950s and 1960s, or for that matter the 1990s when the rising force of New Labour became Blatcherite, then the Lib-Dems could have been considered to be doing the sensible thing, which was pitching their political tent at the very centre of opposing political tendencies and binding them together. However, politics in the second decade of the twenty-first century is not like the consensus politics of earlier decades. The Butskellite consensus was about the social contract of social democracy after the Second World War and was formed by combining the names of the Conservative leader Rab Butler and the Labour leader Hugh Gaitskell. The Blatcherite consensus, if it can be called one and formed by combining Thatcher with Blair, was an agreement on the centrality of the role that the market played in politics. The Lib-Dems perhaps fail to understand the significance of politics today. In other words, what they are doing seems eminently sensible in conventional political terms. But these are not times of conventional politics.

This is where what is happening to the Conservatives and Labour becomes interesting. Brexit seems to have torn apart both the Conservative and Labour parties. The crisis in the Conservatives has been quite serious if one goes by the dismissal of 21 members by Boris Johnson in early September.[28] Prominent among these 21 dismissed conservatives were the former Chancellor Philip Hammond, the Tory grandee and father of the House of Commons, Ken Clarke, and Nicholas Soames, whose name can perhaps never be detached from the looming historical presence of his grandfather, Winston Churchill. These dismissals underlined the manner in which the Conservatives were being transformed from being something of a capacious broad-church one-nation Tory party to a right-wing party of narrow English nationalism.

The reason why this was happening was to take recourse to a pithy quote from Ed Miliband, used in another context, that they were trying to 'out-Farage, Farage'.[29] This witty quote, from a politician generally not known for a quick repartee, captures the predicament of the Conservatives in the sense that every single step that has been taken, at least since 2013, by the Conservatives has been done with one eye on their Euro-sceptic backbench. It is a backbench that in turn seems to work in close tandem with the political antics of Nigel Farage. The thing about Farage's politics is that it is confined to the obsessive single-point agenda of Europe. The rather nasty insularity and thoughtless single-mindedness of Farage's politics are reflected in his own move from the United Kingdom Independence Party (UKIP), a party that he defined with his leadership and presence, to the eponymous Brexit Party.[30] The fact that Brexit had been done led to the party changing its name to Reform UK.[31]

While Brexit has posed a deep crisis for both Conservatives and Labour, the crisis is graver for the Conservatives, in the sense that it is no longer recognizable to many prominent Conservative Party Members. In the case of Labour, while Corbynism is often dismissed as emerging from the left-wing lunatic fringe, this viewpoint overlooks the manner in which Corbynism can reshape the agenda of the Labour Party and thereby irreversibly move the party away from its 1990s and 2000s Blairite moorings. Labour leadership has, of course, moved to the more centrist and pro-Europe position upheld by Keir Starmer, but Corbynism is likely to exert a significant leftward gravitational pull, preventing any possibilities of reverting to the Blairite centre–left. In the opening days of his leadership, Keir Starmer seems to be doing a good and efficient job and looking very potentially prime ministerial as his approval ratings have climbed, with his serious demeanour a study in contrast to Boris Johnson's buffoonery.[32]

This leftward movement of the Labour party under the auspices of Corbynism needs to be seen in the more immediate backdrop of the rather dismal disaster that Ed Miliband's leadership, at least in electoral terms, was all about. This dismal disaster happened despite the recruitment of American strategist David Axelrod, who, of course, could not match up with the Conservative's Australian strategist Lynton Crosby.[33] The lesson that most people, including Labour sympathizers, tend to draw from this is that Labour's continued movement to the left from Miliband[34] and now to Corbyn suggests that Labour basically made itself unelectable. The argument seems premised on the idea of an Overton window which refers to the narrow bandwidth of acceptable politics that political parties must tune into in order to be electable.[35] One of the important elements of the narrow bandwidth is the question of free markets, light touch regulation and capitalism. All these parameters were set by Thatcherism, and the most significant achievement of this, by Mrs Thatcher's own admission, was that it even moulded New Labour to give us 'Blatcherism'. In 2010, when famously the Miliband brothers fought it out for

12 Brexit

Labour Party leadership, the elder sibling, David Miliband, would have been the natural Blairite successor, but that of course was thwarted by the more left-wing trade union-supported Ed Miliband, in many ways bringing to an end the New Labour of Tony Blair.

The younger Miliband was almost paranoid about being condemned as too left wing to be outside the pale of the Overton window. What he seems to have most feared was being termed 'Red Ed', even going to the extent of posing in a picture with *The Sun*, apparently endorsing this red raging bull of a tabloid that has so often decisively influenced the course of British politics in the last four decades. Miliband had to apologize for this decision.[36] Miliband would always make it a point to suggest that he was reforming capitalism, almost saving it from itself and its worst inner instincts and outer excesses. There has always been the lament that Labour got the wrong brother. That the other sibling, David, should have taken charge rather than the younger, geekier, and nerdier Ed.[37] Labour could then have capitalized (pun intended) on the lack-lustre performance of the Cameron-led coalition government, whose most significant and abiding legacy in the over five years that it ruled, between 2010 and 2016, was Chancellor George Osborne's swingeing austerity cuts that almost reached to the point of savagery.

To reiterate, the logic of this is that a political party needs to win elections and that, in order to do so, its politics must tail the larger logic of the free market. Blair did that and was successful. The same logic would continue that everyone after him will likely be unsuccessful, and Jeremy Corbyn, with his unapologetic socialism, many paces to the left of Ed Miliband's reform of capitalism, is only an example of the Labour party walking away into the political wilderness. In doing so, it may be merely re-creating the infamous 1983 'longest suicide note in history', this being a reference to the manifesto written under Michael Foot's leadership of the Labour party. What this analysis fails to consider is that politics need not just be a tailing of the economic logic of the free market. There can be times when politics can creatively rework the possibilities that exist. The argument of this book is that the response to Brexit, understood as a crisis with global ramifications, would need to be one of this kind, where politics in the more traditional Aristotelian sense of an authoritative master science that circumscribes and sets limits to all other activities in society, rather than its ends being set by those other activities, needs to be invoked.[38] In doing so, it can creatively rework possibilities and thereby widen and break out of the constrictions of the Overton window within which it has been made to oscillate and operate. This imperative for politics to take over the economics, and thereby stop genuflecting to 'the economy' and 'the market', becomes all the starker in the light of the Coronavirus pandemic.

Was Corbyn the problem?

Part of the Brexit mess can be understood through the personality of Jeremy Corbyn and his rather obstreperous political attitudes that some believe led to Labour simply being unable to ever form a government. To Corbyn's credit, it can be said that his lifelong left-wing Euroscepticism has an element of the honest and the honourable in it. This can certainly not be said about the opportunistic switching from Remain to the Leave side of the Brexit argument that many Conservative members effected right after the referendum result, including notably the former Prime Minister Theresa May and the one after her, Boris Johnson. Corbyn's attitude towards the European Project reflects his own socialist commitment and his opposition to the kind of capitalism that the European Project supports. On the other hand, the much talked about Euroscepticism of the Conservatives arises from a certain understanding of English nationalism and the full-blooded sovereignty that, in their view, must accompany it.

It is here that the visceral hostility that Corbyn elicits from certain sections of British society and political opinion needs to be analysed. The instant reaction of the Lib-Dem leader, Jo Swinson, to a suggestion that Jeremy Corbyn could take over as Prime Minister of a government of national unity was one in which there was almost an equivalence made between the divisiveness of Jeremy Corbyn and Boris Johnson. The inability of Jo Swinson to make a differentiation between the supposed undesirability of Corbyn and Johnson would be a reflection of the kind of Liberal-Democratic blind-spot pointed out a little earlier and which makes it unable to understand the flaws in the EU project, thereby making the Lib-Dem position become an almost unthinkingly reflexive reversion to EU membership. At the same time, there are many Labour Party members who feel that Corbyn was the biggest liability for them in terms of his lack of electability. This attitude would come predominantly from the Blairite rump in the Labour party.

The most astonishing manifestation of this hostility towards Corbyn, if an internal report of the Labour party is to be believed, was a desire within Labour Party ranks to scuttle the possibilities of Labour doing well electorally and repeating the kind of surge that the party experienced under Corbyn in the 2017 elections. In other words, a faction at Labour party headquarters was so completely anti-Corbyn that it was hoping that the party would not do well electorally and was working in that direction before the December 2019 elections. This was the subject of a report written in March 2020 and released in early April, just as Keir Starmer had taken over as Labour leader and presented something of a challenge in terms of party unity for the new leader. The 860-page report prepared internally by the Labour party by drawing on 10,000 emails and a few WhatsApp group chats also had some important things to say about the persistent anti-Semitism allegations against Labour. While some were quick to infer from the report that the anti-Semitism allegations were baseless and meant to harm Labour's electoral prospects, the report itself seems to suggest that the party's mechanism of handling anti-Semitism allegations was far too lackadaisical and casual. Crucially, the report also suggested that Corbyn did not exercise a direct influence or control over this bad handling of the complaints process and is at variance with the July 2019 BBC Panorama documentary, which implied that Corbyn's office was directly responsible for scuttling and delaying complaints of anti-Semitism.[39] A little surprisingly and abruptly, it was reported, towards the end of July 2020, that the Labour Party had decided to settle the anti-Semitism issue out of court in a libel case and had agreed to pay a hefty six-figure sum to seven former staffers in the Labour Party and John Ware, the man who had made the Panorama documentary. This was a decision strongly criticized by Corbyn, the man who was at the centre of the allegations and who believed, on the basis of legal advice he had received, that the party could win the libel case brought against it.[40] Labour's troubles with anti-Semitism allegations showed no signs of going away. Towards the end of October 2020, the Equality and Human Rights Commission (EHRC) put out a damning 130-page report of the Labour leadership's handling of the persistent claims of anti-Semitism. Jeremy Corbyn, while acknowledging the problem of anti-Semitism, suggested that the scale had been overstated as a result of which he was suspended from the party by leader Keir Starmer.[41]

But in the whole analysis, one aspect stands out which perhaps reflects the politics of the last four decades of neoliberalism. Every move to the left by a social democratic party is viewed with a nervous caution by its well-wishers, keeping in mind electoral success. A move to the left then must be done by treading the ground ever so softly, as it were. Now contrast this with the Conservative Party in the UK and the Republicans in the US, or other right-wing ultranationalist parties across the world, such as the Bharatiya Janata Party (BJP) in India, Fidesz in Hungary and the AKP in Turkey.[42] The more recklessly these parties move to the right, as they indeed have been doing so over the last few decades and in a much more accelerated way in recent years, the more their electoral prospects are enhanced. The moral of the story seems to be 'tread cautiously if you are going left, but if you are moving right don't even let the crash barrier hinder you'. Indeed, a 'great moving right show' of a different extremity altogether.

The problem with Leave: yet more reversion to a desired past

As far as the Leave side of Brexit is concerned, it represents an even more extreme case of wanting to go back to a desired past. The desire to revert to something, as it is being referred to here, is most obvious in the slogan 'Let's take back control'. What is left unspecified is what exactly the nature of control to be taken back is. It would seem that there is a reversion to a particular kind of sovereignty of the early nineteenth-century Austinian undivided and inalienable variety, which, it is hoped, would strengthen the hands of the British state that would in turn seal off British borders from further immigrant incursions.

In this sense, the Leave side represents a kind of English nationalism seeking to re-create a particular notion of Englishness. The social constituents that provide a ready substrate for the Leave side to pitch itself on this notion of nationalism are at extreme removes. On the one hand is the extreme wealth generated by Britain's bloated financial elite, whose success is connected to the centrality of the City of London as one of the world's leading financial centres. This kind of elite would be represented by figures such as Nigel Farage, formerly of the UKIP, who later went on to float the single-agenda Brexit party, which has since been renamed as Reform UK; Boris Johnson himself; and Jacob Rees-Mogg, another central character in the Brexit story. The other end of the social extreme, where the Leave side gains traction, is the deprived working class, especially in terms of its location in the de-industrialized North and Midlands. It was here that Labour's Red Wall bastion was successfully breached by Boris Johnson in the December 2019 elections, when many constituencies that had supported the Labour Party for many generations switched to the Conservatives in the hope that Boris would 'get Brexit done' for them. The bizarre nature of Brexit as a phenomenon can be seen in these two vastly differing social locations that have provided anchorage to the Brexit story.

The fact that Brexit should pitch itself on these two social extremities is perhaps one of the great ironies of the process. In addition to this is the continuing disappearance of the middle class in an advanced capitalist democracy such as the UK, where, like the US, the middle class is increasingly squeezed out,[43] prompting the former Greek finance minister Yanis Varoufakis to suggest that the middle class is the dinosaur in the room set for extinction.[44] The take-back control political position is extremely contemptuous of all parliamentary control and has constantly complained of Parliament acting as a kind of hindrance to the executive. Johnson, in his characteristically outrageous manner, prorogued Parliament in the last week of August 2019. While proroguing Parliament is a legitimate act that can be taken recourse to constitutionally, the way Johnson did this effectively suspended Parliament from sitting for five crucial weeks in the run-up to the 31 October Brexit deadline. The intention was, without doubt, to significantly narrow the window of opportunity that the numerous Remain-supporting MPs would have had of legislatively blocking a no-deal Brexit. One would have to be naïve to the point of stupidity not to read this as Johnson's intention. The decision has been variously termed a 'constitutional outrage' and a 'smash-and-grab operation' to hold onto power.[45] The UK Supreme Court's intervention led to the suspension of Parliament being ruled unlawful. Predictably, it was opposed by Johnson's government, and one member of his cabinet, Jacob Rees-Mogg, went to the rather dangerous extent of characterizing it as a 'constitutional coup'.[46] There was an extraordinary combination of daring, gall and gumption in Johnson's move to prorogue Parliament. It was almost as if members of Johnson's old Bullingdon Club at Oxford had dared him, challenging him to show his guts, with Johnson doing precisely what he was being egged on to do. The sheer recklessness of being able to carry out such acts arises from the cocksure sense of privilege that Johnson's background gives him, which pampered members of the Bullingdon Club at Oxford frequently exercise.

Johnson's action in proroguing Parliament is also reflective of the new kind of compulsively reckless and high-wagering style of politics that is evident not just in this specific act but more generally in the casualness with which Johnson made no-deal Brexit an all-too likely possibility. The way no-deal Brexit travelled from a remote, veritably unknown uncertainty to the centre-stage was a reflection of the bankruptcy that lies at the heart of the Brexit process. It is a further reflection

16 Brexit

of the taker of such political decisions, in this case Boris Johnson himself, and the callous contempt and disregard for those lesser mortals who will face the consequences. The politician as decision-maker is only interested in the rich pickings that the high-stakes bet can rake in. Alarm bells had started ringing that the red-wall bastions of erstwhile Labour-supporting constituencies of the North, which Boris Johnson so successfully breached, would be particularly badly hit in the likely event of a no-deal Brexit, owing to their higher than national average dependence on manufacturing.[47]

Johnson, when he was Foreign Secretary, was reported to have used the four-letter expletive with reference to business. What was startling about the 'F★★k business' remark was the readiness with which a Conservative Party Member like Johnson could think of leaving business at sea, when it has traditionally been one of the most natural constituencies of the Conservative Party. Robert Shrimsley, writing in *The Financial Times*, observes 'This is the strategic nihilism of a spoiled child lashing out'. Shrimsley goes on to suggest: 'For a Tory to be declaring "fuck business" should be as unlikely as Labour leader Jeremy Corbyn yelling something similar about the workers'.[48] If Johnson could say this about business, one can only imagine if there has been anything to stop him from muttering under his breath to 'F★★k the people'.

What this demagogic and populist appeal to the people and the proroguing of the British parliament, in the very name of the people, reveals is the twisted notion of sovereignty that lies at the heart of the Leave side of Brexit. 'Let's take back control' was one of the most prominent and potent slogans of the Leave campaign.[49] This was certainly not Parliamentary control but the overriding of Parliamentary sovereignty with what can only be termed a vague and crude populist sovereignty, which could be shaped any which way a demagogue like Johnson chose.

There have been frenzied attempts at preventing such an eventuality, especially from those for whom no-deal is a political and economic catastrophe. The Lib-Dems, most of Labour and many Conservatives wanted to prevent no-deal from happening. One of the most interesting and politically intriguing suggestions that came out in the second week of August 2019 by Labour opposition leader, Jeremy Corbyn, was the idea of pulling down the government through a vote of no-confidence that would then be followed by a kind of interim national unity government led by Corbyn that would call for another extension of Article 50, beyond the 31 October 2019 deadline. It could then call for a general election and a second referendum to decide the future course of Britain's relationship with the EU. Much as they wanted to prevent a no-deal, the Lib-Dem leader, Jo Swinson's opposition to the personality of Corbyn, seemed to stand in the way of taking up the Labour leader's offer.[50]

Brexit as representing a worsening climate of democracy

Brexit is no doubt a manifestation of deep-seated discontent against globalization. At the same time, it needs to be seen in conjunction with political developments across the world that have a similarly audacious and reckless quality to them. Brexit needs to be seen in conjunction not just with the Trump victory, with which it shares many similarities, but also other developments, especially since 2016. That same year the bombastic Rodrigo Duterte became the President of the Philippines and Recep Tayyip Erdogan made a series of moves that strengthened his grip over power. The military coup of July 2016 was used by Erdogan to further consolidate his powers. The following year Erdogan held a referendum that went in his favour by 52 per cent of the vote, a number almost the same as the successful Leave side in the Brexit referendum. The victory in the referendum allowed Erdogan to further consolidate his executive powers and to extend his influence to appointments in the judiciary. The following year, in 2017, the centre managed to hold the ground in elections in countries such as France, Holland and Germany. The UK went through a surprise general election called by Theresa May in the hope of consolidating her majority. This was a hope stoked by a significant 20 per cent lead in the opinion polls that May's Conservatives had over Corbyn's Labour. Yet, Corbyn was able to rally his forces and did better than expected to reduce the Conservative majority, forcing them to rely on the Democratic Unionist Party (DUP) of Northern Ireland to give the government a working majority. The following year, in 2018, election verdicts in Hungary, which gave Mr Viktor Orban a large majority, and the results in Italy continued to confirm a right-wing populist surge across most parts of the world. Mr Jair Bolsonaro's victory in the Brazilian elections seems to again continue the trend of right-wing authoritarianism sweeping to power through toxic and divisive election campaigns that are largely conducted through social media platforms such as WhatsApp. As this Introduction was being written, news was coming in from Poland of the narrow victory in the elections of the ultra-nationalist President Andrzej Duda in mid-July 2020.[51]

These electoral verdicts, viewed in conjunction with the Brexit result, would represent what is referred to in the analysis here as a worsening climate of democracy. The year 2016 almost seems like a base year from which we can easily mark off a worsening and deteriorating situation for the very idea of liberal-democracy itself. The question of liberal-democracy is the first major conceptual component of this study on Brexit, and this is reflected in the main title of the book *Brexit and Liberal-Democracy*. Chapter 5 of this book, 'Brexit and the worsening climate of democracy' goes into this aspect in more detail. The further conceptual components of the study are populism, nation-State and sovereignty, to be found in the latter part of the book's title. While the concept of sovereignty finds itself treated separately in Chapter 4, 'Sovereignty – Let's take back control', the concepts of nation-state and populism are to be found scattered throughout the analysis of the book. The nation-state forms the central conceptual rubric of Chapter 6 on 'Brexit and the sum of all fears: Racism, Islamophobia and Anti-Semitism'.

Populism

The analysis of populism in this book is very much indebted to the cross-country study of the phenomenon in 31 European countries conducted by many academics, prominent among them being political sociologist Matthijs Rooduijn from the University of Amsterdam and Cas Mudde from the University of Georgia. Numerous articles from the study appeared in the British newspaper *The Guardian*, which was one of the organizers of the project.[52] The term populism has acquired some very specific connotations. One of the first of these is an almost insurrectionary anti-elitism that combines itself with anti-intellectualism and that manifests itself further in a very angry anti-Establishment stance. This set of oppositional 'anti-something' stances contrasts with a supposedly very 'pro-people' appeal. There is an almost self-righteous appeal to 'the people', where very often such an appeal tends to override the intricacies of institutional procedures in the political domain. The will of the people is itself portrayed in an extremely unitary manner, as if there can only be one will of the people. Anyone who fails to be part of this unitary peoples' will risks being labelled anti-people, unpatriotic or, as the word with the most resonance in currently BJP-dominated India goes, 'anti-national'. In 2011, the Turkish leader Recep Tayyip Erdogan started displaying his increasing transformation towards populism when, in a speech delivered after an election victory, he actually combined the peoples' will with the will of God with the declaration: 'The tyranny of the elites is over'. He went on to suggest that Turkey would now avoid the rule of 'criminals whose direction has split from God's will and the will of the people'.[53]

This gives us an insight into the populist's exaggerated, affected and almost fetishized appeal to 'the people'. To explain this point, one needs to first contrast the populist's impassioned appeal, which is often met with unthinking impetuosity, with a more deliberated appeal that is found in more Republican quarters. Let me take the example of the Preamble of the Indian Constitution, which, in a stirring sort of way, begins with the words 'We the people of India' and then ends with how those very people have decided to 'adopt, enact and give to ourselves'[54] the very constitution that the Preamble precedes. Here, there is a mediated sort of appeal, where the intrinsically demagogic possibilities and dangers of an appeal to the people are likely to be mediated and thereby eliminated by the procedures and working of the constitution. Such mediation and elimination are ruled out in the raucous appeal to the people by the populist. This is what makes the populist appeal to the people so dangerous. The populist's appeal is really the voice of the demagogue with all its megalomania, masquerading under the garb of democracy. Large sections of the people seem to sense something within themselves resonating to the surround sound of the populist leader booming away. It is then only a short step down the slippery chute-like slope towards authoritarianism. There is perhaps a diaphanous democratic veil that divides the point where individuals take this short step down the slippery slope, giving the wholly mistaken impression that the path being taken is a democratic one.

There is then an unthinking, impulsive quality to the people's voice that is roused deliberately by a leader who becomes a kind of synecdoche of the people that are being spoken about and supposedly represented. Analyses of the speeches given by populist leaders across the world reveal a set of remarkably similar themes.[55] There is dog-whistling, there is hatred that is spread against minority groups and there are remarks that are not just anti-intellectual, but downright unintelligent. In other words, the current phase of populism that we are witnessing across the world, of which Brexit is just one manifestation, stems from a kind of crass philistinism that is ultimately leading down the road to authoritarianism.

Finally, among the set of 'anti-somethings' pointed out earlier, the one that is supposedly most pro-people is anti-elitism. The figures that populist tendencies can catapult to power are themselves the most degenerate instances of what may be so wrong with the respective elites of those countries. One needs to only think of many ardent Brexiteers such as Boris Johnson, Jacob Rees-Mogg, Nigel Farage and Dominic Cummings. All four individuals were privately educated, and three out of the four went to Oxford. Donald Trump's appeal to the simple common sense of the people is ironical given his own status within the American 'power elite'. C. Wright Mills, in his celebrated 1956 book *The Power Elite*, talked about the shadowy collaboration between three components that constituted the power elite.[56] The first of these was the political Establishment, which would subsume the more overtly political executive, legislative and judicial wings of the American government. It would also bring under its ambit the significant agencies entrusted with intelligence and espionage. The second component would be the higher echelons of the military command. The third was, of course, the upper echelons of powerful corporate America. Trump is certainly an instance of the most undesirable aspects of corporate America as his inheritance of his father's extensive real estate businesses and his subsequent presiding over it reveal. For the purposes of our analysis of populism, Trump's ascent to Presidential office has led to a disruption in the manner the power elite operated in the US. Trump's constant feuds with his intelligence Establishment, especially the firing of FBI director James Comey for leading investigations into Russian links to his election campaign, are just one instance of this disruption.[57] Lastly, in the dying days of his presidency, on 6 January 2021, Trump is alleged to have incited a violent insurrection by his supporters when they marched towards and broke into the Capitol, just as legislators were certifying Joe Biden's election victory.[58] This will perhaps become the most abiding memory of just what Trump's populist appeal to the people was capable of doing.

Boris Johnson's populism reveals some of the worst aspects of the British Establishment. His Etonian enunciation, his inane Latin quotes and the vacuous verbosity of his long-winded stuttering sentences reveal a callous devil-may-care attitude towards the impact that his suicidal no-deal Brexit flight path may have. His swaggering self-confidence in the supposed greatness of Britain is evidence of an elitist privilege that can afford to take no notice of the most calamitous consequences, for the simple reason that they won't affect him.[59] All that matters is his own vanity and self-aggrandizement. Much as Johnson has been compared to Trump, and there are obvious similarities, there are also differences. Unlike Trump, Johnson has an extensive political career and experience in government. Prior to that, Johnson was a journalist, which meant that he was proximate to political circles, again, unlike Trump's real estate business interests. Johnson's expensive education at Eton and Oxford ensures that he can write whole books while Trump struggles with spellings in his short, but numerous, tweets that reveal the very limited range of his vocabulary. This is in contrast to Johnson's capacious one that perhaps rivals and certainly reflects his ego.

It seems that the leader's outsized ego expands in inverse proportion to the perceived pettiness and insignificance of the lives of 'the people'. This perceived pettiness in the lives of 'the people' is sought to be eradicated by putting the nation first and making it great. In one of the strangest ironies of populism, it is the leader's outsized ego that supposedly will look after the interest of 'the people'. One could then search for the psychological roots of populism in the manner of Wilhelm Reich's analysis in his book *The Mass Psychology of Fascism*.[60]

There is a strange kind of longing in just wanting to get out of Europe that is difficult to understand. While the liberal commentariat has been aghast at the idea of Brexit itself, and a no-deal Brexit only seemed to add to that intense discomfiture, Johnson's overall strategy is one of appealing to a particular section of the population that wanted Brexit almost desperately. For this section, Brexit was desirable at any cost, 'do-or-die', come 'hell or high water', sledgehammer or yellow-hammer. Johnson's strategy, faithful to his own personality and disposition, seems to be premised upon a populism that rebels against nuanced detail and revels in what can only be called the stupidly simplistic. It was most readily contained in that inane and vapid Brexit slogan that worked so well for him in the December 2019 elections 'Get Brexit Done'.

Johnson's electoral strategy was to posit 'the people', whatever that means, against Parliament that was so completely excoriated by him and the Conservative Party as standing in the way of the will of the people who just wanted Brexit done and dusted. This counter-posing of the people, deciding at the hustings against Parliament, is a dangerously populist strategy. It almost assumes that the people will not be electing a Parliament but will be deciding things for themselves, especially Brexit, in a kind of direct democracy. In fact, one element of Brexit has been the underlying idea that there is an inherent superiority in direct democracy over the indirect Westminster Parliamentary model birthed and mothered in the very country itself.[61] Johnson's strategy of appealing to the people over the head of an institution of such central importance like Parliament is one of the clearest expressions of his populism. More than that, it is calculated to appeal to a certain weariness that seemed to have set in among the populace over the arcane rigmarole of parliamentary procedures and the seemingly never-ending Brexit saga itself. In this manner, the efforts of Parliament to block and thwart Britain's exit on 31 October 2019 was projected as Johnson appealing to the people, suggesting despairingly that he had been trying to 'get on with it' but that he was being frustrated in his efforts by the Parliament.

Brexit: forever in search of closure?

The simplistic straightforwardness among Brexiteers has made many believe that there could be a clean break, that Britain could just 'cut and run' without even having to pay the 39 billion Euros that was part of Theresa May's rather painstakingly drawn-up divorce deal, thrice rejected by Parliament, each time Boris Johnson being on the side of that very same Parliament that he has been so busily railing against after becoming Prime Minister. Johnson was disabused of this notion of Brexit being a clean break by the Irish Taoiseach Leo Varadkar at a joint press conference with Johnson in Dublin in early September 2019. Varadkar, appearing calm, staid and almost sage-like, said: 'The story of Brexit will not end if the United Kingdom leaves on 31 October or even 31 January – there is no such thing as a clean break. No such thing as just getting it done'. More importantly, Varadkar suggested to Johnson that he would like to play the role of Athena to Johnson's Hercules, who has set himself up the impossibly Herculean task of negotiating fresh trade deals with large parts of the world after the UK's departure from the EU. Varadkar was not only giving Johnson a dose of his own medicine with his frequent references to the classics, but he suggested that it was his task as Athena to strike Johnson's Hercules down as he descended into madness to prevent him from doing further harm to himself and those around him, which is what Brexit seems to have become, especially under Johnson.[62]

Intriguingly, just a week after these rather highbrow classical references to Hercules and his madness having to be saved by the intervention of Athena, Johnson seemed to suggest that madness was good. This time he made a reference to the madness of the Incredible Hulk, suggesting that the madder hulk became the more it was possible to get Brexit done by breaking the manacles of the EU.[63] What is remarkable here is the continuation of the theme of madness but more intriguing perhaps was Johnson's quick descent from highbrow classics to lowbrow popular culture of the Incredible Hulk variety that was characteristically infantile as far as Johnson is concerned.

Brexit, it seems, is a process that is forever fated to remain in search of closure. There never can be a clean, 'cut and run' break from Europe as Brexiteers so ardently seem to want. Like any entity that remains in perpetual search of closure, Brexit, it seems, is destined to ghost-like continue to haunt Britain's relationship with Europe. This perpetual lack of closure is made worse by Boris Johnson's vacuous commandeering of the process. By merely saying that he will 'Get Brexit Done', it is hardly likely that Johnson is ever going to conclude a process that, in typically self-deprecatory British humour, has been characterized as the political equivalent of reversing a vasectomy. What can be suggested though is that a hard no-deal Brexit was perhaps hard-wired into the very process itself. Prime Minister Theresa May's reckless dances with no-deal were perhaps meant to get her own party and Parliament to back her deal. She invoked no-deal as a kind of driving to the cliff-edge, only to pull back at the last minute. In Johnson's case, he may have actually intended a no-deal. This intending of a hard Brexit could have been instigated by numerous think tanks on both sides of the Atlantic, in the US and the UK, with access to many members of Johnson's cabinet. These think tanks, many of them part of what is called the Atlas group, represent, advocate and advance particular business and commercial interests and were particularly

22 Brexit

keen on a hard Brexit, which would then have laid the grounds for a trade deal with the US.[64]

One would have thought that the Coronavirus pandemic would encourage some degree of caution in Johnson to set aside Brexit, for the time being, to prolong and postpone the transition period leading to the ultimate departure of the UK. That, however, is very evidently not going to be the case. In the early days of the pandemic, just as Britain rather belatedly went into lockdown, the prominent centre-right European People's Party group in the European Parliament, which brings together parties of 11 EU leaders, including Angela Merkel's Christian Democrats, urged for an extension of the Brexit transition beyond the year.[65] The British side remained obdurate. In fact, by the end of June 2020, Johnson's government allowed the lapsing of the deadline that could have made it possible to postpone the 31 December 2020 deadline for the UK to leave the EU. If Brexit had made the future for Britain and its relationship with Europe uncertain, the Coronavirus pandemic has multiplied the uncertainty manifold.

Notes

1 'Something resembling hell: how does the rest of the world view the UK'. www.the guardian.com/politics/2019/aug/04/how-does-the-rest-of-the-world-currently-view-the-uk-brexit-boris-johnson. Accessed 24 July 2020.
2 Raf Casert, 'May's relationship with EU was often rocky', *AP News*, 25 May 2019. https://apnews.com/6e3d21bfb2f540e38da644338c30f473. Accessed 10 July 2020.
3 www.ons.gov.uk/economy/grossdomesticproductgdp/bulletins/gdpmonthlyestima teuk/august2019. Accessed 12 July 2020.
4 Rowena Mason and Peter Walker, 'Brexit: Johnson says Britain will leave EU on 31 October "do or die"', *The Guardian*, Tuesday 25 June 2019. www.theguardian.com/politics/2019/jun/25/brexit-boris-johnson-britain-will-leave-eu-31-october-do-or-die. Accessed 11 July 2020.
5 'Brexit: operation Yellowhammer no-deal document published', *BBC News*, 11 September 2019. www.bbc.com/news/uk-politics-49670123. Accessed 11 July 2020.
6 Dominic Cummings, 'How the Brexit referendum was won', *The Spectator*, 9 January 2017. www.spectator.co.uk/article/dominic-cummings-how-the-brexit-referen dum-was-won. Accessed 12 July 2020.
7 Aishwarya Krishnan, 'Demonetization anniversary: decoding the effects of Indian currency notes ban', *The Economic Times*, 21 May 2019. https://economictimes.indiatimes. com/tdmc/your-money/demonetization-anniversary-decoding-the-effects-of-indian-currency-notes-ban/articleshow/61579118.cms. Accessed 12 July 2020.
8 'Supreme court: suspending parliament was unlawful, judges rule', *BBC News*, 24 September 2019. www.bbc.com/news/uk-politics-49810261. Accessed 12 July 2020.
9 'Boris Johnson defeated again; no snap UK election', *Al Jazeera*, 5 September 2019. www.aljazeera.com/news/2019/09/boris-johnson-defeated-snap-uk-election-190904201302893.html. Accessed 12 July 2020.
10 'Brexit: Tory MP defects ahead of crucial no-deal vote', *BBC News*, 3 September 2019. https://bbc.com/news/uk-politics-49570682. Accessed 12 July 2020.
11 Steven Levitsky and Daniel Ziblatt, *How Democracies Die: What History Reveals About Our Future*, Viking, New York, 2018.
12 Mark Chou, 'Sowing the seeds of its own destruction: democracy and democide in the Weimar republic and beyond', *Theoria: A Journal of Social and Political Theory*, Vol.

59, No. 133 (December 2012), pgs. 21–49. https://www.jstor.org.stable/41802532. Accessed 2 August 2018. Chou has the following observation to make:

> That all democracies have, by their very nature, the potential to destroy themselves is a fact too rarely documented by the acolytes of democracy. Preferring instead to focus on how sustainable a practice democracy is, democrats have much rather concentrated on the longevity of democracy and not its supposed likelihood to self-destruct (pg. 21).

13 The Netflix documentary *The Great Hack* is a riveting account of how computer technology and data analysis is proving detrimental to the well-being of democracy.

14 Laura Galante and E.E. Shaun, *Defining Russian Election Interference: An Analysis of Select 2014 to 2018 Cyber Enabled Incidents,* Atlantic Council, 2018. https://www.jstor.org/stable/resrep20718. Accessed 9 July 2020.

15 This is how Martin Fletcher, in his article 'How the cult of Jacob Rees-Mogg unravelled' in *The New Stateman*, 10 June 2020, describes him: 'It did not matter that he was a caricature of a toff, an MP who still communicated with his constituents by fountain pen, a *Downton Abbey* relic who once campaigned on the housing estates of Central Fife with his nanny'. www.newstatesman.com/politics/uk/2020/06/how-cult-jacob-rees-mogg-unravelled. Accessed 12 July 2020.

16 Rowena Mason and Heather Stewart, 'Javid resigned after Johnson pushed him to sack advisers', *The Guardian*, Thursday 13 February 2020. www.theguardian.com/politics/2020/feb/13/javid-resigned-after-johnson-pushed-him-to-sack-advisers. Accessed 13 July 2020.

17 Patrick Greenfield, 'Sajid Javid accused of "human fly-tipping" in Shamima Begum case', *The Guardian*, Friday 31 May 2019. www.theguardian.com/uk-news/2019/may/31/sajid-javid-accused-shamima-begum-case-syria. Accessed 13 July 2020.

18 Kamila Shamsie, *Home Fire*, Penguin, London, 2017. Within a few months of the book's publication, Sajid Jawid became the Home Secretary in May 2018. Shamsie's novel is based on the tragedy of Antigone by Sophocles and, like much of Greek tragedy, has had an enduring relevance for political theory. The Antigone story, as retold by Shamsie's novel, suggests that in a clash between a natural law and a more local domestic law, the tragic resolution can only be death as indeed the central characters of the novel Aneeka (based on the original Antigone), Aneeka's brother Parwaiz (Polynices in the original Antigone) and Aneeka's lover Eamonn (Haemon in the original Antigone) all die at the very end. The intransigence of the Pakistani-origin British Home Secretary Karamat Lone (King Creon in the original Antigone) is seen in his refusal to allow Parwaiz's body to be flown back to Britain owing to his decision to join ISIS. Aneeka, who is Parwaiz's twin, in her desperation to get her brother back, befriends and contrives to fall in love with Eamonn, who happens to be Karamat Lone's son as Polynices is the son of King Creon in the original. The intercession on the part of Eamonn proves to be futile, and the novel ends when Eamonn leaves Britain despite his father's best efforts to prevent him from travelling.

This is how Karamat Lone is described by Aneeka's elder sister Isma when it is suggested by Eamonn that she meet and possibly confront Karamat Lone:

'Me? Meet Karamat Lone?'

Mr. British Values. Mr. Strong on Security. Mr. Striding Away from Muslimness. He would say, 'I know about your family. You're better off without your brother, too'. And Eamonn, his devoted son would have to agree (pg. 52).

In the novel, Isma is much older than Aneeka and is protective towards her younger sibling. However, Aneeka is a much stronger character in the novel as her response to trying to get the brother back is more capacious and wide-ranging, whereas Isma, who also tries, remains within the confines of British law.

19 Rajeev Syal and Anushka Asthana, 'Priti Patel forced to resign over unofficial meetings with Israelis', *The Guardian*, Wednesday, 8 November 2017. www.theguardian.com/politics/2017/nov/08/priti-patel-forced-to-resign-over-unofficial-meetings-with-israelis. Accessed 1 February 2021.

24 Brexit

20 'Priti Patel faces unfair dismissal claim from Philip Rutnam', *BBC News*, 20 April 2020. www.bbc.com/news/uk-politics-52356574. Accessed 11 July 2020.

21 Jose Saramago, *The Stone Raft*, Translated from the Portuguese by Giovanni Pontiero, The Harvill Press, London, 2000.

22 'UK would be "insane" to let in chlorinated chicken, farmers say', *BBC News*, 25 February 2020. www.bbc.com/news/business-51626525. Accessed 10 July 2020.

23 Ailbhe Rea, 'What now for the humbled liberal democrats?', *New Statesman*, 17 January 2020. www.newstatesman.com/politics/uk/2020/01/what-now-humbled-liberal-democrats. Accessed 12 July 2020.

24 See Darren McGarvey, *Poverty Safari: Understanding the Anger of Britain's Underclass*, Picador, Published in association with Luath Press, Edinburgh, 2017, pg. 129–130.

25 Andrew Woodcock, 'Swinson urges Corbyn to give up hopes of leading unity government if Johnson is ousted', *The Independent*, Monday 26 August 2019. www.independent.co.uk/news/politics/corbyn-labour-government-of-national-unity-jo-swinson-brexit-boris-johnson-a9078586.html. Accessed 11 July 2020.

26 Kate Proctor, 'Liberal-democrats poised to back revoking article 50', *The Guardian*, Monday 9 September 2019. www.theguardian.com/politics/2019/sep/09/liberal-democrats-poised-to-back-revoking-article-50-brexit. Accessed 10 July 2020.

27 This is taken from the title of Stuart Hall's article 'The great moving right show', in Stuart Hall and Martin Jacques (eds.) *The Politics of Thatcherism*, Lawrence and Wishart, London, 1983.

28 Kitty Donaldson, 'Brexit rips conservative party apart as Johnson expels 21 rebels', *Bloomberg*, 4 September 2019. www.bloomberg.com/news/articles/2019-09-04/brexit-rips-conservative-party-apart-as-johnson-expels-21-rebels. Accessed 13 July 2020.

29 Ned Simons, 'Queen's speech: Ed Miliband tells David Cameron "You can't out-Farage Farage"', *The Huffington Post*, 8 May 2013. www.huffingtonpost.co.uk/2013/05/08/queens-speech-miliband-cameron-farage_n_3237981.html. Accessed 13 July 2020.

30 Paul Lewis, 'Rage, rapture and pure populism: on the road with Nigel Farage', *The Guardian*, Sunday 19 May 2019. www.theguardian.com/politics/2019/may/19/nigel-farage-brexit-party-on-the-road-road-populism. Accessed 12 July 2020.

31 'Nigel Farage's Brexit party officially changes its name', *BBC News*, 6 January 2021. www.bbc.com/news/uk-politics-55566526. Accessed 24 January 2021.

32 Toby Helm, '100 days on, Keir Starmer's quiet revolution takes hold', *The Guardian*, Sunday 12 July 2020. www.theguardian.com/politics/202-/jul/12/100-days-on-keir-starmers-quiet-revolution-takes-hold? Accessed 13 July 2020.

33 Maya Rhodan, 'Obama political guru helping Britain's labour party', *Time*, 18 April 2014. https://time.com/67981/david-axelrod-britain-labour/. Accessed 21 July 2020.

34 According to Richard Seymour, *Corbyn: The Strange Birth of Radical Politics*, Verso, London and New York, 2016,

> For the Blairites who had been plotting to get rid of Brown as soon as he took the leadership, the 2010 Labour leadership election campaign ought to have been their moment of delicious revenge. With a youthful, and by their standards, charismatic candidate in David Miliband, they were confident of victory. But instead the victory was taken by the younger, more neurotic Ed Miliband, who gained the support of trade unionists by cautiously letting it be known that he was slightly to the left of his brother, and would be more receptive to the concerns of trade unionists if he won. 'Red Ed' was always a tabloid conceit, but Miliband was at least someone who recognised the need to decisively close the New Labour era, recover lost working-class votes, and ever-so-slightly push at the boundaries of acceptable neoliberal discourse.
> *(pg. 172–73)*

35 Josh Bolotsky, 'Use your radical fringe to shift the Overton window', in *Beautiful Trouble: A Toolbox for Revolution* by Andrew Boyd and Dave Oswald Mitchell, OR Books,

New York and London, 2012, pgs. 200–201. www.jstor.org/stable/j.ctt1bkm5nd.85. Accessed 24 July 2020.

36 'Ed Miliband apologises for offence over Sun picture', *BBC News*, 13 June 2014. www.bbc.com/news/uk-politics-27829958. Accessed 21 July 2020.

37 See Mehdi Hasan and James MacIntyre, *Ed: The Milibands and the Making of a Labour Leader*, Biteback Publishing, Hull, 2011.

38 Aristotle, *The Nicomachean Ethics*, Translated with an introduction by David Ross, Oxford University Press, Oxford and New York, 1980, pg. 2.

39 Sienna Rodgers, 'Labour's leaked report is a major blow for "party unity"- Keir Starmer has his work cut out', *The Guardian*, Monday 13 April 2020. www.theguardian.com/commentisfree/2020/apr/13/labour-leaked-report-party-unity-keir-starmer-corbyn-faction. Accessed 14 July 2020.

40 Jessica Elgot and Lisa O'Carroll, 'Antisemitism plunges labour party into civil war', *The Guardian*, Thursday 23 July 2020. www.theguardian.com/politics/2020/jul/22/antisemitism-labour-settlement-plunges-party-into-civil-war? Accessed 24 July 2020.

41 'UK's labour party suspends ex-leader Jeremy Corbyn after anti-Semitism failings exposed', *The Hindu*, 29 October 2020. https://thehindu.com/news/international/uks-labour-party-suspends-ex-leader-jeremy-corbyn-after-anti-semitism-failings-exposed/article32974052.ece. Accessed 24 January 2021.

42 Anna Luhrmann, Juraj Medzihorsky, Garry Hindle, and Staffan I. Lindberg, 'New global data on political parties: V party', Briefing Paper No. #9, 26 October 2020, V-Dem Institute, University of Gothenburg.

43 Paul Mason, 'The strange case of America's disappearing middle class', *The Guardian*, Monday 14 December 2015. www.theguardian.com/commentisfree/2015/dec/14/the-strange-case-of-americas-disappearing-middle-class. Accessed 20 July 2020.

44 'As production is mechanized, and the profit margin of the machine-owners becomes our civilisation's driving motive, society splits between non-working shareholders and non-owner wage-workers. As for the middle class, it is the dinosaur in the room, set for extinction'. Yanis Varoufakis, 'Marx predicted our present crisis – and points the way out', *The Guardian,* The Long Read, Friday 20 April 2018. www.theguardian.com/news/2018/apr/20/yanis-varoufakis-marx-crisis-communist-manifesto. Accessed 16 September 2019.

45 'Brexit: U.K. PM Boris Johnson sparks outrage with Parliament suspension', *The Hindu*, 28 August 2019. www.thehindu.com/news/international/brexit-uk-pm-boris-johnson-sparks-outrage-with-parliament-suspension/article29281250.ece. Accessed 26 July 2020.

46 Nick Miller, 'Johnson's government hits back at "constitutional coup" by UK court', *The Sydney Morning Herald*, 25 September 2019. www.smh.com.au/world/europe/johnson-government-hits-back-at-constitutional-coup-by-uk-court-20190925-p52ux9.html. Accessed 26 July 2020.

47 Richard Partington, 'No-deal Brexit would hit "red wall" areas hard, manufacturers warn', *The Guardian*, Thursday 16 July 2020. www.theguardian.com/politics/2020/jul/16/no-deal-brexit-would-hit-red-wall-areas-hard-manufacturers-warn. Accessed 26 July 2020.

48 Robert Shrimsley, 'Boris Johnson's Brexit explosion ruins Tory business credentials', *The Financial Times*, 25 June 2018. www.ft.com/content/8075e68c-7857-11e8-8e67-1e1a0846c475. Accessed 14 July 2020.

49 See Juliette Ringersen-Biardeaud, ' "Let's take back control": Brexit and the Debate on Sovereignty', *French Journal of British Studies*, Vol. XXII, No. 2 (2017).

50 Andrew Woodcock, 'Swinson urges Corbyn to give up hopes of leading unity government if Johnson is ousted', *The Independent*, 26 August 2019. https://www.independent.co.uk/news/uk/politics/corbyn-labour-government-of-national-unity-jo-swinson-brexit-boris-johnson-a9078586.html. Accessed 26 July 2020.

51 'The day of Duda: on Poland election', *The Hindu*, 16 July 2020. www.thehindu.com/opinion/editorial/the-day-of-duda-the-hindu-editorial-on-poland-elections/article32095089.ece. Accessed 17 July 2020.

26 Brexit

52 Caelainn Barr, Sean Clarke and Paul Lewis, 'Measuring populism: how the Guardian charted its rise', *The Guardian*, Tuesday 20 November 2018. www.theguardian.com/world/2018/nov/20/measuring-populism-how-guardian-charted-rise-methodology. Accessed 18 July 2020.

53 Bethan Meckernan, 'From reformer to "New Sultan": Erdogan's populist evolution', *The Guardian*, Monday 11 March 2019. www.theguardian.com/world/2019/mar/11/from-reformer-to-new-sultan-erdogans-populist-evolution. Accessed 5 April 2021.

54 www.constitutionofindia.net/constitution_of_india/preamble. Accessed 23 January 2021.

55 Kirk Hawkins, 'Don't try to silence populists-listen to them', *The Guardian*, Saturday 9 March 2019. www.the guardian.com/world/commentisfree/2019/mar/09/dont-try-to-silence-populists-listen-to-them. Accessed 13 July 2020.

56 C. Wright Mills, *The Power Elite*, Oxford University Press, New York, 1956.

57 Michael D. Shear and Matt Apuzzo, 'F.B.I. director James Comey is fired by Trump', *The New York Times*, 9 May 2017. www.nytimes.com/2017/05/09/us/politics/james-comey-fired-fbi.html. Accessed 17 July 2020.

58 Brian Stelter, 'Now it's sinking in: Wednesday's Capitol Hill riot was even more violent than it appeared', *CNN Business*, Tuesday 12 January 2021. www.cnn.com/2021/01/09/media/reliable-sources-january-8/index.html. Accessed 26 January 2021.

59 Rafael Behr, 'Brexit was a typically English revolution – one that left the elites unharmed', *The Guardian*, Tuesday 19 January 2021. Some lines from Behr's article are worth quoting:

> The Conservative party is a brilliant machine for adapting social pressure from below, remaking itself to absorb new supporters without the established elite having to surrender power. It happened in the early 1980s, with the sale of council houses. It happened with Brexit and the co-opting of working class 'red wall' voters. It is a pattern predating the modern party, going back to the 19th-century reform acts and selective extension of voting rights.
>
> *(www.theguardian.com/commentisfree/2021/jan/19/brexit-english-revolution-elites-ruling-class?CMP=Share_AndroidApp_Other. Accessed 26 January 2021)*

60 Wilhelm Reich, *The Mass Psychology of Fascism*, Aakar Books, New Delhi, 2015.

61 The vague idea or at least the nebulous desire for some form of indirect democracy has been mooted by some of Brexit's ideologues such as Daniel Hannan; see Sam Knight, 'The man who brought you Brexit', *The Guardian,* The Long Read, 29 September 2016. www.theguardian.com/politics/2016/sep/29/daniel-hannan-the-man-who-brought-you-brexit. Accessed 9 September 2019.

62 Martin Belam, 'Why did Varadkar say he wanted to be Athena to Johson's Hercules?', *The Guardian*, Monday 9 September 2019. www.theguardian.com/world/2019/sep/09/leo-varadkar-athena-hercules-boris-johnson-why. Accessed 10 September 2019.

63 Peter Walker, Jennifer Rankin and Daniel Boffey, 'EU dismay as Boris Johnson compares himself to Hulk', *The Guardian*, Sunday 15 September 2019. www.theguardian.com/politics/2019/sep/15/eu-dismay-boris-johnson-compares-himself-to-hulk. Accessed 21 July 2020.

64 Felicity Lawrence, Rob Evans, David Pegg, Caelainn Barr and Pamela Duncan, 'How the right's radical thinktanks reshaped the Conservative party', *The Guardian*, Friday 29 November 2019. www.theguardian.com/politics/2019/nov/29/rightwing-thinktank-conservative-boris-johnson-brexit-atlas-network? Accessed 31 January 2021.

65 'Extension of Brexit transition is the responsible thing to do', European Peoples Parliamentary Party in the European Parliament, 30 March 2020. www.eppgroup.eu/news room/news/extension-of-brexit-transition-the-responsible-thing-to-do. Accessed 21 July 2020.

2

THE THATCHERITE PRELUDE TO BREXIT

Brexit did not happen suddenly, and there is a significant history to the desire to assert Britain's exceptionalism and aloofness from continental Europe. This chapter will look at the Thatcherite prelude to Brexit, the whole of that influential decade of the 1980s 'when the Iron Lady ruled'.[1] The most famous indicator of this was her Bruges speech of September 1988, in which Mrs Thatcher famously proclaimed, 'We have not successfully rolled back the frontiers of the state in Britain, only to see them re-imposed at European level, with a European super-state exercising a new dominance from Brussels'.[2] Mrs Thatcher used the collective 'we' while talking about the rolling back of the frontiers of the state and perhaps foreshadowed an increasingly megalomaniacal self-referencing, a clearer instance of which was on display when she proclaimed 'We have become a grandmother,' after the birth of her first grandchild in 1989.[3] The influence that Mrs Thatcher has had on the British national psyche and not just British politics is huge to say the least.

When Mrs Thatcher was elected the leader of the Conservative Party, she was in favour of Britain's membership of the European Economic Community (EEC). In fact, her elevation to Conservative Party leadership and the referendum initially held to decide Britain's membership happened in the very same year, 1975. What was then the EEC at the time of Mrs Thatcher's assumption of Conservative Party leadership became the European Community (EC) during the course of her premiership and would become the EU with the signing of the Maastricht Treaty in 1992, within two years of her stepping down as Prime Minister. The usual Brexit argument has been that Britain really did not know what she was signing up for when she initially joined the EEC and that the nature of the beast started to become clear very slowly. This is what Mrs Thatcher has to say in her memoirs about this changing nature of the Europe project:

> The wisdom of hindsight, so useful to historians and indeed to authors of memoirs, is sadly denied to practising politicians. Looking back, it is now

28 The Thatcherite prelude to Brexit

possible to see the period of my second term as Prime Minister as that in which the European Community subtly but surely shifted its direction away from being a Community of open trade, light regulation and freely co-operating sovereign nation-states towards statism and centralism. I can only say that it did not seem like that at the time.[4]

Having realized the true nature of the Europe project, it would only be natural to assert that curious Brexit slogan, 'We want our country back'. The idea of wanting the country back is itself reminiscent of Mrs Thatcher's wanting British money back, when she drove a hard bargain in Fontainebleau in June 1984, when she was able to secure the British Rebate, which meant a significant reduction of Britain's contribution to the European budget.[5] Her prolonged argument for the British rebate was an instance of an almost obsessive scrimping and saving on budgetary contributions that came to characterize Thatcherite politics in both its style and substance. It was again to be reflected in the infamous Brexit campaign slogan that was painted on a red bus: 'We send the EU £350 million pounds a week, let's fund our NHS instead'. There was the same obsession to save money and spend it judiciously on our own NHS, rather than wasting it on the Europeans. This obsession with what has been called scrimping and saving is a distinct feature of Thatcherite politics. It reflects Mrs Thatcher's combination of a house-wife's touch to politics along with the book-balancing that is involved in the running of a small-to-medium business, such as her father's grocery store in her native Grantham.

The scrimping and saving, as it has been called, has had devastating consequences. In all these years, it has been this mentality that has eaten away at the vitals of Britain's welfare state. All this was done with the idea that most welfare state provisions were a sheer waste of taxpayers' money, as people with dignity and self-respect needed to be able to pay their way through life. More broadly, the obsessive idea of scrimping and saving when it comes to public expenditure by cutting back on public services and not raising taxation, is a reversal of the opposing logics of public and household expenditure. When it comes to public expenditure, governments can assess the amount of expenditure that needs to be made and then, on this basis, draw up plans for revenue through appropriate taxation. The opposite is the case with households, at least prudent ones. They must be willing to first assess their incomes and then decide expenses accordingly. For households, it would be a case of deciding the coat of their expenditure according to the cloth of their income.

What Mrs Thatcher did was to translate in the crudest and most anti-intellectual manner the abstruse ideas of August von Hayek and the abstract economic thinking of Milton Friedman into the simplistic language of electoral success. Stuart Hall notes that this, 'Translation of a theoretical ideology into a populist idiom was a major political achievement: and the conversion of hard-faced economics into the language of compulsive moralism was, in many ways, the centerpiece of this transformation'. All that Mrs Thatcher had to do was to argue in a convincingly commonsensical manner that one could not spend more than one earned. By putting the argument in this way, Mrs Thatcher was reversing one of the basic distinctions between public government finance and personal household finance – 'the national economy debated on the model of the household budget'.[6]

The remarkable aspect of neoliberal politics has been its advocacy of prudence and austerity for governments, while removing all limits to the expansion and extension of credit for households. Neoliberal economists tend to express a horror at public debt as a result of which austerity measures are advocated to reduce this, and the nation is encouraged to live within its means. At the same time, neoliberal ideas have presided over a massive accumulation of household debt. These stratospheric levels of debt have been accumulated to buy consumer goods that would ordinarily be far beyond the range set by their incomes. The biggest source of this household debt tends to be the housing loans, and the 2007 financial crisis was an outcome of the US subprime mortgage crisis, when banks lent recklessly to individuals who would not be in any position to pay back these loans.[7] In the UK, the after-effect of the 2007 financial crisis was the decade-long austerity measures inflicted upon the populace by Conservative governments of the 2010s, beginning with the Cameron government, in which the architect of austerity, Chancellor George Osborne, through his relentless cuts, transformed in both qualitative and quantitative terms the British welfare state. In an assessment of these austerity measures, it can be said that the 2007 financial crisis provided the pretext for the kind of ideological reduction of the size of the state that Thatcherism has been all about.

Thatcher on the mind

Mrs Thatcher's personality and, by extension, Thatcherite politics came with its mind decisively made up. This is then combined with the hint of a very definite anti-intellectualism, especially when it comes to the humanities and social sciences in universities, which Mrs Thatcher seemed to have a particular antipathy towards as they, in her view, did not contribute towards productive activity in the economy. Notwithstanding this larger anti-intellectualism, Mrs Thatcher attempted to give a veneer of intellectual respectability to her project through appealing to the writings of Friedrich von Hayek and the ideas of economist Milton Friedman. Even as a veneer, there was an almost embarrassing thinness here. Alfred Sherman, head of the influential right-wing think tank, the Centre for Policy Studies (CPS), doubted whether Mrs Thatcher had ever read Hayek and suggested that she came from her hometown, Grantham, with 'her mind made up'.[8]

Mrs Thatcher's 11-year rule had a deeply personal and psychological impact on British political life. Richard Vinen, in his book, suggests that 'There was something about Margaret Thatcher's premiership that cut deeply into the personal lives of many British people'. He goes on to cite an interesting piece of research by psychiatrists about patients suffering from dementia. For most of the post-war period, such patients could recall the name of Queen Elizabeth II as the monarch but failed to recall who the Prime Minister was. That changed with Mrs Thatcher.

Vinen quotes from the *British Medical Journal* study: 'Mrs. Thatcher has given an item of knowledge to demented patients that they would otherwise have lacked: she reaches those parts of the brain other prime ministers could not reach'.[9] Rather ironically, Mrs Thatcher herself suffered from severe dementia, towards the end of her life, a condition that was painfully portrayed by Meryl Streep in the 2012 film *The Iron Lady*.

A similar, deeply psychological effect that Mrs Thatcher and Thatcherism had is a theme that is also taken up by Louisa Hadley and Elizabeth Ho in their edited volume *Thatcher & After: Margaret Thatcher and her Afterlife in Contemporary Culture*. The book looks at the emotionally fraught responses to Thatcher and Thatcherism and examines the former Prime Minister's continued influence on British political imagination. The editors understand Thatcherism as a trauma and a wound, where trauma, unlike a bodily wound, generates an internal wound that is a break in the mind's experience of time, self and the world. The persistent reappearance of Thatcher and her images in recent times are similar to traumatic flashbacks, as the definition of trauma understood by the editors is an event that is experienced 'too unexpectedly, to be fully known and [which] is therefore not available to consciousness until it imposes itself again and again, repeatedly, in the nightmares and repetitive actions of the survivor'.[10]

Thatcherism: a curious combination of Monetarism and Methodism

Intriguingly, there is, in Mrs Thatcher's politics, a strange combination of Monetarism and Methodism. These two distinct systems of thought, one economic and the other theological, come together to give that very characteristic flavour, so distinctive of the politics of Thatcherism. Thatcher's Christian religious belief, specifically her Methodism, was very upfront and formed an important part of her politics.[11] Before proceeding further, it may be useful to step aside and think of the different ways in which successive British Prime Ministers have talked about their faith. Tony Blair was quite open about his beliefs, and this tended to increase as he became closer to ally President George Bush, especially as the US and the UK became more deeply involved in Iraq. When the media pressed a question on this, Blair's famous media adviser Alastair Campbell cut him short by asserting, 'We don't do God'. David Cameron's expression of religious belief tended more onto the side of ambivalence when he talked about his own faith having the come and go variation of 'reception for Magic FM in the Chilterns' but then tended to get stronger as he progressed in his premiership.[12] Cameron actually borrowed the characteristically colourful line from Boris Johnson,[13] whose only religious belief seems a consistency in his own self-aggrandizement.

Graeme Smith argues, 'An essential part of the biography and political science of Thatcher – and by close association, Thatcherism – is theological analysis'. He categorizes Thatcher's political theology as an Anglo-Saxon Nonconformity and complains: 'So far, political scientists have all but ignored Thatcher's Christianity'.[14]

Smith himself offers us an example of how Thatcher was prone to looking at an economic issue such as inflation as an evil.[15] The fact that Smith cites inflation viewed theologically as an evil highlights the argument that is being made in this chapter in looking at Mrs Thatcher's politics as a curious combination of Monetarism and Methodism. One of the main concerns of Monetarism is the control of inflation.

Methodism itself played a very important role in the quiescence of the English working class, as it advocated a complete and unquestioning loyalty to the crown and government. The historian E.P. Thompson, in his monumental work *The Making of the English Working Class*, talks about the influence of sects opposed to the Anglican Establishment such as Deism, Unitarianism and Socinianism and the particular influence that they had on the furthering of dissent. The effects of Methodism, also a nonconformist sect from the Anglican Establishment, on the other hand, are a study in contrast in terms of the impact that they had on the elimination of dissent.[16] There are three further aspects of Methodism that need to be emphasized, with the suggestion that the last two especially seem to be replicated in the politics of Thatcherism. First, there is an ambivalent relationship with reason and the Enlightenment. Second, there is an overall anti-intellectualism that pervades Methodism as a whole. Third, there is the founder John Wesley's overbearing and autocratic manner of operating, which created a situation in which individuals were free of their volition to be led by him, but had to leave if they differed with him.[17] This last attitude could be seen in Mrs Thatcher's cabinet dismissals and resignations. Beginning with the elimination of her rival Tory 'wets', as they were referred to, there was a series of resignations, the last and most significant one being that of Foreign Secretary Geoffrey Howe, whose mild-mannered acceptance of loyalty to Mrs Thatcher often became the butt of the very cruel humour of the British press. His resignation over the issue of Europe and, most dramatically, the resignation speech that he gave in the House of Commons, in which he talked about how he had 'wrestled with his conscience for far too long', are widely believed to have brought about the fall of the Iron Lady. Parts of this speech are worth recalling, for they very clearly bring up the Thatcherite prelude to Brexit very effectively.[18] This chapter concludes with an analysis of Howe's resignation speech, which is widely considered to have brought the curtains down on Mrs Thatcher's Prime Ministership.

Historically then, Methodism had the effect of encouraging the acceptance of subordination among the working class. It was also characterized by its always being kept at an arm's distance by the Establishment and rarely being given admittance to its hallowed portals. There arose then a strange ambivalence between the British Establishment and Methodism. The Establishment itself tended to almost disdainfully keep Methodism away, while Methodism never had the hint of any insurrectionary logic to it unlike other nonconformist sects such as Unitarianism and Socinianism, as a result of which they often drew the unwanted attention of the state. This ambivalence, in terms of mutual relationship between the British Establishment and Methodism, can be seen almost replicated in the politics of

32 The Thatcherite prelude to Brexit

Thatcherism. Thatcher's entry into politics and her rise to the very apex of British politics would represent the Methodism of her own origins and attitudes with respect to the Establishment Tory grandees, the upper-class, aristocratic men that she was up against.

Once she had successfully risen to the Prime Ministership, her very first cabinet was a precarious balance between Tory 'wets' and 'dries', as the two factions were referred to. Mrs Thatcher was able to successfully purge her cabinet of Tory 'wets', which was a reference to the generally older generation of male politicians whose Conservative Party traditions and politics emanated from their far more privileged aristocratic upper-class backgrounds that contrasted starkly with Mrs Thatcher's more humble petit-bourgeois origins. The 'wets' partook of a politics that was more about middle-of–the-road consensus and state intervention, thereby not rocking the boat too much as their own privileged position within the British Establishment seemed secure and safe. Mrs Thatcher challenged and changed that.

Thatcherite politics is a strange kind of interposing between the working class, which it disdains, and the Establishment, which it is disdained by on account of its being, in the Establishment's view, plainly put, arriviste. Simultaneously, Thatcherite politics shares the disdain of the working class towards the poshness of the British Establishment. In this interposing between working class and upper-class Establishment, there is a moral and methodical self-righteousness, the momentum for which it derives from a kind of zeal for rigorous and regular hard work. This almost suggests that the working class below and the upper-class Establishment above do not engage in the kind of methodical and rigorous work captured in a favourite and rather stern Thatcherite expression, 'an honest day's pay for an honest day's work'.

This interposing of Thatcherism, however, did something vital for the British Establishment, which the latter seemed particularly unable to accomplish, especially from 1972 onwards. That year, Conservative Prime Minister Edward Heath suffered a humiliating defeat at the hands of the National Union of Miners (NUM). In February 1974, Heath called for elections in which he rather exasperatedly posed the question to the electorate, 'Who Governs?'[19] The petulant question was posed owing to the increasing powers of the miners' union. The answer received from the electorate was an ambiguous hung parliament, leading to a minority government formed by Labour leader Harold Wilson.

Thatcherite politics, by contrast, was able to quell very decisively working-class agitational politics, and this was most evident in Mrs Thatcher's crushing defeat of the miners led by the once-powerful trade unionist Arthur Scargill. It was the same Mr Scargill who had humbled a Tory grandee like Edward Heath in 1972. What Mrs Thatcher did to the miners during the 1984–1985 miners' strike was so different to what the miners were able to do to a previous Conservative government under Heath in 1972. Obviously, the crushing defeat inflicted by Mrs Thatcher created an almost vehement hatred towards her among large sections of the working class. It also opened up the possibility of a very curious connection between Thatcherism and the working class that needs to be investigated and that arose from the proximity of the petit-bourgeois social basis of Thatcherism with the working class. Thatcherite politics played a strange kind of bridging mechanism with the working class, the material for which it derived from Methodism, and which, unlike most bridging mechanisms, did not have much possibility of reconciliation within it. Reconciliation was never a forte of Thatcherite politics anyway.

Before proceeding further, it is important to point out that Methodism played a significant role in the working class and also the Labour Party. J.A. Jaffe, in an important article, notes how the 'history of Methodism is inextricably linked to the history of the British working class'. His paper analyses what is characterized as one of the 'most dramatic events of early nineteenth-century British history that witnessed the convergence of Methodism and working-class agitation' in the form of the Durham and Northumberland miners' strike of 1831–1832. Jaffe argues that the strike was significant as approximately 10,000 miners, located over 50 different collieries and spread over an area of 350 square miles, were able to achieve their objectives.[20] Despite the strong influence that Methodism played in the working class, it also created a set of hostile attitudes towards them from the classes above. This is amply reflected in the politics of Thatcherism, where there is a distinct tendency to disdain and excoriate the supposed laziness and idleness of the working class. Despite the apparent distancing excoriation, the influence of Methodism, historically speaking, did uniformly create loyalty towards the Establishment in both the working class and the adjacent lower-middle class.

This uniformity, in terms of simultaneous loyalty to the Establishment yet disparagement towards its poshness, is just one aspect of the strange bridging mechanism created by Methodism. Perhaps an even more crucial aspect of the bridge, which is more relevant for our consideration of Thatcherite politics, is its optically illusory encouragement of one-way traffic out of the decrepitude of the working class and into the neat respectability of the lower middle class, if not further beyond. It is illusory owing to its encouragement of the vision of upward mobility for the working class, yet blind to the precarious positioning of people who can, at any time, fall into deep financial and social troubles.

The illusory bridging mechanism created by Thatcherism suggests that there is no reason why anyone should remain working class. With hard work, and again the idea of 'an honest day's pay for an honest day's work', people can determinedly pull themselves up by their own bootstraps. This attitude is further typical of neoliberal politics, which tends to deny the very existence of the working class, suggesting that the only class that exists in isolation is the middle class, which makes it a kind of 'class of no class'.[21] The absurdity of a class existing in isolation is brought out at the very beginning of E.P. Thompson's book *The Making of the English Class*, when he suggests that class is an inherently relational concept. A class is a middle class in relation to a working class below and an upper class above. In Thompson's own words: 'Moreover, we cannot have two distinct classes, each with an independent being, and then bring them into relationship with each other'.[22]

In electoral terms, what this Thatcherite bridging mechanism does is to guarantee the continuing electoral success of the Conservative Party. The Conservative

34 The Thatcherite prelude to Brexit

Party, through its long periods of being in power, has come to be viewed as the natural party of governance in Britain. In contrast, the Labour Party's periods in power seem to look almost like isolated, island-like interludes. Historically, the preponderance of the Conservatives, in terms of their ability to be voted into power, is bolstered by two sets of working-class voters who tend to swing towards them and apparently at odds with their class interests. On the one hand are a small and perhaps increasingly disappearing set of 'deference voters', working class in their origin but likely to support Conservatives as the men who have the ability to run the country as they are the gentlemen of the ruling class. On the other is the 'aspiring voter', again working class, but likely to be lured by the brighter prospects of advancement that Conservatives have on offer and hoping to see themselves catapulted into the ranks of the middle class and out of their present working-class conditions.[23] This kind of 'aspiring voter' from the working class may have proved especially important for Mrs Thatcher's particular brand of politics.

Thatcherism as a break from one-nation Conservatism

Within the Conservative Party, the Thatcherite takeover of the party can be contrasted with the older, grander Tory tradition inspired by the nineteenth-century Benjamin Disraeli, with its spirit of *noblesse oblige*, which undergirds the idea of one-nation Conservatism. The purpose here is not to, in any way, valorize the *noblesse oblige* in one-nation Conservatism, but to contrast that more paternalistic attitude towards the working class, with the changed attitude towards the working class fostered through the politics of Thatcherism that makes it generally more antagonistic and hostile. Such aggression and hostility is enough to cleave the very possibility of one nation into two nations, which Thatcherism has been accused of. The divide is one characterized by polar oppositions of the good and bad, giving variations such as 'productive/parasitic, rich/poor, North/South, employed/unemployed, etc.'. Jessop et al. observe that, far from making at least the minimal attempt earlier at acknowledging and integrating the less privileged through 'one nation' Toryism, there was instead something else that happened under Thatcherism:

> Increasingly Tory populism is taking the form of unification of a privileged nation of "good citizens" and "hard workers" against a contained and subordinate nation which extends beyond the inner cities and their ethnic minorities to include much of the non-skilled working class outside the South East.[24]

The Thatcherite cleaving into two nations is worsened with a further cruel condemnation of the other half. This would often take the form of Mrs Thatcher pointing to scroungers, those despicable individuals who lacked the self-esteem and self-respect to go out and look for a job, preferring to idle their time away at state expense. The pursuit of the scrounger was taken up by one of Mrs Thatcher's most loyal ministers, Norman Tebbit, when, in 2011, he felt the unemployed should get on their bikes and look for work, an idea he first talked about in 1981, when he recalled his father never complaining about unemployment in the 1930s and getting on his bike to look for work.[25] Echoing similar sentiments in late 2012, Chancellor of the Exchequer George Osborne, of grinding austerity fame, took recourse to the old distinction between 'strivers' and 'skivers'. The strivers were the honest individuals who were up early in the morning and were well on their way to work, by which time the 'skivers' had still got their curtains drawn and were snugly asleep under their duvets.[26]

The kind of hostility fostered towards the working class is effectively captured by Owen Jones in his highly readable book, *Chavs: The Demonisation of the Working Class*.[27] The acronym Chavs when expanded becomes Council housed and violent. Notice here the attitude towards public council housing, as if it were the festering sore from which the undesirability of the working class emerges. It is no accident then that one of the early and major components of the Thatcherite project was the sale of public council housing and the consequent privatization of housing in the efforts to create a property-owning democracy that, just a few years later, would be combined with the idea of a shareholding democracy, as major British public utilities such as British Telecom and British Gas started to be sold off.

The literature on Thatcherism: From culturalist 'authoritarian populism' to the political economy of 'failed Fordism'

The literature and analysis that has developed around Thatcherism on the British Left has been distinguished and of an exceptionally high intellectual quality. Perry Anderson, in an extensive survey of the effects of Thatcherism on the intelligentsia and academia, has suggested that the political adversity of those years led to the emergence of 'the liveliest republic of letters in European socialism'.[28] The term Thatcherism was itself coined by Stuart Hall, whose other major contribution to the understanding of Thatcherism is the term 'authoritarian populism'. Despite the high intellectual quality of the analysis, there was a tendency for a Gramscian and hence overly cultural understanding of Thatcherism to prevail. In terms of the class basis of Thatcherism, the fact that this was very different from earlier, more upper-class, one-nation Conservatism was an aspect that initially the Gramscian analysis captured. This largely Gramscian analysis was also able to effectively train the focus on the social terrain of Thatcherism, arising from where the petit-bourgeois, lower middle class shaded off into the upper layers of the working class, just below it.[29]

Yet, the use of the Gramscian theoretical lens and its concept of hegemony imparted in the analysis an excessive element of 'ideologism'. This excessively cultural tilt was corrected by the intervention of Bob Jessop et al. by taking issue with the concept of 'authoritarian populism' put forward by Stuart Hall. The question that Jessop et al. were asking was less to do with the actual emergence of Thatcherism, but what made it continue. This was despite the far-from-glorious start that the Thatcher premiership had got off to. In the first two years of Mrs Thatcher's

36 The Thatcherite prelude to Brexit

first term in office, unemployment was rising and inflation far from under control, and there were the infamous summer urban riots in Toxteth in Liverpool and Brixton in London. While not entirely dismissive of the concept of authoritarian populism and the Gramscian theoretical framework from where it arose, Jessop et al. felt that it had been stretched too much, resulting in its being 'overused in discussing Thatcherism'.[30]

Among the many advantages of Jessop's intervention was that it enhanced the conceptual and theoretical repertoire by bringing in the formulations of the Greek structural Marxist Nicos Poulantzas. What was now illuminated was the distinct nature of the British state, the different classes and fractions of capital that provided the props to Thatcherism, the room for manoeuvre that the relative autonomy of the British state gave to Mrs Thatcher, thereby bringing out the interesting and crucial 'Bonaparte in petticoats' aspect of the phenomenon. More importantly, Jessop was able to bring in the uniqueness of the British transition from Fordism to post-Fordism, in fact, to look at the plight of Britain arising from the country's 'failed Fordism'.[31]

In terms of the transition to post-Fordism, Henk Overbeek's writings stepped in to highlight the difference in the British experience and phase of Fordism from that of the US and Europe. Fordism was more prolonged and drawn out and hence more influential in the US, where it was introduced much before the Second World War. The impact of Fordism was more decisive and indeed more dramatic in Western Europe in the immediate aftermath of the Second World War, as the economies of Western Europe were more drastically transformed by the impact of the Second World War, thereby creating the conditions for a rapid phase of economic growth. The Fordist transformation of Britain was not so decisive, and this finds expression in a number of 'specificities' unique to Britain and one of the most important consequences of which was that the overall productivity and economic growth lagged far behind more dynamic economies such as West Germany and Japan. These specificities, according to Overbeek, were first, the heterogeneity of the productive apparatus leading to an accumulation of problems in the essential sector of the production of the means of production; second, the separation between banking capital and industrial capital; third, the inefficiency and paralysis of the state; and fourth, the originality of industrial relations and the trade union practices of the British salariat (wage earners).[32]

Thatcher's monetarism reconsidered

Thatcher's monetarism had a uniqueness of its own. The idea of monetarism argues that controlling inflation should be the priority of economic policy rather than full employment, which Keynesianism seemed to emphasize, so much so that it was willing to tolerate a mild degree of inflation. By contrast, there has been an almost militant zeal to contain inflation in monetarism. There has been a tendency of equating monetarism with Thatcherism with the consequence 'that Margaret Thatcher continued to be attacked for being in hock to the theory long after its ideologues were mourning the fact that her government had wandered off the monetarist path'.[33]

Monetarism was not brought into UK economic policy by Mrs Thatcher, and there were elements of what most certainly were monetarism in the policies of the Labour Chancellor of the Exchequer, Denis Healey, in James Callaghan's government of the late 1970s. Healey's recourse to Monetarist measures was a more tactical one compared to the more conviction-oriented touting of Thatcher's monetarism. Even then, the most striking observations of the monetarism that preceded Thatcher's rule have been provided by the political journalist Peter Riddell, who argued: 'If there was a Thatcher experiment it was launched by Denis Healey'.[34] Similarly, Henk Overbeek argues that it is justified to conclude that the essentials of the Thatcher government's later monetary strategy were already contained in Denis Healey's letter of intent to the International Monetary Fund in December 1976.[35] The important conditions of the $3.5 billion IMF loan extended to Britain were the maintenance of high interest rates to attract foreign funds, sizeable cuts in public spending, stern wage restraints and the sale of $500 million worth of government-held shares in British Petroleum. All this sounds very much like the subsequent recipe for Thatcherism.

If one went even further back to 1958, the resignation of Chancellor Peter Thorneycroft, Financial Secretary Enoch Powell and Economic Secretary to the Treasury Nigel Birch from Harold Macmillan's Conservative government would be an even earlier instance of a monetarist stirring against the dominance of Keynesianism. The resignation of these three individuals resulted from their demand for a further £50 million reduction of public expenditure beyond what the cabinet had decided. The role of Enoch Powell is significant, as he was one of those individuals who consistently championed free markets and monetarism in the 1960s and was admired by none other than the economist and ideologue of monetarism, Milton Friedman himself.[36] Enoch Powell forms a kind of important and interesting precursor to the politics of Thatcherism, made more intriguing by the fact that he left the Conservative Party in February 1974, the year before Thatcher's elevation to the party leadership. In a chapter that he contributed to a volume edited by Denis Kavanagh and Anthony Seldon, *The Thatcher Effect*, Powell suggests that, as a result of his much talked about relinquishing of Conservative Party membership and his backing of the Labour Party, he has 'no direct knowledge of events or movements of opinion within that party after Mrs Thatcher was elected leader a year later'. He does, however, try to trace up to the year of his leaving, those 'antecedents of tendencies and changes in government policy' that have become more manifest and obvious in the Thatcher premiership.[37] Not surprisingly, Powell has much to say about monetarism. He further connects monetarism to the ability of the Thatcher government being able to bring under control the earlier dominance of the trade unions, for which of course he expresses profound admiration.

Given the combination of Methodism and Monetarism that has been talked about, it almost seems as if Mrs Thatcher's political philosophy and economic ideas assumed the form of a religious belief derived from an unread book. In 1975, on a

38 The Thatcherite prelude to Brexit

visit to the Conservative Research Department, Mrs Thatcher interrupted a presentation by someone who was arguing for a pragmatic steering of a middle path to avoid the extremes of left and right. She reached into her suitcase, took out a copy of Friedrich Hayek's book *The Constitution of Liberty* and displayed it to everyone. She proclaimed that this was what they believed in, before proceeding to slam the book down on the table.[38]

Europe: so near, yet so far

Thatcher's Conservative predecessor, Edward Heath, was enthusiastic about Britain joining Europe. In the decade of the 1960s, there was great opposition to the idea of Britain entering the EEC, and this opposition came from across the English Channel, most famously in the form of France's Charles de Gaulle. What is it about Europe that makes Britain want to so much turn its back on the continent and look increasingly towards the United States across the Atlantic? The answer may well be a deep-seated, almost atavistic desire to continue to rule the waves, far beyond Albion's shores, and of course much beyond the continent of Europe, which becomes a mere myopic barrier to such far-reaching ambitions. There coexists with this tendency the desire to withdraw into a Little England, the one characterized by a bucolic ideal of 'the country of long church shadows on county (cricket) grounds, warm beer, invincible green suburbs, dog lovers and pool fillers'.[39]

Ironically, there is hidden within the politics of Brexit two contradictory and almost irreconcilable tendencies. There is, on the one hand, the little England tendency, which, in Mrs Thatcher's case, would be her idealization of her father's grocery shop in the Lincolnshire town of Grantham. On the other hand, there is the 'rule Britannia' sentiment and its swashbuckling desire to revive the glory of the British Empire and ensure the continuation of Britain's extended role across the globe. In the Brexit view, this extension of Britain's influence across the globe must not be mediated by membership in the EU. However, it would have no problem seeing an extension of this role even if it meant, riding subordinated to the coattails of the United States.

As a result of these two conflicting tendencies, there seems to be an inability among Brexiteers to reconcile themselves to living in good neighbourly proximity with Europe. The famous Roman Emperor and Stoic philosopher Marcus Aurelius had the following advice to give, which might sum up the unhappiness of many Brexiteers: 'Adapt yourself to the environment in which your lot has been cast, and show true love to the fellow mortals with whom destiny has surrounded you'.[40] The problem of Brexit seems to be one of not wanting to live cheek by jowl with Europe and to not have immigrants as neighbours, the frequent complaint being that there are just 'too many of them here', on an already crowded island. There seems almost a desire for the British Isles to float off across the Atlantic to be moored closer to America.

Graeme Smith, in his theological reading of Thatcher's politics, cites her 1977 Iain Macleod Memorial Lecture, where she talks about the Christian idea of 'loving thy neighbour as thyself'. This idea is especially evident at the rooted level of the local community of which one is a part. In its outward extension, the idea, in Thatcher's view, is bounded by national culture. Beyond the bounds of the national culture, it tends not to embrace the whole of humanity and emphasizes instead in a more particularistic manner cultural bonds such as the Anglo-Saxon one between Britain and the US. As a result of this shared cultural bonding, the EU is not favourably looked upon by Mrs Thatcher, even though it is more proximate in geographical terms. Smith notes: 'In other words, the limits of the individual's neighbourly responsibilities are cultural rather than geographical, based, rather dangerously, on the idea of those others who are recognized as fellow human beings'.[41]

The central axis that undergirds the EU is, of course, Paris–Berlin, and somehow London just doesn't seem to fit as rivalries with the French and the Germans keep surfacing. One aspect of the rivalry that this chapter will emphasize is the question of manufacturing industry, which, it is suggested, is one of the key issues to understand Brexit itself. British manufacturing was at the height of its powers when the sun never set on the British Empire. However, as the twentieth century progressed, especially in its second half, and as the Empire was gradually wound up, what also regressed and declined was British manufacturing. After the Second World War, the rise of US hegemony may have rankled for the British in the beginning, but pales in comparison to the resentment created by the advance of West German and Japanese manufacturing industries that, in their export-drivenness, ate into the US and UK markets.

The crisis of the British industry became especially acute in the 1970s, and the winter of discontent of 1978 is widely, but perhaps not entirely correctly, understood as the last straw that heralded Mrs Thatcher's entry as Prime Minister. Mrs Thatcher's solution to the crisis of Britain's economy, especially the one that stemmed from manufacturing, can be captured in five words: 'Stop making and start doing'. Mrs Thatcher, in order to throw out the bathwater of trade unionism that was so much the bugbear of Conservative governments, also threw away the baby of manufacturing. Britain's prosperous future was envisioned on the back of financial services, and the 1986 Big Bang reforms of the City of London captured this.

The politics of Thatcher in the UK and Reagan across the Atlantic in the US was to transform these advanced industrial economies into even more advanced, post-industrial economies. The prosperity of these two societies throughout the decades of the 1980s, 1990s and all the way up to the financial crisis of 2007 was to be built on the fleeting back of financial services rather than the solid footing of manufacturing industry. That seemed to have been left to the losers of the Second World War and the laggards of the industrial revolution, Japan and West Germany. The Thatcherite prelude to Brexit seemed to be set in the decline of manufacturing and deliberate deindustrialization that this politics entailed.

The Iron Lady's myopic short-termism

Despite Mrs Thatcher's cultivated image of a determined Iron Lady who would not brook any sign of weakness such as dependence on the state, Thatcherite politics

40 The Thatcherite prelude to Brexit

created a nagging short-termism that has been detrimental to long-term economic advantage. This is most obvious in an area where Mrs Thatcher's government was just plain lucky when it came to manage a beleaguered economy such as the British one. The proceeds from North Sea oil production, which, in the year 1985 had peaked to above £20 billion, were used by Mrs Thatcher in that particular obsession of right-wing economics of balancing the budget, rather than investing in the faltering infrastructure of early 1980s Britain. The proceeds from North Sea oil were a stroke of good fortune for Mrs Thatcher, something that was not available to her predecessors or her successors. The success that has been attributed to her as a major western politician needs to take this windfall into account. There is merit to the argument that the money from North Sea oil production was squandered and as one view rather crudely put it, 'pissed it up against the wall'. The 1994 Channel 4 documentary 'Wasted Windfall' also captured effectively in its title the way in which Thatcher's Britain allowed a remarkable opportunity for the regeneration of industry and infrastructure to just pass by without any sign being left behind, except for a rather sordid legacy. The short-termism displayed by the Thatcher government failed to secure a better, brighter future for the UK.

The best way to contrast what the UK did with North Sea oil would be to look at the other major North Sea Oil producer, Norway.[42] Norway invested part of its North Sea oil revenue to create a national pension fund that had grown by the year 2008, when the world economy was being roiled by the financial crisis, to 2 trillion Kroner.[43] In the Brexit debate, Leavers have often expressed the desire of being like Norway when it comes to not being part of the EU. Leavers also tend to be ardent, almost fanatical free marketeers, and it is unlikely that they would agree with the manner in which Norway handled its North Sea oil proceeds with a far more dirigiste role through its state-owned company Statoil.[44]

Revisiting Thatcher's Britain of 1986

If there is one year during Mrs Thatcher's premiership that can be taken as decisive to the course that British capitalism took and which would also set the terms of the Brexit debate, then it is 1986, exactly three decades before the year of the fateful Brexit referendum in 2016. One of Shane Meadows' *This is England* movies is set in 1986, when, a mere four years after the euphoria created by the victory over Argentina in the Falklands War, Diego Maradona's Argentina beat England in the FIFA World Cup held in Mexico through his infamous 'hand of god' goal.[45] Meadows' movie bleakly depicts the depressing and dysfunctional lives of a set of youngsters in an unidentified midlands town, far away from the swagger and excitement that London was about to witness in the same year as a result of the Big Bang financial reforms that would catapult the City of London into becoming the world's largest financial centre. This section of the chapter will look at three separate events in the year 1986 in order to understand the year better and the decisive role that it played in the unfolding of recent British history. These are the Westland Helicopter affair in January, the opening of the Nissan car plant in Sunderland in the north east of England in September and the October Big Bang reforms in the City of London.

The Westland affair

The year 1986 itself opened rather disastrously for Mrs Thatcher. The glorious victory over the Argentinians in the Falklands War, which helped her win a second election, seemed to be far away, and even the victory at the end of the yearlong miners' strike in March 1985 was paling. The crisis for Mrs Thatcher was over the embattled Westland Helicopters, a small company located in Yeovil in the southwest of England, and two rival takeover bids. One was from across the Atlantic in the form of the American helicopter company Sikorsky and the other was across the English Channel, from a European-backed consortium. The crisis over Westland Helicopters had been brewing since October 1985 but was to really come to a head in January 1986. Mrs Thatcher herself was in favour of the American helicopter firm Sikorksy, although she denies this in her memoirs. Her great rival in the Cabinet, Defense Secretary Michael Heseltine, was backing the European bid and, to his detractors at least, was doing so to the point of obsession.[46] Heseltine's concern seemed to be that the American takeover would undermine the manufacturing capacity of a British company. This particular concern about protecting and promoting British manufacturing by tilting towards Europe has, in fact, had a consistent quality in Heseltine and was reiterated almost three decades later in the report commissioned by the David Cameron government, which he wrote, called *No Stone Unturned*.[47]

The Westland controversy led to two significant cabinet resignations that really shook Mrs Thatcher's government, almost endangering her Prime Ministership. One was that of Heseltine himself and the other was the Thatcher faithful, the trade and industry secretary, Leon Brittan. Eric Evans suggests that it is reasonable to date the background of Mrs Thatcher's ultimate downfall not to 1990, the year of her resignation, but to 1986, the year of the Westland controversy.[48]

Mrs Thatcher was quick to dismiss the Westland affair as a storm in a teacup, brewing perhaps with political egos. Henk Overbeek, in an insightful article on the Westland affair, has argued that it is important not to look at the episode as a mere clash of egos and personalities in the Thatcher cabinet, but more decisively as an event that was to determine the course that British capitalism took. The course taken was a further distancing from continental Europe as a potential market for British manufactured goods and a greater inspiration from American capitalism. This distancing from Europe and the leaning towards the US has been a significant and recurrent theme in British foreign and industrial policy and is another instance of the Thatcherite prelude to Brexit.

Those who have advocated a greater leaning and openness to Europe have argued that the benefits of this would accrue to domestic British manufacturing as the goods produced would find a ready market in Europe. They have been the voices that have represented the interests of British manufacturing, and this

42 The Thatcherite prelude to Brexit

would have implied a strategy for rationalization, modernization and hence re-industrialization of British industry. Within the Conservative Party, this would very much be the consistent position taken by the pro-Europe Michael Heseltine.

The strategy upheld by Mrs Thatcher and most of the rest of her cabinet was of not doing much about British manufacturing, allowing the running down of traditional manufacturing industries located especially in the North, and emphasizing instead the interest of internationally oriented British capital in the City of London and high-technology services more generally in the south-east. Overbeek is quick to emphasize that 'the populist appeal of Thatcherism should not blind us to the fact that beneath the surface the fractional interests of circulating capital were more directly served by the rise to power of Thatcherism than those of any other fraction'.[49] Pointing to the distinction between capital engaged in production and capital engaged in circulation, Overbeek has argued that the post-Fordist transition of the 1970s was a transition from productive capital to circulating capital, and Mrs Thatcher represents in the crudest form the dominance of the latter circulating money capital.

The Westland affair underlines Mrs Thatcher's determination to take Britain down the road of a capitalism premised more on the vagaries of money, circulation and finance (circulating capital) rather than a sturdier capitalism built upon the foundations of manufacturing and industry (productive capitalism). Interestingly, in 1985, the very year in which the Westland affair exploded on the British political scene, a select committee of the House of Lords 'came to conclusions which were devastating for the economic policies of the Thatcher government and called for "urgent action" in order to "revive manufacturing and stimulate trade in manufactured goods"'.[50]

After all the ructions that it created, the Westland affair seemed to melt away in the early part of 1986 with the board of the helicopter company voting in favour of the American-backed Sikorsky bid. In the cauldron of the controversy, an interesting Indian role needs to be mentioned, perhaps as an aside. In her memoirs, Mrs Thatcher mentions that in early October 1985 her trade and industry secretary Leon Brittan had made a thorough assessment of the Westland Helicopters situation and had warned that if the issue was not resolved by the end of November, then the company would go into receivership. Mrs Thatcher writes that Leon Brittan 'urged me to take up the issue of India's proposed helicopter order with Rajiv Gandhi when he visited Britain in October'.[51] The Indian government duly obliged by placing a £65 million order in December 1985 for 21 helicopters, just before Christmas, even as the political crisis in the UK was reaching a tipping point. The money itself came out of Britain's aid budget and seemed to be tied to the purchase of the helicopters. Very soon after this, in April 1986, the Indian government bought the British Naval Carrier HMS Hermes for $63 million.[52] HMS Hermes was commissioned into the Indian navy as INS Viraat in May 1987 and had seen action in the Falklands War of 1982 and was decommissioned by the Royal Navy in 1985.

Then, almost three decades later, there was a ghost-like reappearance of Westland Helicopters when controversy arose in early 2013 over the Indian government's placing of orders from what had now become Agusta Westland, a reincarnation of the earlier helicopter company that was now owned by the Italian firm Finmeccanica.[53] This time, the political storm was to erupt in India and was to add to the increasing woes of the Manmohan Singh-led United Progressive Alliance (UPA) II government as it was to be accused of corruption that would lead on to a huge electoral defeat, the next year in 2014.

The Nissan car plant in Sunderland

The same year, on 11 September 1986, much before that date was to acquire synonymy with the World Trade Centre attacks in New York, the Japanese car manufacturer Nissan opened a plant in Sunderland in the north-east of England. John Holloway, in an article on the setting up of the car manufacturing plant, echoing points about the flawed Fordism of Britain made by Bob Jessop and Henk Overbeek, observes that the nature of Thatcherism is of a transitional type of government that is well-suited to destroying the vestiges of Fordism/Keynesianism but would fall short of being able to provide the basis of a post-Fordist state.[54] The really interesting part of Holloway's article, however, is the analogy that he makes between changing managerial strategies at the beleaguered British Leyland car manufacturer throughout the 1970s and early 1980s to the setting up of the Nissan car plant in 1986 and the British state in this same period. Holloway suggests that the British state under Mrs Thatcher was borrowing, almost copying, these strategies with management leading and the state following.

The analysis begins in 1974 and the commissioning by the Labour government of a report by Sir Don Ryder, chairman of the National Enterprise Board. The Ryder Plan was published in April 1975 and acknowledged in typically Keynesian fashion of affirming trade union power, the strength of the shop stewards within British Leyland. It sought the cooperation of the shop stewards with management through a process called 'mutuality', whereby management would necessarily have to get the agreement of the unions for every technical change introduced. The strategy of the Ryder Plan had a clear parallel with the Social Contract of the mid-1970s, the parallel lying in the attempt in both to placate and accommodate the powerful trade unions. It was precisely in this placation and accommodation that union power was hollowed out. By 1977, when it was clear that the Ryder Plan was not working in terms of increasing productivity, a more openly aggressive 'macho management' style was introduced in October 1977 with the appointment of Michael Edwardes as Chairman and Chief Executive of British Leyland. There was an aggression, almost a ruthlessness, in terms of the assertion of the management's prerogatives and powers, ending the process and practice of mutuality mentioned earlier. This aggression, Holloway suggests, clearly foreshadows Thatcher's own Iron Lady determination variant of crushing the miners' union in 1984.

44 The Thatcherite prelude to Brexit

The Big Bang reforms in the city

Finally, the last instance taken from the year 1986 is a consideration of the 27 October reforms, which resulted in the city of London becoming the world's largest financial centre. The city has been treated with kid gloves by successive governments, especially from Thatcher onwards and notably by New Labour under both Tony Blair and Gordon Brown. It has almost been treated like the golden goose that promises to lay so many golden eggs in the form of ever-higher tax receipts that the government receives from the vibrancy, vitality and competitiveness of its financial markets and trading activities.

The ability of the City of London to reinvent itself and remain relevant as a major international financial centre is quite a remarkable story. This becomes especially so, keeping in mind the story of the continuous decline of domestic British economy. The contrast between an economically depressed hinterland and a vibrant capital city suggests a mismatch and a widening gap as the ever-dynamic London seems to pull away from the deadweight of its hinterlands.[55] The story would actually be of London being created very deliberately into some kind of offshore haven whose very vibrant existence is premised on and promoted by the laggard quality of its midlands and northern hinterlands.

In 1963, the German Jewish banker Siegmund Warburg created a huge market in Eurobonds, which have nothing to do with the currency Euros, which of course was a good four decades away from being formed. Eurobonds emerged on account of regulations that existed in the US and as a result of which the London market provided significant opportunities for trading in dollars. London and its Eurobond market provided the possibility of investment and raising funds for many major European projects. All this happened despite the prevalence of exchange controls in the UK that did not, however, prevent trade in non-sterling business. The exchange control restrictions were to be lifted 16 years after 1963, in the year 1979, constituting one of the earliest decisions taken by Chancellor Geoffrey Howe under the first Thatcher government, allowing Britons to bring in and out of the country larger sums of money. In this manner, two years, 1963 and 1979, immediately stand out as prominent in the re-emergence of London as the world's leading financial centre after the Second World War.

The October 1986 Big Bang Reforms were themselves an outcome of decisions taken in 1983, when the Thatcher government had been voted back into power for a second term. One of the most significant aspects of these reforms was the introduction of new computerized trading, and this was to open the kinds of possibilities that the initiators of the reforms themselves could not have fathomed at the time. Mrs Thatcher herself seems to have understood little of the implications of the major reforms that would be in the offing. It was the conservative politician and member of the Thatcher cabinet, Cecil Parkinson, who took the early vital decisions that created the possibilities of the Big Bang. Intriguingly, the Big Bang Reforms have become synonymous with Thatcherite deregulation of free markets. The obscenely high amounts of money-making that the Big Bang reforms created may have unnerved the Methodist instincts of Mrs Thatcher and her dictum of an 'honest day's pay for an honest day's work'. Memos released after 30 years reveal the debates that went on in Mrs Thatcher's policy unit where concerns about financial instability, 'boom and bust', getting rich quickly and making money unscrupulously were aired.[56] She is known to have voiced her concerns about this, but certainly never enough to put this gigantic, financial bubble of a genie back into its bottle. It seemed to be fulfilling the promise of making Britain rich, great and important in the world all over again, and that seemed too tempting a prospect to shun. Surely, the grounded nature of an 'honest day's pay' could be set aside for launching the greatness of Britain all over again on the back of a financial bubble.

The success of the City of London is of a piece with a general British sentiment that seems to have set in after the Second World War and the loss of Empire, which is to latch on to the slightest signs of the 'world beating' quality of British enterprise. The success of the City of London would be one of the more prominent instances of this obsession with 'world beating'. The satisfaction derived does not consider the cost that success may have for other sectors of British life. Despite the lionization of the City of London as contributing so many jobs and providing so much revenue from taxation, there is ample evidence that the bloated nature of Britain's financial sector is actually harmful to the rest of the economy.[57] Stephen G. Cechetti and Enisse Kharroub raise questions about the almost definitive manner in which it is accepted that finance is good for growth. In much the same manner that a person who eats too much, could it be the case that a bloated financial system becomes a drag on the economy and draws talented people who could have been scientists into becoming hedge fund managers?[58]

The Big Bang Reforms, the financial deregulation and the creation of London into the foremost financial centre in the world are usually looked upon as reflective of the dynamism that Thatcherite politics unleashed in an economy that was widely considered the sick man of Europe towards the end of the 1970s. The Reforms are themselves connected to the wave of privatizations of state enterprises unleashed by the Thatcher government, especially the sale of British Gas, which happened just after the Big Bang. The city thus complemented these often mammoth sales of shares to the public by readily offering its expertise in the area. A quite remarkable aspect of Thatcherite reforms, especially in the sale of public enterprises and the Big Bang financial reforms, is how British companies and conglomerates have been often sidelined. Large swathes of former public utilities are thus owned by foreign hands as a result of privatization. The same can be the story of the city of London, where once British-owned banks have been taken over one after the other, by foreign ones. The most curious case would be Warburg Bank itself, started by Siegmund Warburg, the man who created the Eurobond market and set the ball rolling for the revival of London's fortunes as the world's financial capital after the Second World War. In May 1995, Warburg was sold to Swiss Bank Corp for $1.37 billion. Siegmund Warburg had himself died by this time.[59]

Inevitably, the Big Bang reforms are bound to be seen through the prism of the 2007 financial crisis and the austerity that was imposed as result of the colossal

46 The Thatcherite prelude to Brexit

failures of the banks, who famously, because they were too big, could not be allowed to fail.

Curtains for the Thatcher Prime Ministership

It was the issue of Europe which brought down the Thatcher government. The speech that really signalled the end of her long 11 years as Prime Minister came from her Foreign Secretary Geoffrey Howe. The British media had for long caricatured Howe as someone who, owing to his mild-mannered nature, was prone to being bullied by Margaret Thatcher. The 18-minute speech that Howe delivered in early November 1990 deserves close attention, especially for what it has to say about Mrs Thatcher's increasingly impetuous attitude towards Europe. There was much that Howe had to say on monetary policy and what he believed was the Thatcher government's successful fight against inflation. He began striking a critical note on the question of Britain's membership of the Exchange Rate Mechanism (ERM) of the European monetary system that he had always been in favour of and which he believed that Britain had been late in joining. The ERM was a range or band between which European currencies were allowed to fluctuate and which Howe felt was a further external help in controlling inflation that would supplement the many domestic decisions that had been taken in this regard. The ERM was itself part of the wider scheme of European Monetary Union (EMU) and the preparing of the grounds for the introduction of a single European currency. Britain was to crash out of the ERM in September 1992, just a little before the signing of the Maastricht treaty.

Every single word of Howe's speech holds true for Brexit, close to three decades after it was delivered. Howe raised the issue of Britain's early dithering with respect to Europe, as a result of which the country was unable to bring its influence to bear on the framing of the rules and principles of the EC. Invoking the former Conservative Prime Minister Harold Macmillan, Howe warned against the dangers of retreating into a 'ghetto of sentimentality about our past and so diminish our own control over our destiny in the future'. Those are ringing words, which should perhaps be heeded by contemporary Brexiteers. Howe accused Mrs Thatcher of creating a 'nightmare image' of Europe, and he was especially critical of Thatcher's tendency to depict Europe as 'teeming with ill-intentioned people' and 'scheming, in her own words, to "extinguish democracy"'.

Howe seemed particularly perturbed by Mrs Thatcher's intransigence on and outright dismissal of ultimate monetary union. He suggests that he was not necessarily in favour of a future single currency, but he was more concerned about Britain being actively involved in all manner of negotiations. Mrs Thatcher's position seemed to be one of giving up the option of shaping a European future by simply not being part of it, another clear instance of the Thatcherite prelude to Brexit. Howe seems to complain about the Iron Lady's almost ironic indecisiveness on monetary union, of a kicking of the can down the road of the future when he says 'it was extraordinary to hear her assert that the whole idea of EMU might be open for consideration only by future generations'. Howe, in the very next sentence, adds – very pertinently it must be said – 'Those future generations are with us today'. A little later there is a warning that may prove relevant as Britain has engaged in protracted negotiations with the EU over a trade deal. In the warning, Howe took recourse to a cricketing metaphor by suggesting that when it came to negotiations with Europe, Mrs Thatcher's attitude seemed to be one of sending the opening batsmen out to the crease, only for the batsmen to discover before the first ball had been bowled that their bats had been broken by the team captain. The current team captain, Boris Johnson, another cricket enthusiast, seems to have done precisely that, of breaking bats to prevent the possibility of any possible trade deal with the EU. It goes without saying that a no-deal Brexit may have appeared, very true to Boris Johnson's immature persona of a child-like petulance of crying out that his team was not interested in playing any more.

Howe raised the issue of sovereignty, and the current crude Brexit obsession with a rather simplistic notion of sovereignty, as taking back control appears particularly stark and denuded. Howe suggested it was too simplistic to think in terms of 'surrendering sovereignty' and warned against looking at the European enterprise as 'some kind of zero sum game'.[60] It may be that tendency among Brexiteers that makes them look at the EU as an all or nothing extremity: of either one extremity of being ensnared in the clutches of a European super state or to just cut and run and thereby assert an absolute British sovereignty. With the current Brexit obsession of 'taking back control' and the invocation of an almost absolute sovereignty, there is the very real possibility of Britain being continuously denuded of influence. The more thoroughly Britain invokes an uncompromising stance on sovereignty, the less influential and consequential she is likely to become. Geoffrey Howe died in October 2015, a little over two and a half years after Margaret Thatcher's death.

Notes

1 This is from the title of Robert Chesshyre's book *When the Iron Lady Ruled*, Revised and Expanded Edition, Alma Books, Richmond, Surrey, 2012.
2 David Willets, 'How Thatcher's Bruges speech put Britain on the road to Brexit: she believed that the vision of a "social Europe was a bridge too far', *Financial Times*, 31 August 2018. www.ft.com/content/0b0afe92-ac40-11e8-8253-48106866cd8a. Accessed 27 January 2021.
3 www.bbc.co.uk/worldservice/learningenglish/specials/2013/04/130417_thatcher_phrases.shtml. Accessed 24 June 2020.
4 Margaret Thatcher, *The Downing Street Years*, Harper Collins, London, 1995, pg. 536.
5 Derek Brown, 'Thatcher settles for 66pc rebate', *The Guardian*, 27 June 1984. www.theguardian.com/politics/1984/jun/27/past.eu. Accessed 27 January 2021.
6 Stuart Hall, 'The great moving right show', in Stuart Hall and Martin Jacques (eds.) *The Politics of Thatcherism*, Lawrence and Wishart, London, 1983, pgs. 29–30.
7 Adam Tooze, *Crashed: How a Decade of Financial Crises Changed the World*, Vintage, New York, 2018.
8 Quoted in Andy Beckett, *When the Lights Went Out: Britain in the Seventies*, Faber & Faber, London, 2009, pg. 280.

48 The Thatcherite prelude to Brexit

9 Richard Vinen, *Thatcher's Britain: The Politics and Social Upheaval of the 1980s*, Simon & Schuster, London, pg. 2.

10 Louisa Hadley and Elizabeth Ho (eds.), *Thatcher & After: Margaret Thatcher and Her Afterlife in Contemporary Culture*, Palgrave Macmillan, Basingstoke and New York, 2010, pg. 4.

11 Florence Sutcliffe-Braithwaite, 'Neo-liberalism and morality in the making of Thatcherite social policy', *The Historical Journal*, Vol. 55, No. 2 (June 2012), pgs. 497–520. https://www.jstor.org.stable/23263347?seq=1&cid=pdf-. Accessed 5 April 2021.

12 Nicholas Watt, 'David Cameron ignores Alastair Campbell's advice as he does God', *The Guardian*, Wednesday 27 April 2011. The article observes at the beginning: 'Prime Minister's pious Easter message contrasts with joke that his Christianity is like patchy reception of Magic FM'. www.theguardian.com/politics/wintour-and-watt/2011/apr/27/davidcameron-easter. Accessed 27 January 2021.

13 Brian Wheeler, 'Politicians, pulpits and god', *BBC News*. www.bbc.com/news/uk-politics-27112774. Accessed 12 June 2020.

14 Graeme Smith, 'Margaret Thatcher's Christian faith: a case study in political theology', *The Journal of Religious Ethics*, Vol. 35, No. 2 (June 2007), pgs. 233–257. https://www.jstor.org/stable/40014868. Accessed 5 April 2021. These significant observations are made by Smith at the beginning of his article on pg. 236 and play a vital role in the unfolding of the argument.

15   In terms of ethics and national economics, I should like to refer to what I believe is an evil; namely, sustained inflation. For over thirty years the value of our currency has been eroding. It is an insidious evil because its effects are slow to be seen and relatively painless in the short run. Yet it has a morally debilitating influence on all aspects of our national life. It reduces the value of savings, it undermines financial arrangements, it stimulates hostility between workers and employers over matters of pay, it encourages debts and it diminishes the prospects of jobs. . . . It is, in my view, a moral issue, not just an economic one.

(Margaret Thatcher quoted in Graeme Smith, 'Margaret Thatcher's Christian faith', pg. 243)

16 See E.P. Thompson, *The Making of the English Working Class*, First Vintage Edition, Vintage Books, New York, 1963. This is what Thompson has to say:

This surrender was implicit in Methodism's origin – in the Toryism of its founder and in his ambivalent attitude to the Established Church. From the outset, the Wesleyans fell ambiguously between Dissent and the Establishment, and did their utmost to make the worst of both worlds, serving as apologists for an authority in whose eyes they were an object of ridicule or condescension, but never of trust (pg. 350).

17 Henry D. Rack, 'A man of reason and religion? John Wesley and the enlightenment', *Wesley and Methodist Studies*, Vol. 1 (2009), pgs. 2–17. https://www.jstor.org/stable/42909772. Accessed 24 June 2020.

18 Most notably, Geoffrey Howe said that Mrs Thatcher had conjured up 'a nightmare image' of Europe. Even more striking was how he feared the 'very real tragedy' of the Prime Minister's 'attitude towards running increasingly serious risks for the future of our nation'. Perhaps most famous was how he ended: 'I've done what I believe to be right for my party and my country. The time has come for others to consider their own response to the tragic conflict of loyalties which I have, myself, wrestled for perhaps too long'. Olivia Blair, 'Geoffrey Howe dead: watch how the former Chancellor's historic resignation speech sparked the downfall of Thatcher', *The Independent*, Saturday 10 October 2015. www.independent.co.uk/news/uk/politics/geoffrey-howe-dead-watch-the-former-chancellor-s-historic-resignation-speech-a6688961.html. Accessed 20 June 2020.

19 Lewis Baston, 'Elections past: who governs?', *The Guardian*, 4 April 2005. www.theguardian.com/politics/2005/apr/04/electionspast.past9. Accessed 27 January 2021.

20 J.A. Jaffe, 'The "chiliasm of despair" reconsidered: revivalism and working-class agitation in county Durham', *Journal of British Studies*, Vol. 28, No. 1 (January 1989), pgs. 23–42. https://www.jstor.org/stable/175416. Accessed 5 April 2021. Jaffe makes these

observations on page 25 where he further notes: 'Between June 1831 and April 1832, the miners and their union leaders exercised an unprecedented degree of control over work and employment in the northern coal mines'.

21 Philip Mirowski, *Never Let a Serious Crisis Go to Waste: How Neoliberalism Survived the Financial Meltdown*, Verso, London and New York, 2014, pg. 117. Mirowski observes:

One major cultural development over the last three decades is that the only permissible mention of 'class' in the economic sense has been the utterly superfluous habit of treating oneself and others as solidly 'middle class'. In the late 1990s, in Britain, New Labour proclaimed 'We're all middle class now' on the grounds of the evaporation of industrial jobs. In this, they were parroting their putative Tory opponent: 'Class is a Communist concept,' Margaret Thatcher told *Newsweek* in 1992. 'It groups people together and sets them against each other'.

22 E.P. Thompson, *The Making of the English Working Class*, pg. 9.

23 For the distinction between 'deference voter' and 'aspiring voter', see Geoffrey Ostergaard, 'The transformation of the British labour party', *The Indian Journal of Political Science*, Vol. 24, No. 3 (1963), pgs. 217–238. https://www.jstor.org/stable/41853974. Accessed 13 June 2020. While a rather dated article, it does contain insights relevant for more contemporary times. See pg. 220 for the distinction between 'deference voter' and 'aspiring voter'. The article also contains very relevant points about the debates around Clause Four of the Labour Party constitution subsequent to the party's 1959 electoral defeat (pg. 226) and which foreshadows Tony Blair's deletion of it in 1994 when he assumed the leadership of the Labour Party.

24 Bob Jessop, Kevin Bonnet, Simon Bromley and Tom Ling, *Thatcherism: A Tale of Two Nations*, Polity Press, Cambridge, 1988, pg. 87.

25 Nathan Rao, 'Get on your bike, Norman Tebbit says – again', *Daily Express*, Wednesday 23 February 2011. www.express.co.uk/news/uk/230675/Get-on-your-bike-Norman-Tebbit-says-again. Accessed 20 June 2020.

26 George Monbiot, 'Skivers and strivers: this 200 year old myth won't die', *The Guardian*, 23 June 2015. Osborne invoked the distinction at the Conservative Party conference in early October 2012. www.theguardian.com/commentisfree/2015/jun/23/skivers-strivers-200-year-old-myth-wont-die. Accessed 10 June 2020.

27 Owen Jones, *Chavs: The Demonisation of the Working Class*, Verso, London, 2011.

28 Perry Anderson, 'A culture in contraflow-I', *New Left Review*, No. 180 (March/April 1990), pgs. 40–78.

But whatever the strains imposed by political adversity in these years, with its train of muffled frictions or misfired arguments, basic solidarity on the intellectual Left was rarely breached; and out of the trial emerged the liveliest republic of letters in European socialism.

(pg. 44)

29 Andrew Pearman, in his book *The Politics of New Labour: A Gramscian Analysis*, Aakar Books, New Delhi, 2015, makes the following observation:

As a form of 'authoritarian populism', with a primarily petit bourgeois social base and crucial linkages to the 'respectable', 'aspirational' upper working class or 'labour aristocracy', Thatcherism has more in common with the earlier right-wing currents like fascism and Poujadism. It is not, however, equivalent to them; it has some shared characteristics, but these are set within a wholly distinctive and historically specific English 'national-popular' context.

(pg. 57)

30 Bob Jessop, Kevin Bonnet, Simon Bradley and Tom Ling, *Thatcherism: A Tale of Two Nations*, pg. 92.

31 Bob Jessop, 'Thatcherism: the British road to post-Fordism', *Essex Papers in Politics and Government*, Department of Government, University of Essex, Colchester, Number 68, November 1989.

50 The Thatcherite prelude to Brexit

32 Henk Overbeek, *Global Capitalism and National Decline: The Thatcherite Decade in Perspective*, Unwin Hyman, London, pg. 137.
33 Graham Stewart, *Bang! A History of Britain in the 1980s*, Atlantic Books, London, 2013, pg. 49.
34 Quoted in Andrew Gamble, *The Free Economy and the Strong State: The Politics of Thatcherism*, Macmillan Education, Basingstoke, 1988, pg. 201.
35 Henk Overbeek, *Global Capitalism and National Decline*, pg. 172.
36 See Daniel Stedman Jones, *Masters of the Universe, Hayek, Friedman and the Birth of Neoliberal Politics*, Princeton University Press, Princeton, NJ, 2012, pgs. 190–197.
37 Enoch Powell, 'The conservative party', in Denis Kavanagh and Anthony Seldon (eds.) *The Thatcher Effect*, Clarendon Press, Oxford, 1989, pg. 80.
38 John Ranelagh, *Thatcher's People: An Insider's Account of the Politics, the Power and the Personalities*, Harper Collins, London, 1991, pg. xi.
39 'Leading article: what a lot of tosh', *The Independent*, Saturday 24 April 1993. https://www.independent.co.uk/voices/leading-article-what-a-lot-of-tosh-1457335.html. Accessed 6 April 2021. The words are from the then British Prime Minister John Major, who, in a speech, was talking about the future of Britain in Europe and suggesting that the character of Britain would 'survive unamendable in all essentials'. The following part of the article is worth quoting:

> So where does Mr Major derive his lyrical certainties? The answer is George Orwell, who supplied the quote in Mr Major's speech about 'old maids bicycling to Holy Communion through the morning mist' as another unamendable emblem of Britishness. Orwell depicted these old maids in his long essay, 'The lion and the unicorn: socialism and the English genius', which was published in 1941, post Dunkirk and pre-Pearl Harbour, when Britain stood alone against Germany. Orwell pondered the unique attributes of 'English civilisation' and concluded that it was 'somehow bound up with solid breakfasts and gloomy Sundays, smoky towns and winding roads, green fields and red pillar-boxes'. Ah yes: that solid breakfast known as muesli, that winding road called the M25, that gloomy Sunday spent in Tesco, that bright-yellow field of rapeseed, that old mill town where the only smoke is on bonfire night, that pillar-box which may be privatized. Our case rests.

40 https://practicalphilosophy.org.au/adapt-yourself-to-the-environment-in-which-your-lot-has-been-cast-and-show-true-love-to-the-fellow-mortals-with-whom-destiny-has-surrounded-you-marcus-aurelius/. Accessed 26 January 2021.
41 Graeme Smith, 'Margaret Thatcher's Christian faith', pg. 244.
42 Terry Brotherstone, 'A contribution to the critique of post-imperial British history: North Sea oil, Scottish nationalism and Thatcherite neoliberalism', in John-Andrew McNeish and Owen Logan (eds.) *Flammable Societies: Studies on the Socio-Economics of Oil and Gas*, Pluto Press, London, 2012, pgs. 70–97. https://www.jstor.org/stable/j.ctt183pbx9.7. Accessed 19 June 2020. On page 85, Brotherstone writes:

> In drawing up a balance sheet of the social impact of UK North Sea oil, the most obvious comparator is Norway, and its long-term strategy to harbour oil revenues to help meet the challenges of a post-oil economy. In 2010 a BBC Scotland reporter visited Norway to reflect on the contrast and on how a similar policy might have affected Scotland's – and the United Kingdom's – ability to weather the international financial crisis. But the UK failure cannot be explained simply as a conjunctural 'mistake' in decision making: it has to be seen in the context of the historical determinations – the point arrived at in British post-imperial history – underlying the direction of policy not simply in the Thatcherite 1980s but in the whole period from the collapse of British social democracy during the Wilson governments of 1964–76 onwards.

43 Graham Stewart, *Bang! A History of Britain in the 1980s*, pgs. 193–194.

The Thatcherite prelude to Brexit **51**

44 Andrew Cumbers, 'North Sea oil, the state and divergent development in the United Kingdom and Norway', in John-Andrew McNeish and Owen Logan (eds.) *Flammable Societies: Studies in the Socio-Economics of Oil and Gas*, Pluto Press, London, 2012, pgs. 221–242. https://www.jstor.org/stable/j.ctt183pbx9.13. Accessed 19 June 2020. On page 227, Cumbers notes:

> The 'developmentalist' state perspective has therefore also shaped the Norwegian state's dealings with foreign oil companies in the 1970s and 1980s, most notably through insistence on Norwegian ownership throughout the oil industry and its supply chain and the establishment of Statoil, with the intention of developing a fully fledged national oil champion.

45 Amy Raphael, 'Shane Meadows's this is England gang will give channel 4 a kick up the 80s', *The Guardian,* Saturday 4 September 2010. www.theguardian.com/film/2010/sep/04/this-is-england-86-shane-meadows. Accessed 19 June 2020.
46 Margaret Thatcher, *The Downing Street Years*. This is what Mrs Thatcher has to say:

> I still do not understand why anyone later imagined that the Westland board, Leon Brittan and I were all biased against a European option. In fact, the Government bent over backwards to give that option and Michael Heseltine every opportunity to advance their arguments and interests. Yet in the frenzy which followed there was almost no limit to the to the deviousness and manipulation we were accused of employing to secure Sikorsky its minority holding.

> *(pg. 427)*

47 The Rt. Hon the Lord Heseltine of Thenford CH, *No Stone Unturned*, October 2012. https://assets.publishing.service.gov.uk/government/uploads/system/uploads/attachment_data/file/34648/12-1213-no-stone-unturned-in-pursuit-of-growth.pdf. Accessed 20 June 2020.
48 Eric Evans, *Thatcher and Thatcherism*, Second Edition, Routledge, Taylor and Francis Group, London and New York, 2004, pg. 113.
49 Henk Overbeek, 'The Westland affair: collision over the future of British capitalism', *Capital and Class*, No. 29 (Summer 1986), pg. 22.
50 Henk Overbeek, 'The Westland affair: collision over the future of British capitalism', pg. 15.
51 Margaret Thatcher, *The Downing Street Years*, pg. 426.
52 Rashmi Rajput, 'As Scrap, retired Naval aircraft carrier Viraat finds no takers', *The Economic Times*, 19 December 2019. https://economictimes.indiatimes.com/news/defence/as-scrap-retired-naval-aircraft-carrier-viraat-finds-no-takers/articleshow/72862015.cms. Accessed 19 June 2020.
53 K.T. Jagannathan and Anuj Srivas, 'The ghost of the helicopter past', *The Hindu*, 24 February 2013. https://www.thehindu.com/news/national/the-ghost-of-the-helicopter-past/article4446909.ece. Accessed 6 April 2021. The helicopters that India bought back in 1985 were a disaster. Two crashed in accidents in August 1988 and February 1989, killing over 10 passengers. The article further notes:

> In 1991, the helicopters were withdrawn from service on safety grounds, after a number of subcommittee reviews, by the Director-General of Civil Aviation. In 1993, Pawan Hans, the state-owned helicopter firm that operated the Westland copters, put out a global tender for the defective helicopters. Eventually, British firm AES Aerospace emerged as the sole bidder, and the entire fleet of Westland helicopters was packaged off to Britain for the scrap value of just £900,000.
>
> During the period of operation of those helicopters, Pawan Hans incurred an aggregate loss of Rs. 95.67 crore, while the British national audit office concluded that its government lost more than £105 million due to the deal.
>
> British firm GKN acquired Westland in 1998, and merged it with Finmeccanica's subsidiary Agusta in 2000. In 2004, Finmeccanica acquired GKN's stake in the joint venture.

52 The Thatcherite prelude to Brexit

54 John Holloway, 'The Red rose of Nissan', *Capital and Class*, No. 32 (Summer 1987).
55 John Plender, 'London's Big Bang in international context', *International Affairs* (Royal Institute of International Affairs 1944-), Vol. 63, No. 1 (Winter, 1986–1987), pgs. 39–48. https://www.jstor.com/stable/2620231. Accessed 27 June 2020.
56 Jim Pickard and Barney Thompson, 'Archives 1985 & 1986: Thatcher policy fight over "Big Band" laid bare', *Financial Times*, 30 December 2014 www.ft.com/content/f3c0d500-8537-11e4-bb63-00144feabdc0. Accessed 19 June 2020.
57 Nicholas Shaxson, 'The finance curse: how the outsized power of the City of London makes Britain poorer', *The Guardian*, The Long Read, Friday 5 October 2018. www.theguardian.com/news/2018/oct/05/the-finance-curse-how-the-outsized-power-of-the-city-of-london-makes-britain-poorer. Accessed 19 June 2020.
58 Stephen G. Cecchetti and Enise Kharroubi, 'Reassessing the impact of finance on growth', Paper presented for the Reserve Bank of India's Second International Research Conference in Mumbai, India on 1–2 February 2012.
59 Iain Martin, *Crash, Bang, Wallop: The Inside Story of London's Big Bang and a Financial Revolution that Changed the World*, Sceptre, London, 2016, pgs. 257–258.
60 All quotes from Geoffrey Howe's speech are taken from the Hansard website. https://api.parliament.uk/historic-hansard/commons/1990/nov/13/personal-statement. Accessed 10 July 2020.

3

BREXIT, THE 2007 FINANCIAL CRISIS AND AUSTERITY

The Warwick University academic Thiemo Fetzer has argued that it was the deleterious effects of austerity policies introduced by the David Cameron-led Conservative government of 2010–2015 that led to the Brexit referendum swinging to the Leave side. Fetzer suggests that the political landscape of the UK changed significantly in a few years between 2010 and 2015 as a result of austerity. He further attempts to make a direct connection between the effects of austerity policies in certain areas and how this translated into support for Leave. His analysis relies, to a great extent, on looking at the increase in the vote share of the UKIP, a populist, single-issue party created in the 1990s and obsessed with the issue of Europe.[1]

Fetzer's argument suggests the need to understand more closely the effects of austerity measures introduced in the aftermath of the 2007 financial crisis and its impact on British politics. To begin with, the term austerity is quite a misnomer for the kind of effects that it has on the people in general. The axe of austerity cuts hits the *already austere* working class the most and especially the public services on which the working class is most dependent, such as public health, social housing and public transportation. Austerity measures can be understood as a particularly brutalized and savage extension of economic neoliberalism that accelerates the latter's tendency to commoditize social and public goods such as health, housing and education. In terms of understanding austerity as an extension of economic neoliberalism, this chapter will look at the 2007 financial crisis as precipitating this austerity-induced extension of neoliberalism, which in turn is premised heavily upon a continuing financialization of the economy. The British economy is a clear example of one that is especially lopsided in terms of its excessive tilt towards finance.

The austerity measures analysed here will refer specifically to the ones introduced after the 2007 financial crisis that began with the sub-prime mortgage catastrophe in the US and spread rapidly to the UK and the Eurozone.[2] The analysis

54 Brexit and austerity

will ultimately come to rest the focus squarely on the UK. The focus will not be on historically earlier forms of austerity that were introduced by, say, the Ramsay Macdonald government in the UK in 1931 or in periods thereafter.[3]

Austerity is understood as a very crucial culmination of the neoliberal project. The neoliberal project has itself spurred on the kind of globalization that the contemporary world is most familiar with and large parts of which seem to be revolting against. Brexit has been understood as a revolt against globalization. In a very skeletal fashion, contemporary globalization can be characterized as the unhindered and unimpeded flow of trade, investment, goods and services across international boundaries.[4] The unimpeded flows of globalization suddenly, and perhaps a little curiously, harden when the question of labour flows comes knocking on national borders. In addition, neoliberal-driven globalization has an excessively financialized component to it, as result of which vast sums of money are moved around the globe. London itself emerged, with the 1986 Big Bang economic reforms introduced by the Thatcher government, as the largest of such international financial centres. Its advantageous time zone played a central role to ensure that trading was on in full swing in London as it closed for the day in Tokyo and as the day began in New York (see the chapter on 'The Thatcherite Prelude to Brexit').

The pre-eminence of London as a global financial centre has, however, existed at the expense of domestic manufacturing industry, deep in the British hinterland. This is where demands for Brexit have emerged most vociferously. The centrality of London as a financial centre has meant the maintaining of the British Pound Sterling as an over-valued international currency, making British exports more expensive and less competitive. Brexit has quite rightly been understood as a revolt of the de-industrialised Midlands and North. These are parts of the country ravaged by the Thatcher government and its deliberate deindustrialization. It has again been quite rightly compared to the Trump presidential victory in 2016 arising out of blue-collar discontent in the American rust belt states of Wisconsin, Michigan and Pennsylvania and more generally of rising levels of inequality creating a sense among many of being left behind by globalization.[5]

As against the kind of services-based economy, heavily dependent on finance that the UK has become, the emphasis on productivity and manufacturing has often been associated with greater alignment with Europe. The most prominent representative of such an attitude can be found in a Conservative politician and former member of the Thatcher cabinet, Michael Heseltine. Heseltine has been vocal in his more recent criticism of his own Conservative Party on the Brexit issue. He lost the Tory whip after saying that he voted for the Lib-Dems in the May 2019 European Parliament elections.[6] A lifelong Europhile, Heseltine resigned from the Thatcher cabinet in early 1986 over the now largely forgotten Westland Helicopter controversy. The manoeuvrings of Mrs Thatcher and her cabinet colleagues in that controversy are explored in the previous chapter on 'The Thatcherite prelude to Brexit' as one of the early stirrings towards Brexit itself. More recently Heseltine wrote, *No Stone Unturned: In Pursuit of Growth*, a report on industrial strategy commissioned by the David Cameron government in 2012.[7]

Keynesian, but not quite

The introduction of austerity policies consequent to the financial crisis assumed the form of a mass bail-out of the banks that had themselves created the mess in the first place. This intervention of the state to bail out the reckless banks at the centre of the crisis was done on the infamous plea that they were 'too big to fail', making at least some of them, even bigger than they were before the financial crisis.[8] This would also be a classic case of the socialization of losses, with its concomitant being, of course, the privatization of profits.

The bail-out took the form of massive infusions of money into the economy, through a process called quantitative easing. It bore a twisted resemblance to the fiscal stimulus of Keynesian kick-starts to depressed economies. However, the resemblance to Keynesianism went only thus far and no further. This has led Alex Callinicos to observe of that time: 'One might regard the present economic and financial crisis as, from a Keynesian perspective, a happy tale in which an activist policy response prevented the kind of protracted collapse in output and employment that occurred between 1929 and 1933'. Callinicos immediately observes that there was 'a sting in the tail', which very soon led to calls for rolling back the increase in budget deficits that had been created. He further explains, 'but my concern here is with the puzzle represented by the speed with which policy makers shifted from an apparently Keynesian response to the prospect of economic and financial collapse to an agenda dominated by deficit cutting'.[9] The apparently Keynesian infusions of money into the economy were not done to stimulate productive economic activity but channelized to the banks and financial institutions. This underlines the point about financialization made earlier, and which broadly refers to the ever-increasing proportion of financial transactions to the total transactions in the economy.[10] Even if the activities of governments in their response to the financial crisis bore a resemblance with Keynesianism, it can be said to be a caricatured one at that.

Austerity: a bit rich coming from the ruling class

It is a bit rich for a policy to be termed austerity when it is enforced by a political Establishment, backed by a powerful banking and financial sector and the painful effects of which are far more likely to be felt by the working class. George Osborne, the Chancellor of the Exchequer in the Cameron government and thereby, the 'enforcer-in-chief' of austerity policies, suggested in what can only be called a cruel cocking a snook at solidarity that, 'We're all in this together'.[11] Austerity policies are obsessed with balancing the books. This compulsive preoccupation with reducing and eliminating the public debt is, however, done on the backs of the most vulnerable. It was a bit of irony then to hear Rishi Sunak, Osborne's successor by a few removes, and chancellor at the time of the Coronavirus pandemic, revive the slogan of 'we're all in this together'. It was of course the same slogan but, almost eight years apart, had a completely different ring to it.[12]

56 Brexit and austerity

The term austerity is ironical as an economic policy that promotes a kind of supposed disciplinary fiscal belt tightening that is likely to hurt the more vulnerable at the behest of the powerful political and financial Establishment. Gary Dymski, in his article on 'The Logic and Impossibility of Austerity', has gone into the origins of the word and, citing the Oxford English Dictionary, notes how the word can be traced to Old French in the fourteenth century. Three meanings of the word are available. The first 'Harshness to the taste, astringent sourness' (1634), then from 1340 we have, 'Harshness to the feelings; stern, rigorous or severe treatment or demeanor'. From a 1590 meaning we have something which, Dymski notes, is relevant for the word as it has been parachuted into economic policy: 'severe self-discipline or restraint; moral strictness, rigorous abstinence, asceticism'.[13] He cites Sue Konzelmann to take note of the origins of the concept's application to economic policy, which happened as a result of Great Britain using public borrowing to fund military expansion. A rather humiliating naval defeat at the hands of the French in the Battle of Beachy Head in 1690 led to a determination to build a powerful navy. As the funding could not be done through taxation, this led to the setting up of the Bank of England as a private institution in 1694 to provide the King with money.[14]

Interesting and ironical though the term austerity may be, what is of greater interest for our purposes here is how austerity measures, as an extension of neoliberalism in the wake of the 2007 financial crisis, were also able to give another lease of life to economic neoliberalism, which many had hoped would just die out. Perhaps a little petulantly Alex Callinicos queried: 'So why didn't the situation force a move away from neoliberalism after 2008?' It is precisely this kind of petulant query that seems to be the burden of Philip Mirowski's extremely readable book *Never Let a Serious Crisis Go to Waste: How Neoliberalism survived the Financial Meltdown*. This is how he begins his book:

> Conjure, if you will, a primal sequence encountered in B-grade horror films, where the celluloid protagonist suffers a terrifying encounter with doom, yet on the cusp of disaster abruptly wakes to a different world, which initially seems normal, but eventually is revealed to be a second nightmare more ghastly than the first. Something like that has become manifest in real life since the onset of the crisis which started in 2007.

Mirowski then spools forward to 2011 to suggest that

> as the year ended, it slowly dawned upon most of us that the natural presumption that we were capable of rousting ourselves from the gasping nightmare, that we might proceed to learn from the mistakes and fallacies of the era of Neoliberal Follies, was itself one more insidious hallucination.

Continuing the gloom, Mirowski notes: 'Austerity became the watchword in almost every country; governments everywhere became the scapegoats for dissatisfaction of every stripe. In the name of probity, the working class was attacked from all sides, even by nominal "socialist" parties.'[15]

The London riots of 2011, austerity and 'feral youth'

In August of 2011, there was major rioting that happened in London, and the then British Prime Minister David Cameron was quick to dismiss this disorder as arising from the lack of discipline and complete immorality on the part of those active in the looting and arson. Cameron, of course, had to deny that the riots were in any way remotely connected to his government's recently introduced austerity cuts.

> These riots were not about race: the perpetrators and the victims were white, black and Asian. These riots were not about government cuts: they were directed at high street stores, not Parliament. And these riots were not about poverty: that insults millions of people who, whatever the hardship, would never dream of making others suffer like this.[16]

Cameron went on to bewail 'the slow-motion moral collapse' that has overtaken the country over the past few generations. Having shifted the cause from collective structural problems such as economic inequality and class deprivation, he proceeded to pin the blame on individual moral agency:

> Irresponsibility. Selfishness. Behaving as if your choices have no consequences. Children without fathers. Schools without discipline. Reward without effort. Crime without punishment. Rights without responsibilities. Communities without control.[17]

Perhaps the most notable comment from the political Establishment, in terms of its haranguing of the youngsters involved in the rioting, came from then Deputy Mayor of London Kit Malthouse, who, some years later, gave his name to the 'Malthouse compromise' formula that attempted to bring together different factions of the Conservative Party over Theresa May's Brexit withdrawal agreement.[18] Malthouse suggested at the time of the London riots that 'feral youth were to blame for the violence in London'. This was a resounding statement to make on the supposed dysfunctionality of British working-class culture that did not seem to know how to raise children into fine young adults.

In sharp contrast to the repeated attempts on the part of Establishment politicians to shift the blame away from the structural problems of capitalism, Jeffrey Stevenson Murer, in an interesting analysis, attempts to 'examine the aesthetics of this high moment of consumerism in a time of increasing state austerity'. His paper explores 'how the events of the summer of 2011 were a moment marked by the spread of affective capitalism, complemented by welfare state contraction and shrinking state responsibility'. The strength of Murer's paper is the fact that he can view the riots as the culmination of the vacuous consumerism that has been

58 Brexit and austerity

encouraged under the aegis of British capitalism, with its collapse of manufacturing and the concomitant loss of gainful employment that this lost manufacturing could have brought about. This is of course complemented by a consumer credit-fuelled economic expansion. Murer coins the interesting term 'lumpen-consumerate' to characterize riotous British youngsters. His paper begins in a riveting manner when he draws parallels between the rampaging behaviour of desperate shoppers on Black Friday with the riotous youngsters going on the rampage during the London riots.[19]

The thing about the London 2011 riots is that they have not been sufficiently analysed in relation to the cycle of roughly 10-year outbreaks of violence that have so often rocked the blighted British urbanscape. There is thus the 1981 Brixton and Toxteth rioting. Then in 1991 there was the rioting in Leeds. In 2001 there was the summer of urban rioting in the northern former mill towns of Bradford, Leeds, Burnley and Barnsley. Comparisons were inevitably made between 2001 and 1981. Also, the 2001 riots happened just as Tony Blair's extended honeymoon period was clearly coming to a juddering halt. Breaking these 10-yearly cycles have been the 1985 Broadwater Farm violence and the 1958 Notting Hill violence.

While those on the Conservative Right were quick to dismiss the 2011 London riots as nothing but irresponsible and badly reared youngsters going on the rampage, there were those on the left who saw this in terms of a kind of proto-proletarian uprising that was happening just as the British political Establishment was making its best efforts to tide over the 2007 financial crisis. This was dismissed by observers who suggested that the motivating emotion or the subjective feeling behind most of the rioters was to catch up in terms of consumption. It was all about consuming at its crassest, and it would be difficult to read into or find any profounder political point in the rioters.[20]

Perhaps the inevitably in-between reality of the London riots was nailed by Slavoj Zizek's highly readable account in the *London Review of Books*, where, at the very beginning of his article, he suggests that the recurrence of something like the 2011 riots was clearly symptomatic of a deeper structural crisis. However, as the article reaches its penultimate paragraph, Zizek makes a point that could just as effectively sum up the Brexit crisis itself, though of course it was still a few years away from erupting:

> And this is the fatal weakness of recent protests: they express an authentic rage which is not able to transform itself into a positive programme of socio-political change. They express a spirit of revolt without revolution.

As suggested, these lines, especially the words 'authentic rage', could just as well capture Brexit and the genuine grievance that undergirds it. Somewhere in the middle of the article, Zizek captures, with his somewhat unpredictable brilliance, the truth about the London riots with this line: 'On British streets during the unrest, what we saw was not men reduced to "beasts", but the stripped-down form of the beast produced by capitalist ideology'.[21]

The reason why the London riots of 2011 are crucial to an understanding of Brexit is on two counts. First, they prefigure Brexit itself in terms of the hopeless discontent that they seem to be giving rise to and the subjective response to them by people in terms of the objective conditions that they find themselves mired in.

Second, riots and civil war seem to have become part of the Brexit narrative.[22] The government's document, Operation Yellowhammer, suggested that there was the likelihood of civil disorder on the streets in case the UK crashed out without a deal on 31 October 2019.[23] This part of the warning that was being served by a government report has been very craftily twisted by Leavers to suggest that were Brexit not to happen on schedule on the 31 October deadline, then there would be real danger of violence and civil unrest. The most glaring example of this was *Spiked* editor Brendan O'Neill actually suggesting on a BBC television programme that he was surprised that no rioting had happened as a result of Brexit being denied to the British people. He went on to further suggest that there 'should be' riots in the way that the *gilets jaunes* or Yellow Vest movement protestors went on the rampage in France. He also tried to justify his appeal to violence by invoking the fine historical legacy in Britain of radical political action such as the Levellers in the 1640s and the Chartists in the 1840s to the Suffragettes.[24] The very same Brendan O'Neill made his acute displeasure felt during the violence of the 2011 London riots when he condemned all those commentators who were connecting the violence to the unfairness of capitalism, choosing to make an earlier reference to the Levellers and the Suffragettes, though, on this occasion, a tad disparagingly it would seem:

> Painting these riots as some kind of action replay of historic political street-fights against capitalist bosses or racist cops might allow armchair radicals to get their intellectual rocks off, as they lift their noses from dusty tomes about the Levellers or the Suffragettes and fantasise that a political upheaval of equal worth is now occurring outside their windows. But such shameless projection misses what is new and particularly deeply worrying about these riots. The political context is not the cuts agenda or racist policing – it is the welfare state, which, it is now clear, has nurtured a new generation that has absolutely no sense of community spirit or social solidarity.[25]

From a wider perspective, the 2011 London riots could also be seen in relation to the 1992 Los Angeles riots. Comparisons could be made to the 2005 violence in the suburbs of Paris. Worthwhile comparisons could also be made to the violence that occurred at the end of the Obama administration when towns such as Ferguson, Missouri, were jolted by violence to spark the Black Lives Matter movement. There were the riots that spread across many US cities in the immediate aftermath of the death of George Floyd in late May 2020, with the sense of disquiet emerging from Floyd's death rapidly spreading to many other parts of the world and the UK resonating especially to these events across the Atlantic. More to the point, the initial provocation for the 2011 London riots was the killing by

60 Brexit and austerity

the London Metropolitan Police of Mark Duggan, a black man. This initial spark became quickly transformed into an orgy of consumerism and did not seem to have much hint of racial backlash within them.

There ain't no black in Brexit

What other way to invoke this lack of black in the London riots that acted as a more immediate prelude to Brexit and, for that matter, in the whole Brexit process itself, than Paul Gilroy's extremely famous book *There Ain't no Black in the Union Jack*.[26] The Brexit process has been powered by a recrudescent English nationalism that has simply whitewashed all elements of Blackness. The lack of discussion of black politics or, for that matter, the black presence itself gives one a clue to the politics of Brexit. This can only be brought into bolder relief by noting that the Brexit saga has unfolded almost in parallel with the revelations of the Windrush generation and how callously and cruelly official Britain treated its Black citizens from the Caribbean. Olivia Petter, writing in *The Independent* observed, 'In April 2018, a political scandal of such significance emerged that it almost took people's minds off of Brexit for a period of time'.[27] The controversy is named after the ship, the HMT Empire Windrush, which was the first vessel to carry large numbers of people from the Caribbean to the shores of England, a flow that was to continue from 1948 to 1973, carrying around 500,000 people. The Windrush controversy led to the resignation of Home Secretary Amber Rudd in Theresa May's government. The build-up to something as insensitive as this controversy was prepared by Theresa May when she was Home Secretary in David Cameron's government and the 'hostile environment' that she deliberately created towards supposedly illegal immigrants, as a matter of policy. In many cases this involved asking individuals who had come to the UK in their childhood, who had worked and built-up their lives in the country, to go back to places that they were only familiar with in the form of a vague distant memory, as countries and places left far behind in the past.

The London riots of 2011 would almost suggest that earlier lawlessness could be taken as the early warning sign for the discontents of Brexit itself. Boris Johnson was then still Mayor of London. The disorder on the streets of London back in 2011 might portend the civil disorder that a government report such as Operation Yellowhammer has suggested could happen in the event of a no-deal Brexit. Among the many controversial things that Johnson did as Mayor was the acquisition in 2014 of the first water cannon for use on the British mainland. This was purchased from the German federal police at a cost of £218,000 to the taxpayer. Natalie Sedacca notes that the required prior approval from the Home Secretary was not taken.[28] Johnson's justification for the haste at which the water cannon had been acquired was in terms of the reasonably low price at which they were available and the fact that they might be useful in the summer months ahead, when urban rioting seems to be more common. Natalie Sedacca writes:

> It is also hard to understand why in a time of austerity, when cuts are being made to front line community policing, a substantial sum of money would

be spent in instruments which are expected to be used extremely rarely and to have no impact on those protesting against cuts.[29]

The distance and arrogance of the British Establishment can be seen from the fact that its own members, such as David Cameron and George Osborne, who are quick to condemn the bad behaviour of misguided youngsters, reveal no hint of any vague recollection of the Bullingdon Club-induced 'feral' behaviour of Oxford undergraduates. Boris Johnson, in a sign of the far worse populist times that we live in, seems to want to stoke that very same general lawlessness on the streets to bolster his own vulnerable political position, setting people against Parliament.

The shift from Cameron and Osborne's attitudes towards street violence back in 2011 to Johnson's Prime Ministerial attitude towards such street violence in 2019 is a sign of how Brexit is an outcome of an isolated political Establishment seemingly safe in its Whitehall bubble, creating the conditions for Brexit to ripen and happen across the land. Brexit has been allowed to happen because of the British political Establishment and its cosy relationship with the financial heft that exists in the City of London that can let a larger nation go to waste. The populism of Johnson, himself a part of that very elitist Establishment, gives him the audacity to speak in the name of the people, the very same people whose conditions were worsened and aggravated by a Conservative government supported by the Liberal-Democratic Party as it continued to grind them down with austerity. Brexit is the culmination of the neoliberal project inaugurated by the Thatcher government in 1979. This continued with the consensus on neoliberalism and its connected commitment to financialization under the Blair government of 1997–2007. The Brown government, which seemed to have a slightly better sense of the impending financial crisis and seemed to want to take counter measures in the face of it, was voted out of power in 2010. Cameron's coalition government brought in a full decade of austerity that was not just an extension of neoliberalism but served to give it a new lease of life. Not only was austerity about giving a new lease of life to a neoliberal politics that deserved to die much earlier, but it also served the ideological agenda of significantly hacking away at the perceived expanses, not to forget expenses, of the British welfare state and thereby shrink the state, that almost obsessive concern of neoliberal politics.

Who wants a no-deal Brexit? Cui bono?

The Johnson government's first few months in office showed an almost single-minded obsession with achieving Brexit, whatever that may have meant. Time and again it was suggested that Britain should just 'get on with it' and 'get Brexit done'. The political posturing of the Johnson government made the likelihood of a no-deal Brexit, a palpable reality, perhaps the only possibility, ruled out at the last minute, perhaps owing to a Biden victory in the US Presidential election. There was a certain callous irresponsibility in the way Johnson and other members of his cabinet could even countenance the possibility of no-deal, let alone express

62 Brexit and austerity

enthusiasm. There were of course many Conservative Party MPs who resigned or had their whips removed as a result of the boorish behaviour of the leadership.

Who wanted the hardest of no-deal Brexits, despite the dire economic warnings against it? The further question to pose is *Cui bono*, or who benefits from a no-deal Brexit? The former Chancellor of the Exchequer Philip Hammond had suggested that a small group of unscrupulous hedge-fund speculators were betting on the odds of a no-deal Brexit and were likely to make large sums of money out of it. Curiously, the use of the word 'speculator' was construed by a Hammond critic, Toby Toung, as being anti-Semitic, as he felt or assumed that all financial speculators are Jewish. Thankfully, this accusation was withdrawn with an apology to Hammond, when the latter threatened legal action.[30] (See chapter on Brexit, Anti-Semitism and Islamophobia.)

On the question of who benefits from a no-deal and who is behind the idea, analysis is led to the workings of numerous right-wing think tanks on both sides of the Atlantic in the US and the UK. The prominent ones in the UK would be the Institute of Economic Affairs (IEA) and the Legatum institute, and in the US, they would be the American Enterprise Institute (AEI) and the Heritage Foundation. They have significant access to many members of Boris Johnson's cabinet, with many members making regular trips to the US for lectures and seminars. More significantly, the numerous think tanks form an influential group in the form of the Atlas Network, which has its headquarters in Arlington, Virginia.[31]

The organization known as the think tank is itself a vehicle that has been unique to the extension and propagation of neoliberal ideas. Daniel Stedman Jones in his book, *Masters of the Universe: Hayek, Friedman and the Birth of Neoliberal Politics*, has devoted a whole chapter to understanding the workings of these often shadowy organizations that are funded generously by large business corporations. He has noted two waves of their existence. The first wave of think tanks was set up in the 1940s and 1950s, just as the Keynesian consensus was being firmed up in the US and the UK. The presence and consolidation of Keynesianism was the sparring partner for the kind of initially intellectual shadow-boxing that the first wave of neoliberal think tanks engaged in. Among the first wave of neoliberal think tanks set up in the 1940s and 1950s were the AEI and the Foundation for Economic Education (FEE) in the US and the IEA in Britain. The second wave of neoliberal think tanks was established in the 1970s and included the CPS and the Adam Smith Institute (ASI) in the UK and the Heritage Foundation and the Cato Institute in the US.[32] The second wave of think tanks not only proved to be far more influential in terms of actually influencing the policy of the Thatcher and Reagan governments but would serve the knock-out blow to Keynesianism in the 1970s, in contrast to the shadow-boxing with Keynesian ideas that the first wave of think tanks was confined to earlier. Jones has also noted the proclivity of these think tanks to form transatlantic networks across the 'pond', as the wide expanse of the Atlantic is so fondly referred to on either side.

The particular proclivity of right-wing think tanks to form transatlantic alliances is fascinating. In 1951 a small group of Conservative politicians created the Bow

Group, strictly speaking not a think tank. It tried to rival the Fabians on the left in terms of its intellectual exertions. Jones has noted that while membership was open to Conservatives of all stripes, the chairmen of the group in the 1950s, 1960s and 1970s included men such as David Howell, Leon Brittan, Michael Howard, John MacGregor, Norman Lamont and Peter Lilley, who would all go on to become cabinet ministers in Thatcher governments. The 'leading light' of the Bow Group was Geoffrey Howe, who crucially served as Mrs Thatcher's Chancellor in her first government and was the one cabinet minister who seemed to survive until the very end of the Thatcher premiership, before contributing, most crucially, to her downfall. In terms of transatlantic influence, the Bow Group was replicated by the Ripon Society of the Republican Party in the US in 1961.[33]

In the various think tanks mentioned, the UK-based IEA, set up in 1955 by businessman Anthony Fisher, creator of the first factory-style chicken farm in Britain, was especially influential in terms of intellectual orientation and trans-Atlantic networking. Fisher was also behind the creation of the Atlas Foundation, which knitted together the burgeoning phenomenon of the think tank, many modelled on the IEA.[34]

While the think tank is now a familiar part of the political and intellectual landscape of many countries across the world, the influence that it has exercised in terms of pulling the UK out of the EU presents a kind of contrast that represents the anti-democratic instincts of the Brexit process at its worst. There is, on the one hand, the dumbed-down Brexit rhetoric dispensed through the shallow superficiality of slogans such as 'Get Brexit Done', multiplied and proliferated through the right-wing British press and algorithm-driven social media platforms. On the other hand, there is the cloistered world of think tanks with their battery of intellectual entrepreneurs writing their abstruse policy papers that prove decisive and influential in moving government policy. The contrast, once again is that the more rarefied is the intellectualism of think tanks, the thicker seems to be the dumbed-down, wider public discourse. A measure of Fisher's influence, and by extension that of right-wing think tanks, can be had by looking at the Atlas Network's website. In the section on the beginnings of the organization, British MP Oliver Letwin is quoted:

> Without Fisher, no IEA; without the IEA and its clones, no Thatcher and quite possibly no Reagan; without Reagan, no Star Wars; without Star Wars, no economic collapse of the Soviet Union. Quite a chain of consequences for a chicken farmer.[35]

The hypocrisy of household homilies

Quite remarkably, the Conservatives were able to deflect the blame of the 2007 financial crisis away from the greed of the London bankers and the financial Establishment onto the fiscal profligacy of the Labour government from 1997 to 2010.

64 Brexit and austerity

They did so by taking recourse to a series of household homilies. Cameron accused the Labour government of bringing on the 2007 financial crisis because Labour did not, in his famous words, 'mend the roof when the sun was shining', a phrase repeated by his successor Theresa May.[36] The fact that this kind of argument can wash with the electorate, that the Conservatives can always be trusted with the economy in a way that no Labour government ever can, reveals the depth and pervasiveness of the roots that neoliberal thinking has sunk in the minds of people. It has almost become, to use the words of Philip Mirowski, 'the ideology of no ideology'.[37] Mirowski goes on to explain the all-pervasive acceptance of neoliberal doctrines by suggesting:

> The tenacity of neoliberal doctrines that might have otherwise been refuted at every turn since 2008 has to be rooted in the extent to which a kind of 'folk' or 'everyday' neoliberalism has sunk so deeply into the cultural uncon-scious that even a few rude shocks can't begin to bring it to the surface long enough to provoke discomfort.[38]

In chapter 3 of his book, Mirowski quite rightly suggests that there is an 'everyday neoliberalism' that is very difficult to escape as it swaddles and engulfs us in a vice-like grip. The vice-like grip makes itself almost natural and acceptable as it has acquired an unquestionable common-sense character. This rather crass neoliberal common sense is reinforced by a set of homilies that Conservative governments have served to people who seem to have readily accepted them hook, line and sinker. Perhaps worse is how this crass common sense is characterized by a streak of 'everyday sadism' as Mirowski refers to it: 'It underpins the argument that the poor must of necessity bear the brunt of austerity now, because it will only get worse for them later if they do not'.[39]

In taking recourse to some rather earthy and supposedly genuine homilies, suc-cessive Conservative governments have been successful in translating the language of household finance and bringing it to bear on the public finances of govern-ment.[40] Cameron's suggestion that Labour did not 'mend the roof while the sun was shining', in reference to the days before the 2007 financial crisis, is an instance of an apparently earthy prudence speaking. The sensible thing would be to call 'the thatcher' (pun unavoidably intended) to mend the roof while the sun of the economy was still favourably shining. This kind of household homily is like the point that Mrs Thatcher would make back in the late 1970s, when she made a parallel between a housewife managing domestic expenses and the government doing something similar. The political intent and impact of the idea was Thatcher's suggestion that Britain could no longer afford the 'cradle to grave' welfare state, and the sensible thing to do would be to roll it back.

This rolling back and capping of benefits was continued with Cameron's brutal austerity measures. These apparently sensible, simple and straightforward house-hold homilies swap the principles of household finance for public finance, and more importantly serve as an ideological inversion intended to shrink the state. In

Brexit and austerity **65**

other words, when households budget, they must prioritize income by first looking at the money flowing in and only then can they consider the various expenses that can be made. This is obviously good, plain common sense. The economist Simon Wren-Lewis calls this kind of fiscal prudence contained in the household homilies referred to, as a form of 'deficit fetishism' and suggests that it is very difficult to counter as such talk is a form of 'political bullshit'. With the help of Princeton philosopher Harry Frankfurt, Wren-Lewis argues that bullshit is distinct from lying in that it has no reference to the truth. There is a futility in countering political bullshit with facts and reason as political bullshit does not reside in the 'court of truth'.

> In the case of fiscal policy, deficit fetishism as bullshit involves appeals to 'common sense' by invoking simple analogies with households, often coupled with an element of morality: it is responsible to pay down debts. The point in calling it bullshit (in this technical sense) is that attempts to counter it by appeals to facts or knowledge (for example, the government is not like a household, as every economist knows) may have limited effectiveness. Instead it might be better to fight bullshit with bullshit, by talking about the need to borrow to invest, or even that it is best to 'grow your way out of debt'. (If you think the latter is nonsense, you are still in the wrong court: the court of truth rather than bullshit. As long as the phrase contains what I have sometimes called a 'half-truth', it has the potential to be effective bullshit.)[41]

Many of these homilies were repeated in all their inanity by Johnson's Home Secretary, Priti Patel, at the Conservative Party Conference held in October 2019 at Manchester. Patel invoked the legacy of Margaret Thatcher when she suggested simple straightforward ideas such as an honest day's pay for an honest day's work, not spending more than you can afford, paying your bills and supporting the police.[42] On a completely different Conservative note would be the household homily put forward by the former Conservative Prime Minister Harold Macmillan. In the late 1950s, as the British economy was recovering from the ravages of the Second World War and was on the verge of entering the decade of the swinging sixties and Beatles mania, he is known to have famously opined that 'our people have never had it so good'.[43] This was more in the nature of a self-congratulatory pat on his own back to talk about the improving conditions of people's lives under the Conservative Party. More pertinent to our purposes in the analysis here is what he said when he critiqued Mrs Thatcher's privatization policies in the 1980s. Macmillan suggested that the selling of shares in British public enterprises, such as British Telecom and British Gas, was like 'selling off the family silver'.[44] The household in this homily was more of an aristocratic one, forced onto bad times. It also gives a clear indication of the changed nature of the British Conservative Party from its more subdued old-moneyed days of *noblesse-oblige*, one-nation Toryism to the more rambunctious new money years of Mrs Thatcher's Conservative Party.

66 Brexit and austerity

Just a little thought reveals the inherent deception and hypocrisy in many of these Conservative homilies. Worse, there is a reversal effected between the principles of household expenditure and public expenditure. While fiscal prudence has been advised for the government, through the easy supply of credit to households, a rather reckless fiscal profligacy is encouraged for them. The UK's household debt stands at a staggeringly high rate with the Trade Union Congress (TUC) reporting in early January 2019 that it had touched a new high of £428 billion. What this meant was that, excluding mortgages, the average debt per household rose in the year 2018 to a peak of £15,385. This figure was up by £886 from the previous year. This included student loans that the Bank of England does not factor in when it considers household debt and so gives a figure that is half of the TUC's estimate. The TUC's general secretary Frances O'Grady said: 'Household debt is at crisis level. Years of austerity and wage stagnation has pushed millions of families deep into the red'.[45]

This point about the sucking in of the working class and the middle class into credit markets would be worthwhile, keeping in mind a point that Alex Callinicos makes, which is that financialization does not mean merely the expansion and ballooning of the banks and the disproportionate power that they command. More importantly, financialization is understood as a much larger social and economic phenomenon in which larger and larger segments of the middle and working class are sucked into credit markets.[46] It would also hold a key to understanding the unmaking of the working class, which has, in the very evocative rendering of its culture in Richard Hoggart's book *The Uses of Literacy*, been traditionally averse to being indebted as this passage so insightfully reveals:

> I know several families which have elected to keep their electricity supply on the shilling-in-the-slot system. They pay more that way and frequently find themselves in the dark because no one has a shilling: they have enough money coming in now to pay quarterly bills easily. But they cannot bear the thought of having a debt outstanding longer than a week.[47]

Take another of these household homilies, this time straight from Mrs Thatcher herself, who would talk about 'an honest day's pay for an honest day's work'. Now contrast the apparent simplicity of this statement with the obscene amounts of money made by bankers in the City of London. These changes that were brought about by Mrs Thatcher in terms of the slightly insensitive celebration of wealth have been captured in Graham Stewart's book *Bang: A History of Britain in the 1980s*, which is an expansive effort to capture the social changes that Thatcherism was unleashing.[48] Iain Martin's book on the 1986 Big Bang reforms that unleashed the monster of the financial revolution that created in London the world's largest financial centre notes: 'In dress, mores and willingness to talk about wealth, for those intimately involved it was an intoxicating moment of liberation. For those not invited, it looked rather different'.[49] It can be added that the English working class was of course never invited to the party. This has been really rubbed in by the callous contrast created by recent stern dispensations of austerity by Conservative governments throughout the decade of the 2010s.

Perhaps the most glaring instance of the hypocrisy of the household homily is 'Fat Cat Day', an idea created by the High Pay Centre think tank and the Chartered Institute of Personnel and Development. Every 4 January underlines the fact that in merely 3 days into the new year the money made by a typical FTSE 100 company chief executive exceeds the average annual UK salary. In other words, in a mere 3 days the average FTSE 100 chief executive has drawn in more money than the average salary in the UK over the course of the whole 365 days.[50] So much for an honest day's pay for an honest day's work!

Brexit and the unmaking of the English working class

The Brexit process cannot be understood without a reference to and a clear understanding of the working class. What has happened to the English working class since the onslaught of the Thatcher era, the supposedly Labour Blair interlude and the grinding austerity of Conservative governments beginning with Cameron's in 2010, can be captured by tweaking the title of E.P. Thompson's classic work to make it *The Un-making of the English Working Class*. One of the most straightforward ways in which the working class has been unmade since the Thatcher era has been simply by denying it the possibility of work and holding up the ever-present danger of unemployment. This straightforward and cruel manner of upholding the threat of unemployment and often carrying it through was further compounded with the tendency to subject the working class to abject humiliation by depriving them of their long tradition of dignity and pride. The rather sadistic manner in which the Conservatives have done this is to ridicule people for not looking hard enough for work. Back in the early days of Thatcherism in the 1980s, Norman Tebbit suggested that unemployed people should just get on to bikes and start looking for work, an admonishment he decided to repeat 30 years later.[51] This is a kind of derision and subjection to ridicule that has continued. In 2012, Chancellor George Osborne, as he continued to enforce his swingeing austerity cuts, made a distinction between 'skivers', who shirk work, and 'strivers', who are out on their way to work even as the skivers still have their curtains tightly drawn together.[52]

Another classic work already mentioned a little earlier, Richard Hoggart's *Uses of Literacy: Aspects of Working Class Life*, talks about the immense significance of solidarity for the working class in the UK.[53] It was this element of collective working-class solidarity that Thatcherism battered down with its Ayn Randian pull-yourself-up-by-your-own-bootstraps variety of individualism. It can perhaps be suggested that the very same Ayn Randian individual aspiration unleashed by Thatcherism was so corrosive, perhaps on account of this observation that Hoggart makes in his book: 'The solidarity is helped by the lack of scope for the growth of ambition'.[54]

This particular line from Hoggart's book is by no means meant to celebrate or romanticize the difficult and hard-pressed nature of working-class life in England or, for that matter, any part of the world. It is merely meant to indicate that there was spontaneous and genuine warmth that prevailed among the English working class. This spontaneous warmth could be something to be retrieved in the reordering of societies in order to make individuals happy and contented. In this manner, the way out of the economic crisis, compounded by the Coronavirus pandemic, may not be the hackneyed mainstream economic one of stimulating economic growth, boosting consumption and demand in the economy, but to reorder societies less on the lines of *homo economicus* and more on the lines of communities of individuals that flourish on account of less consumption and more fellow-feeling for those around.[55]

In an assessment of Brexit and the anger of the British working class, a contrast can be made with an earlier quiescence that was induced by a combination of admirable stoic resignation that could sometimes lapse into a less desirable kind of fatalism. Perhaps, in a twisted sort of way, Thatcherism changed that. It infused an angry discontent that has manifested itself in Brexit.

Thatcherism seems to possess a horror at the slightest whiff of collectivity as it would seem to suggest socialism. Her opposition to any notion of the collective is contained in that famous 1987 interview, with its relentless methodological individualism, when Mrs Thatcher famously opined that there is 'no such thing as society. There are individual men and women and there are families'.[56] Thatcherite free-market capitalism, with its pretty picture of perfectly rational individuals, was thus inherently corrosive of working-class solidarity and could be considered one of the further elements in the class war that Thatcher waged against the working class, once she had deprived them of their livelihood, work and dignity.

The question of solidarity

Solidarity is not confined just to the cohesiveness of the working class. In addition to working-class solidarity, which has already been mentioned, there would be the solidarity at the level of the unwritten British constitution that has kept the UK and its four nations – England, Scotland, Northern Ireland and Wales – together. Then there is the solidarity that has been created by the extensive British welfare state, designed to take care of the citizen from 'cradle to grave' and the foundation for which was laid by the Beveridge Report of 1942. One would have to mention the remarkable solidarity that has been created by the NHS set up in 1946.[57] The politics of Thatcherism has undermined solidarity at all these levels. Not only has it undermined the solidarity of the working class, but Thatcherism was a clear jettisoning of the one-nation Tory tradition that could be considered another one of those ties of solidarity that served to bind, this time in a kind of class-transcending manner, connecting the ruling class and the British Establishment, notionally committing them to look after the working class, in a spirit of *noblesse oblige*.

Austerity and the consequent Brexit process that it has given rise to have undermined solidarity at all these levels that have been mentioned, thereby endangering the very framework that has held the UK together over the centuries. Hard-line nationalisms of the kind that inspire a phenomenon like Brexit are likely with their extreme insistence on centralizing, pulling inward forces to disturb the balance that hitherto may have existed between opposing, yet complementary, centripetal and centrifugal forces. What Brexit threatens to do is to break into pieces and fragments the union, a truly broken Britain. Brexiteers might want to heed a bit of Oriental advice. The first Umayyad ruler Muawiya, when he was asked how he kept his territories together, suggested that what connects him to his countrymen was as fragile as a strand of hair. 'And even if there be one hair binding me to my fellow-men, I do not let it break: when they pull I loosen, and if they loosen I pull'.[58]

Notes

1 Thiemo Fetzer, *Did Austerity Cause Brexit?* Working Paper Series No. 381, Centre for Competitive Advantage in the Global Economy, Department of Economics, University of Warwick, June 2018. See also Alan Sked, 'The case for Brexit', *The National Interest*, No. 140, The GOP Civil War (November/December 2015), pgs. 41–50. https://www.jstor.org/stable/44028506. Accessed 16 September 2019.

2 See George Ross, 'Austerity and new spaces for protest: the financial crisis and its victims', in Marcos Ancelovici, Pascale Dufour, and Heloise Nez (eds.) *Street Politics in the Age of Austerity: From the Indignados to Occupy*, Amsterdam University Press, 2016, pgs. 43–65. https://www.jstor.org/stable/j.ctt1d8hb8t.5. Accessed 13 September 2019.

3 See John D. Fair, 'The conservative basis for the formation of the national government of 1931', *Journal of British Studies*, Vol. 19, No. 2 (Spring 1980), pgs. 142–164. https://www.jstor.org/stable/175497. Accessed 5 November 2019. The Ramsay Macdonald government had come to power in 1929 and by August 1931 was assailed by a full-scale financial crisis that necessitated a recourse to austerity measures. Macdonald has been criticized for accepting austerity measures, especially given the fact that he was a Labour politician. His government fell that same year to be succeeded by the Conservatives, who would remain in power until the beginning of the Second World War.

4 For the difficulties involved in defining globalization, see, Manfred B. Steger, *Globalization: A Very Short Introduction*, Oxford University Press, Oxford, 2017, chapter 1 especially the section in the chapter on 'Towards a definition of globalization'.

5 Chris Holden, 'Confronting Brexit and Trump: towards a socially progressive globalization', in Hudson John, Needham Catherine, and Heins Elke (eds.) *Social Policy Review 29: Analysis and Debate in Social Policy*, Bristol University Press, Bristol, UK and Chicago, IL, 2017, pgs. 63–82. https://www.jstor.org/stable/j.ctt1t8953p.9. Accessed 1 August 2020.

6 Peter Walker, 'Heseltine: imposing no-deal Brexit "intolerable" attack on democracy', *The Guardian*, Sunday, 11 August 2019. www.theguardian.com/politics/2019/aug/11/heseltine-imposing-no-deal-brexit-intolerable-attack-on-democracy. Accessed 21 August 2020.

7 The Rt. Hon the Lord Heseltine of Thenford CH, *No Stone Unturned*, October 2012. https://assets.publishing.service.gov.uk/government/uploads/system/uploads/attachment_data/file/34648/12-1213-no-stone-unturned-in-pursuit-of-growth.pdf. Accessed 20 June 2020.

8 Patrick Jenkins and Ian Bott, 'What happened to the "too big to fail" banks?', *The Financial Times*, 24 August 2017. www.ft.com/content/0bd8f4d4-76de-11e7-a3e8-60495fe6ca71. Accessed 31 July 2020.

9 Alex Callinicos, 'Contradictions of austerity', *Cambridge Journal of Economics*, Vol. 36, No. 1, Special Issue: Austerity: Making the same mistakes again – Or is this time different? (January 2012), pgs. 65–77. https://www.jstor.org/stable/24232380. Accessed 13 September 2019.

70 Brexit and austerity

10 See Robert Skidelsky, 'How austerity broke Britain – and how we can recover', *New Statesman*, 12–18 October 2018. www.newstatesman.com/politics/uk/2018/10/how-austerity-broke-britain-and-how-we-can-recover. Accessed 31 July 2020.
11 David Blanchflower, 'Autumn statement: George Osborne claims we're all in this together. But we're not', *The Independent*, Wednesday 3 December 2014. www.independent.co.uk/news/business/comment/david-blanchflower/autumn-statement-george-osborne-claims-we-re-all-in-this-together-but-we-re-not-9902008.html. Accessed 13 September 2019.
12 John Harris, 'Coronavirus means we really are, finally, all in this together', *The Guardian*, Sunday 29 March 2020. www.theguardian.com/commentisfree/2020/mar/29/coronavirus-means-we-really-are-finally-all-in-this-together. Accessed 31 July 2020.
13 Gary Dymski, 'The logic and impossibility of austerity', *Social Research*, Vol. 80, No. 3, Austerity Economics: Failed Economics but Persistent Policy (Fall 2013), pgs. 665–696. https://www.jstor.org/stable/24385688. Accessed 13 September 2019. Quoted lines on pg. 669.
14 Sue Konzelmann cited in Gary Dymski, 'The logic and impossibility of austerity', pg. 669.
15 Philip Mirowski, *Never Let a Serious Crisis Go to Waste: How Neoliberalism Survived the Financial Meltdown*, Verso, London and New York, 2014, pgs. 1–2.
16 Joe Bennett, 'Moralising class: a discourse analysis of the mainstream political response to Occupy and the August 2011 British riots', *Discourse & Society*, Vol. 24, No. 1 (January 2013), pgs. 27–45. https://www.jstor.org/stable/24441656. Accessed 3 October 2019.
17 Joe Bennett, 'Moralising class: a discourse analysis of the mainstream political response to Occupy and the August 2011 British riots', pg. 36.
18 Robert Hutton, 'The tory "malthouse compromise" and what it means for Brexit', *Bloomberg Quint*, 29 January 2019. www.bloombergquint.com/politics/the-tory-malthouse-compromise-and-what-it-means-for-brexit. Accessed 31 July 2020.
19 See Jeffrey Stevenson Murer, 'The emergence of a Lumpen-Consumerate: the aesthetics of consumption and violence in the English riots of 2011, *International Journal of Politics, Culture and Society*, Vol. 28, No. 2 (June 2015), pgs. 161–178. https://www.jstor.org/stable/24712997. Accessed 3 October 2019. This is how Murer begins his paper:

> It's midnight, and the crowd outside of the hip, new clothing store is growing, clamouring for the gates to be opened, pressing against one another. A triumphant cheer goes up, as the barrier to their entry into the store gives way, and the steel gate rises; young people squeeze under the barrier, rush inside the store before others can get there and grab all they can. Throughout the store, people run for what they want, stacking their loot in their arms.

Having rather graphically depicted this disorderly scenario, he suggests:

> Chaos, greed, pandemonium and violence, surely these must have been the scenes from Tottenham to Croydon in London from 2011. Yes these events did not occur in the UK, but rather in the US, and they are not meant to be condemned, but celebrated.

(pg. 162)

20 See James Treadwell, Daniel Briggs, Simon Winlow and Steve Hall, 'Shopocalypse now: consumer culture and the English riots of 2011', *The British Journal of Criminology*, Vol. 53, No. 1 (January 2013), pgs. 1–17. https://www.jstor.org/stable/23639965. Accessed 3 October 2019.
21 Slavoj Zizek, 'Shoplifters of the world unite', *London Review of Books*, 19 August 2011. www.lrb.co.uk/2011/08/19/slavoj-zizek/shoplifters-of-the-world-unite. Accessed 30 July, 2020.
22 Polly Toynbee, 'A civil war state of mind now threatens our democracy', *The Guardian*, Wednesday 28 August 2019. www.theguardian.com/commentisfree/2019/aug/28/proroguation-parliament-boris-johnson-brexit. Accessed 30 July 2020.

This is one of the arguments that Toynbee makes:

> The aggressive prorogation of parliament widens the Brexit debate into a civil war state of mind. This is the battleground Johnson seeks – himself as roguish, freewheeling, representative of the people's will, defender of referendum versus the Westminster establishment and the elite, as represented by MPs elected in Parliament.

23 'Brexit: operation Yellowhammer no-deal document published', *BBC News*, 11 September 2019. www.bbc.com/news/uk-politics-49670123. Accessed 11 July 2020.

24 Jonathan Read, 'Brexiteer says that "there should be riots" over Brexit in the style of gilets jaunets', *The New European*, 27 September 2019. www.theneweuropean.co.uk/top-stories/brendan-o-neill-on-politics-live-1-6294304. Accessed 4 October 2019.

25 Brendan O'Neill, 'Made by the welfare state', *Spiked*, 9 August 2011. www.spiked-online.com/2011/08/09/londons-burning-a-mob-made-by-the-welfare-state/ Accessed 4 October 2019

26 Paul Gilroy, *There Ain't No Black in the Union Jack: The Cultural Politics of Race and Nation*, Routledge, New York, 1992.

27 Olivia Petter, 'Windrush scandal: everything you need to know about the major political crisis', *The Independent*, Monday 22 June 2020. www.independent.co.uk/life-style/windrush-generation-scandal-sitting-in-limbo-anthony-bryan-documentary-a95522881.html. Accessed 31 July 2020.

28 Natalie Sedacca, 'Water cannon: In June the metropolitan police bought a supply of water cannon from Germany. Natalie Sedacca asks if it is for preventing disorder or quelling democratic rights?', *Socialist Lawyer*, No. 68 (October 2014), pgs. 20–22. https://www.jstor.org/stable/10.13169/socialistlawyer.68.0020. Accessed 3 October 2019.

29 Natalie Sedacca, 'Water cannon: In June the Metropolitan police bought a supply of water cannon from Germany. Natalie Sedacca asks if it is for preventing disorder or quelling democratic rights?', pg. 22.

30 'Ally of British PM apologized for accusing former minister of anti-Semitism', *The Times of Israel*, 30 September 2019. www.timesofisrael.com/ally-of-british-pm-apologizes-for-accusing-former-minister-of-anti-semitism/. Accessed 20 July 2020.

31 Felicity Lawrence, Rob Evans, David Pegg, Caelainn Barr and Pamela Duncan, 'How the right's radical thinktanks reshaped the Conservative party', *The Guardian*, Friday 29 November 2019. www.theguardian.com/politics/2019/nov/29/rightwing-thinktank-conservative-boris-johnson-brexit-atlas-network? Accessed 21 July 2020.

32 Daniel Stedman Jones, *Masters of the Universe: Hayek, Friedman and the Birth of Neoliberal Politics*, Princeton University Press, Princeton, NJ, 2012, pg. 134.

33 Daniel Stedman Jones, *Masters of the Universe: Hayek, Friedman and the Birth of Neoliberal Politics*, pg. 149.

34 On Anthony Fisher's tireless efforts, Jones, in his book *Masters of the Universe: Hayek, Friedman and the Birth of Neoliberal Politics*, has the following observations to make:

> Through what he called the Atlas Foundation, think tanks such as the Fisher Institute in Dallas, the Fraser Institute in Vancouver, the Manhattan Institute in New York City, and the Cato Institute, first in San Francisco and then removed to Washington, D.C., all modeled on the IEA, (Institute of Economic Affairs) were established across North America. Many more sprang up all over the world after 1980, especially in Eastern Europe and the countries of the former Communist bloc. John Redwood, once a member of Margaret Thatcher's Policy Unit and a cabinet minister in John Major's Conservative Government, has described the neoliberal breakthrough into Eastern Europe in the 1990s after the fall of the Berlin Wall as a "revolution". By the 1990s, it was clear that Fisher's legacy had contributed to the reforms that followed the collapse of the Berlin Wall in 1989. Fisher was a visionary who saw his project as international in scope and aimed at spreading free market, neoliberal ideas all over the world.
>
> *(pg. 158)*

72 Brexit and austerity

35 www.atlasnetwork.org/about/our-story. Accessed 2 August 2020.
36 'Theresa May borrows from David Cameron to slam Labour saying they "failed to mend the roof when the sun was shining" at PMQs', *The Scottish Sun*, 28 February 2018. www.thesun.co.uk/video/news/theresa-may-borrows-from-david-cameron-to-slam-labour-saying-they-failed-to-mend-the-roof-when-the-sun-was-shining-at-pmqs/. Accessed 2 August 2020.
37 Philip Mirowski, *Never Let a Serious Crisis Go to Waste*, pg. 28.
38 Philip Mirowski, *Never Let a Serious Crisis Go to Waste*, pg. 89.
39 Philip Mirowski, *Never Let a Serious Crisis Go to Waste*, pg. 131. In fact, Mirowski suggests that

> the culture of everyday neoliberalism tends to foster a set of attitudes reminiscent of Nietzsche's creditor psychology, and has plumped for a different morality: it extends beyond a defensive schadenfreude of the Great Contraction, if only because it predates the crash. Since the 1990s, not just the rich, but almost everyone else who still has a job has been galvanized to find within themselves a kind of guilt pleasure in the thousand unkind cuts administered by the enforcers of trickle-down austerity.
> *(pg. 130)*

40 See Robert Skidelsky, 'How austerity broke Britain – and how we can recover'. Consider what Skidelsky has to say:

> Of all the arguments supporting the Cameron and Osborne austerity policy (backed by the Liberal Democrats in government), the one that resonated most was that the government was like a private household. Everyone knows, so ran the argument, that if a household's income falls it has to reduce its consumption. It can borrow temporarily, but the loan must be paid back by saving even more. The same was true for a government. If its revenue falls, as a result of the slump, it needs to cut its own consumption. Any temporary borrowing should be repaid as quickly as possible. This was the logic of Osborne's austerity programme.
> *(www.newstatesman.com/politics/uk/2018/10/how-austerity-broke-britain-and-how-we-can-recover)*

41 Simon Wren-Lewis, *The Lies We Were Told: Politics, Economics, Austerity and Brexit*, Bristol University Press, Bristol, pgs. 142–143. https://www.jstor.com/stable/j.ctv7h0v2h.12. Accessed 1 August 2020.
42 www.youtube.com/watch?v=p1mJFJDPdOQ. Accessed 5 August 2020.
43 Harry McPhail, 'Throwback Thursday: Harold Macmillan's "never had it so good" speech', *Bedford Independent*, 5 September 2019. www.bedfordindependent.co.uk/throwbackthursday-harold-macmillans-had-is-so-good-speech/. Accessed 5 August 2020. The speech was made in July 1957 in Bedford.
44 Polly Toynbee, 'Selling off the family silver? Cameron and Osborne have gone way beyond that', *The Guardian*, Thursday 28 January 2016. www.theguardian.com/commentisfree/2016/jan/28/selling-family-silver-cameron-osborne-thatcher. Accessed 5 August 2020.
45 'UK household debt hits new, peak says TUC', *BBC News*, 7 January 2019, Business. www.bbc.com/news/business-46780279. Accessed 21 August 2020.
46 Alex Callinicos, 'Contradictions of austerity', pgs. 65–77. This particular point regarding financialisation of the economy is to be found on pg. 68.
47 Richard Hoggart, *The Uses of Literacy: Aspects of Working Class Life*, Penguin Modern Classics, London, 2009, pg. 63.
48 Graham Stewart, *Bang: A History of Britain in the 1980s*, Atlantic Books, London, 2013.
49 Iain Martin, *Crash, Bang, Wallop: The Inside Story of London's Big Bang and a Financial Revolution That Changed the World*, Sceptre, London, 2016, pg. 146.
50 Joe Sommerlad, 'What is Fat Cat Friday? The date exposing the yawning pay gap between CEOs and their employees', *The Independent*, Wednesday, 2 January 2019.

www.independent.co.uk/news/business/news/fat-cat-friday-ceos-executive-pay-gap-workers-salary-wages-a8707596.html. Accessed 21 August 2020.

51 Nathan Rao, 'Get on your bike, Norman Tebbit says – again', *Daily Express*, Wednesday 23 February 2011. www.express.co.uk/news/uk/230675/Get-on-your-bike-Norman-Tebbit-says-again. Accessed 20 June 2020.

52 George Monbiot, 'Skivers and strivers: this 200 year old myth won't die', *The Guardian*, 23 June 2015. Osborne invoked the distinction at the Conservative Party conference in early October 2012. www.theguardian.com/commentisfree/2015/jun/23/skivers-strivers-200-year-old-myth-wont-die. Accessed 10 June 2020.

53 Richard Hoggart in *The Uses of Literacy*, notes:

> In any discussion of working-class attitudes much is said about the group-sense, that feeling of being not so much an individual with 'a way to make' as one of a group whose members are all roughly level and likely to remain so. I avoid the word 'community' at this stage because its overtones seem too simply favourable; they may lead to an under-estimation of the harsher tensions and sanctions of working-class groups.
>
> *(pg. 64)*

54 Richard Hoggart, *The Uses of Literacy*, pg. 66.

55 See Amitai Etzioni, 'Politics and culture in an age of austerity', *International Journal of Politics, Culture, and Society,* Vol. 27, No. 4 (December 2014), pgs. 389–407. https://www.jstor.org/stable/24713303. Accessed 13 September 2019.

56 These famous lines have always been quoted in a truncated sort of way, so they deserve to be quoted in full:

> They are casting their problems at society. And you know, there's no such thing as society. There are individual men and women and there are families. And no government can do anything except through people, and people must look after themselves first. It is our duty to look after ourselves and then, also, to look after our neighbours.

(Mrs Thatcher said this in an interview in *Women's Own* in 1987. 'Margaret Thatcher: a life in quotes', *The Guardian*, Monday 8 April 2013. www.theguardian.com/politics/2013/apr/08/margaret-thatcher-quotes. Accessed 3 August 2020)

57 Tom Montgomery and Simone Baglioni, 'The United Kingdom', in Veronica Federico and Christian Lahusen (eds.) *Solidarity as a Public Virtue? Law and Public Policies in the European Union*, Nomos Verlagsgesellschaft mbH, 2018. https://www.jstor.org/stable/j.ctv941sdc.11. Accessed 16 September 2019.

58 Philip Hitti, *History of the Arabs: From the Earliest Times to the Present*. Revised Tenth Edition with a new Preface by Walid Khalidi, Palgrave Macmillan, Basingstoke, 2011, pg. 197.

4

'LET'S TAKE BACK CONTROL'

Brexit and the assertion of sovereignty

This chapter begins by considering yet another instance of the verbal vacuities that have characterized the Brexit process. In this instance the process of leaving the EU has been captured under the inanity of the slogan to 'take back control', which has been made at varying stages of the unfolding Brexit saga.[1] This desire to take back control contains within it the assertion of a rather confused and unformulated sovereignty. More specifically, it contains an almost archaic notion of Austinian sovereignty formulated in the early nineteenth century, whose premises may simply be unavailable in the interconnected globalized world of the twenty-first century. The Austinian conception is premised very centrally on, first, being able to identify a distinct individual such as the monarch or a body of individuals such as Parliament, to whom, second, habitual obedience is rendered by the vast bulk of people with, third, the sovereign itself not being in the habit of obeying someone or anything above itself.[2] British Prime Minister Boris Johnson, as he tried to push through his Brexit Withdrawal Agreement Bill soon after he had secured a deal with the EU in late October 2019, stated that the Bill would be the 'the greatest single restoration of national sovereignty in parliamentary history'. With his Etonian enunciation, Johnson attempted to present this supposed restoration of sovereignty as one of the most significant constitutional landmarks that Britain would experience for many years to come.[3]

However, there is a very crafty twist to the concept of an essentially Austinian sovereignty that has been invoked as a result of the Brexit process. Parliamentary sovereignty has been clearly undermined and, in its stead, there has appeared a crassly populist appeal made by Boris Johnson on behalf of 'the people'. Johnson's appeal to a vague notion of 'the people', which is straight out of the populist's playbook, is a crafty sleight of hand to give his consolidation of power a veneer of democratic legitimacy. The supposed democratic appeal on behalf of 'the people' can very quickly degenerate into a riotous mob. The fact that the crassly populist appeal on behalf of 'the people' has the potential to be transformed into a mob further reverberates to the demand for a strongman and powerful leader that supposedly emanates from 'the people' themselves. Who better to fit this role but 'ballsy Boris', who can even taunt the opposition Labour leader Jeremy Corbyn to 'man up' and face him in an election?[4] Boris Johnson's appeal to 'the people' is a classic instance of a member of the entitled Etonian elite temporarily making common cause with the mob. This alliance between the elite and the mob is a point that Hannah Arendt discusses several times in her book *The Origins of Totalitarianism*.[5]

Severe sovereignty versus soft sovereignty

A crucial aspect of the Brexit conundrum can be captured by framing the issue as an appeal to a particular kind of 'severe' sovereignty. With the creation of a European Parliament that issues legislation, the distinct and discernible nature of the sovereign to whom the bulk of the population are habituated to obeying has become obscured. As far as the Leave side of Brexit is concerned, like much else in the campaign, the appeal to sovereignty in the form of the slogan 'Let's take back control' is at best an empty and rhetorical one, and at worst a political programme for greater concentration and centralization of power. In starker terms, it is a path leading to authoritarianism. As the arguments in this chapter progress, it will be suggested that insights into the Brexit issue can be gained through adjusting the lens of sovereignty by moving it away from the 'severe' sovereignty associated with John Austin to a 'soft' sovereignty found in the writings of early twentieth-century English pluralists such as Harold Laski, J.N. Figgis, G.D.H Cole and George Unwin.

We begin with Laski, who was critical of the monistic theory of the modern state and offered instead the idea of a pluralist one. The monistic state came bundled with a particular notion of sovereignty that, according to Laski, in its 'scientific statement', went back to Jean Bodin, who in turn 'became the spiritual parent of Hobbes, and thence, through Bentham, the ancestor of Austin'.[6] Laski suggests that there is a remarkable manner in which the monistic state stands head and shoulders above all private and individual concerns that are rendered into pettiness in front of the majesty and supreme sovereignty of the state. What is not mentioned by Laski is the fact that this looming large of the state in supreme isolated sovereignty over the pettiness of private concerns should be so ironical, as the sovereignty of the state itself flows out of these self-same aggregated private individual concerns. What Laski does say about the emergence of the monistic state out of the petty squabbling concerns of private individual interests is this insightful point:

> The state is an absorptive animal; and there are few more amazing tracts of history than that which records its triumph over the challenge of competing groups. There seems, at least today, no certain method of escape from its demands. Its conscience is supreme over any private conception of good the individual may hold. It sets the terms upon which the lives of trade unions may be lived. It dictates their doctrine to churches. . . . The area of

its enterprise has consistently grown until today there is no field of human activity over which, in some degree, its pervading influence may not be detected.[7]

This is a profoundly insightful point about the way the state emerges and then stands in splendidly supreme and sovereign isolation above all other lower, narrower, pettier and more provincial concerns. It seems to emphasize the state standing apart, over and above, detached, and in an aloofness that would guarantee its being a neutral arbiter in the resolution of conflicts. What it does not bring out clearly, and perhaps misses out completely, is to reiterate the irony of this sovereignty that supposedly stands over and above in its resplendent isolation. The irony is that this sovereignty of the state is a seamless extension that emerges from lower, supposedly pettier, private individual concerns. This is a point that again Hannah Arendt brings out effectively in her book *The Origins of Totalitarianism*, a work that has resonated so much in recent times, when the world appears to have been on the brink of descent into totalitarianism. The world has started appearing since 2016 as reliving the experience of the 1930s.[8] Arendt's insight regarding the supremely public nature of the state's sovereignty emanating seamlessly from lower down private concerns is emphasized here on account of her reading of Thomas Hobbes:

> It is significant that modern believers in power are in complete accord with the philosophy of the only great thinker who ever attempted to derive public good from private interest and who, for the sake of private good, conceived and outlined a Commonwealth whose basis and ultimate end is accumulation of power. Hobbes, indeed, is the only great philosopher to whom the bourgeoisie can rightly and exclusively lay claim, even if his principles were not recognized by the bourgeoisie class for a long time. Hobbes's Leviathan exposed the only political theory according to which the state is not based on some kind of constituting law – whether divine law, the law of nature, or the law of social contract – which determines the rights and wrongs of the individual's interests with respect to public affairs, but on the individual interests themselves, so that 'the private interest is the same with the publique'.[9]

In bestowing a special status to the state, this conception of sovereignty almost denies, or at best significantly undermines, the existence of associations and groups that exist within its territorial ambit. Contrast this view of the state, standing in splendid isolation, to the view that the English pluralists held of looking at the state as one association among many others. The English pluralists offered a kind of antidote to the severity of Austin's sovereignty by drawing from the Germanophile writings of F.W. Maitland and the inspiration that he in turn drew from the German theorist, Otto Gierke.[10] The conclusion that one might arrive at is that the state, for the purposes of *coordinating* the possible conflicting functions of different associations, has a kind of special status, possibly *primus inter pares*, or first among equals, when it comes to a gradation of associations. This is, however, a conclusion that at least one figure among the English pluralists, G.D.H. Cole, certainly does not reach, and the reasons for this will be taken up a little later in the section of this chapter that deals with his writings.

What a consideration of severe and soft sovereignty tells us about Brexit

This initial consideration of sovereignty with respect to those who support leaving the EU does four things. First, it brings out the desire to bring about the restoration of sovereignty vis-à-vis the EU, as stated by Prime Minister Johnson. It represents a desire to reassert the viability of the nation-state in the face of the much-hated supranational entity that is the EU. The Brexit-obsessed politician Nigel Farage has often made this point in terms of the rebirth of the nation-state.[11] Second, these monistic claims of sovereignty go against the grain of the devolution of powers to the constituents of the UK, Scotland, Wales and Northern Ireland that were made in the series of landmark constitutional changes by the Blair government soon after assuming power in 1997, and more specifically have to do with the creation of the Northern Ireland, Welsh and Scottish assemblies.[12] Third, the more robustly hard Brexit postures are struck, the greater is the possibility of the union that is the UK breaking apart, a point made at the end of the previous chapter. Perhaps to the chagrin of Brexit supporters, the viability of the UK as a political entity is reinforced through the EU. A breaking away from the EU that Brexit is all about could mean the breaking up of the UK. The proclivity of the EU to favour the constituents of the UK is obvious from the way the EU has consistently stood up for the Republic of Ireland and crafted the earlier backstop arrangement as an insurance policy to prevent a hard border on the island of Ireland. Similarly, politicians of the Scottish Nationalist Party (SNP) have frequently made their case of breaking apart from the union of the UK to remain aligned with the EU. Fourth, and finally, Brexit, understood as an atavistic striving of English nationalism, underlines the reasoning behind the creation of the EU in the first place, especially by its continental architects such as Jean Monet. It was an outbreak of virulent strains of nationalism on the continent that led to the ravages of the Second World War, which particularly affected France and Germany. The memories of that seem to have been lost upon more hard-line Brexiteers.

Perhaps the wrong lessons of history have been learnt by Brexiteers. Some of them, such as Boris Johnson, have referred to the EU as a kind of Nazi project of totalitarianism.[13] In its stead they have emphasized that Britain is better off as a lone-ranger island nation with its buccaneering spirit of free trade with large parts of the world that were once its colonies and where famously the sun never set. The fact that this supposed free trade was actually enforced with the captive markets that British colonies became is completely missed in the history lessons that Johnson and his fellow Brexiteers like to draw. As Brexit Britain re-embarks on its farcical swashbuckling capture of world markets through 'trade agreements on WTO terms', as Brexiteers so cavalierly describe it, without seeming to fully understand the implications, the enduring relevance of Marx's hauntingly beautiful lines at the beginning of the *Eighteenth Brumaire of Louis Bonaparte*, about history repeating itself the first time as tragedy and the second time as farce, is particularly apt. In other words, a hard-line Brexit in the image of Johnson and his ilk is a farcical re-embarking of the swaggering spirit of the initial tragedy that was the British Empire.[14]

The framing of the Brexit issue in terms of the severe sovereignty inspired by Austinian British legal positivism and the softer sovereignty of the English pluralists does the following. It brings out the stark contrast between the homogeneous English nationalism crafted by the Leave side and the perhaps more heterogeneous, pluralist, possibly multicultural view of the Remain side. In addition, taking recourse to the English pluralists achieves something else in terms of coming to closer grips with the Brexit phenomenon, especially as it has manifested itself in the form of discontent stamped by the resilient culture of the working class of the North of England.[15] The English pluralists, especially someone like G.D.H. Cole and a relatively lesser-known George Unwin, represent the celebration of associational life through economic groupings such as the guild and the trade union.[16] A large part of the Brexit story can be told as the breaking up of such associations, beginning with the assault on trade unionism during the Thatcher years. This, combined with the more deleterious effects of austerity enforced by more recent Conservative governments such as that of David Cameron, has created an isolation that tends to corrode the possibilities of working class and trade union solidarity that many strands of English pluralism seem to have especially revelled in.

There may be a question mark raised over the contemporary significance of two rather dated perspectives on sovereignty, the nineteenth-century Austinian one and the early twentieth-century English pluralist one. However, the 1975 referendum that led to the UK joining what was then the EEC may need to be recalled. Both left and right of the political spectrum, in the form of Michael Foot and Enoch Powell, seemed to fold back and unite in calling for a no vote based on protecting parliamentary sovereignty.[17] The sovereignty associated with the English pluralists seems far more conducive to a more supranational arrangement as envisaged by the EU.

'Let's take back control'. Control of what?

The slogan 'let's take back control' immediately gives rise to the question of just exactly what is going to be controlled? And who is going to be doing the controlling? For ardent Brexiteers, it certainly does not mean the British Parliament taking control of Brexit. Indeed, Parliament has tried to do just that on several occasions. The businesswoman Gina Miller, in a successful petition to the Supreme Court in September 2017, ensured that any ultimate decision on the UK leaving the EU would be subject to Parliament passing an act. This was a step deeply resented by Brexiteers.[18]

Despite the Johnson government's repeated efforts to bypass, then undermine and thoroughly discredit it, Parliament and the House of Commons in particular has been successful in running rings around Boris Johnson. The attorney general Geoffrey Cox in September 2019 suggested that the commons were 'a disgrace' and that they had lost the moral right to sit on those famous green benches. This was of course echoed by the callous and coarse rhetoric of Prime Minister Johnson, who has kept insinuating that Parliament is a saboteur and wrecker of 'the people's' will contained in the Brexit referendum and that it has surrendered power to the EU.[19] What was further witnessed was the extraordinary spectacle of Johnson turning against Parliament by attempting to prorogue it for an extended 5-week period. All appearances suggested an intention on the part of Johnson to stymie the possibility of legislative scrutiny. The controversial move was thwarted by the UK Supreme Court in late September 2019. In uncharacteristically strong language, it ruled that the proroguing was not in order. Parliament promptly reconvened the very next day.[20]

Parliament had also passed the Benn Act, which placed a further constraint on Johnson by legally obliging him to approach the EU to request an extension of Article 50 (which involved the process of a member state leaving the EU), if a deal had not been arrived at by the 31 October 2019 deadline for Britain's exit from the EU. This was done to prevent the possibility of a calamitous no-deal British crash-out from the EU.[21] This was likely to create endless customs queues at the UK's borders, lead to food and medicine shortages and, more ominously, the possibility of violence and civil disorder on British streets. These rather dire warnings were contained in a government-commissioned report, Operation Yellowhammer.[22]

Even these warnings were not enough to deter Brexit adventurists, who seem to derive a thrill from the mere idea of leaving the EU. Johnson was characteristically leading from the front in terms of maintaining a steady barrage of irresponsible statements, as he kept suggesting that he would rather 'be dead in a ditch' than approach the EU for another extension and delay.[23] This can hardly be said to have helped in the negotiation process with the EU. Further, Johnson and his Cabinet colleagues seemed to be rather blasé about no-deal possibilities, with many cabinet members suggesting that Britain was ready even for the eventuality of a no-deal Brexit. This rather unbelievable attitude can again be captured in yet another empty and vacuous Brexit slogan: 'No deal, no problem!' Apparently, Nigel Farage is responsible for this addition to the series of Brexit inanities. Ellen Berry, writing in *The New York Times*, has this very valid observation to make, which indeed could very well capture my own reason for writing this book:

> One of the mysteries of Brexit – one that will be studied by political scientists for generations – is how, for much of the country, a gradualist goal of achieving a less-restrictive relationship with Europe was replaced by an extreme and risky one: walking away with no deal at all.[24]

80 'Let's take back control'

All that seemed to matter to Johnson and friends was the tearing rush to get out of the EU on 31 October. The apocalyptic manner in which the 31 October deadline was invoked was meant to raise electoral expectations to fever pitch, as by this time Johnson seemed to be almost itching to hold a general election as the best, and perhaps the only, way to consolidate his hold over power. Here again he was being thwarted by Parliament and the Labour opposition, which was making it clear that it would only countenance an election if the prospect of no-deal was taken off the table. What followed was a rather immature taunting of the opposition by Johnson, almost daring it to come and play the election game. This could give us an insight into the way Johnson conducted himself in the playground as a child, by which time he had of course already expressed a desire to be 'world king'.[25]

The taunting has, of course, not been confined to the opposition but extended to a general disdain of Parliament as an institution itself. Johnson kept referring to the Benn Act on the floor of the House of Commons as the 'surrender bill'. This disparagement of a Bill that had been passed by Parliament is just one indicator of the contempt in which Johnson holds Parliament. What was worse, and unbelievably so, was the language that the Prime Minister used that many opposition Labour MPs such as Jess Phillips suggested simultaneously mirrored and stoked the divisive and dangerous language out on the streets. In the face of criticism about his divisive rhetoric, Johnson dismissed it as 'humbug' and remained unrepentant by defending his use of what he called 'military metaphors' as being perfectly justifiable. Worse, he suggested that the best way to honour the murder of Labour MP Jo Cox a few days before the June 2016 Brexit referendum was by 'getting Brexit done'.[26]

The divisiveness of Johnson's language, especially with respect to the way he was running down Parliament, was suggestive of his desire to set up not just a crudely populist election campaign on the lines of the 'people versus Parliament', but more dangerously signalled an alliance between his own elitism and the riotous mob on the streets, a point that has already been made at an earlier stage in this chapter with a reference to the work of Hannah Arendt. This alliance between Johnson's Etonian elitism and the mob signalled impatience with parliamentary procedures and the desperate desire contained in the already voiced Brexit catchphrase to 'get on with it'. However, there was a further Brexit vapidity that Johnson was to about to coin, 'Get Brexit done'. It is interesting that after Johnson had used this latest vacuity, it seemed to catch on, with the words becoming the slogan of the Conservative Party conference held in Manchester in late September 2019 and being plastered onto every single available surface in the city.

This particularly vapid slogan, 'Get Brexit done', revealed something else and perhaps more insidious, which was the tendency to blackmail and hold the country to ransom. If people were disturbed by the divisiveness of the language, then they had only to 'Get Brexit done', and this divisiveness would go away. This language of blackmail and holding to ransom was evident not just in Johnson himself as he sparred with opposition MPs in the House of Commons. It came out clearly in a viral video in which a Labour MP, Karl Turner, confronted Johnson's powerful adviser, Dominic Cummings. As the visibly agitated Labour MP confronts him about the tone of the Prime Minister's language and the death threats that he had received, Cummings remains nonchalantly leaning against a pillar, and calmly tells the Labour MP to 'get Brexit done'.[27] In other words, in the face of the Brexit mob, there is no other option but to get the thing done and the death threats will go away. What we have then is not just a coarsening of the political discourse as a result of the divisive rhetoric that Brexit has introduced but a kind of menacing thuggishness.

Boris Johnson has been not just dismissive of Parliament but positively avoids the scrutiny that the institution is supposed to carry out on legislation. He was in a tearing rush to avoid parliamentary scrutiny of his Brexit Withdrawal Agreement Bill with his 31 October deadline fast approaching. His haste was more than evident in the programme motion that was tabled in the House of Commons that wanted to confine legislative scrutiny of the Bill to just 3 days, when it was obvious that a document of its bulk would need at least a few weeks of legislative attention. For a bill of such bulk and constitutional significance to receive such limited parliamentary scrutiny of 3 days meant that it would have received the same amount of attention as the 'Wild Animals in Circuses Act 2019'.[28] The defeat of the programme motion was preceded by just a few minutes when, in a rare Parliamentary success for Johnson, his Withdrawal Agreement Bill was passed by a majority of 30, thereby moving it to the second reading stage of legislation. This was no mean achievement, given the successive legislative defeats that Johnson had suffered in the House of Commons. Yet, as soon as the programme motion to confine the debate on the Bill to a mere 3 days was defeated, Johnson, in almost child-like petulance, decided to pause the bill altogether.[29] This was almost suggestive of a child who had lost interest and now wanted to play another game, this time the game of an election contest. This really is the problem with a politician like Boris Johnson. It is all a game that must be won and even in losing, the consequences are to be borne by someone else. There then immediately followed, talk of a general election before Christmas. Given Labour's lack of preparedness and perpetually bad state in the opinion polls, any statement of readiness for elections from them was viewed as 'turkeys voting for Christmas'.[30]

The question again arises, 'control of what'? The answer is not much. The simple reason is that the kind of Brexit envisaged by Boris and friends was always a deregulated low-tax regime that would depart from the high food, environmental and labour protection standards of the EU and move the UK into closer alignment with the US. The implications of this low-regulatory regime would be especially felt on the question of protection of workers' rights. Johnson made vague promises about protecting workers' rights as he defended his withdrawal agreement Bill in parliament in order to win over a few Labour MPs to support his bill, and he was, to an extent, successful. The nature of the Brexit phenomenon would also suggest that control does not mean regulating the market. The word control is actually deceptive as it implies the need to loosen many regulations such as environmental ones or, for that matter, social protection afforded to workers, many coming from the EU itself. The Brexit notion of control would also mean very centrally, exiting the jurisdiction of the European Court of Justice and the European Court of Human Rights. Brexit then has huge implications for the protection, or rather non-protection, of workers' rights, and this aspect of Brexit can again be understood by looking at the writings of another important figure of the English pluralists, G.D.H. Cole.

G.D.H. Cole and guild socialism

Ardent Brexiteers are likely to make fervent appeals to reclaiming sovereignty captured in the hollowness of the slogan 'take back control'. So far, this chapter has considered the external aspect of sovereignty, which is the problem of how the UK as a nation-state can possibly relinquish sovereignty of the Parliament in Westminster and surrender part of this to the European Parliament. The time has now come to consider an internal dimension of sovereignty. This pertains specifically to the proclivity on the part of the monist state to give minimal recognition to groups and associations below and it and within the boundaries of its territorial jurisdiction. This minimal recognition is itself an outcome of what some English pluralists have critiqued as the 'concession theory', whereby groups and associations below the state exist at the behest of the state that deigns to recognize them and could, by that logic, even de-recognize them. The monist state seems to give this strictly minimal recognition through the concession theory, almost as if it is jealously guarding its own hard fought severe sovereignty. It reinforces a point that was made earlier with reference to the works of Harold Laksi, whereby the monist state portrayed itself as standing way above all other groups and associations. This was despite the fact that the modern social contract state emerges almost directly out of individual private interests.

The problem with this severe sovereign view of the state is that it denies the vibrancy and vitality of associational life that exists immediately below the state. As against the monist theory of the state, the pluralist one would tend to look at the state as one association among many others. One would ordinarily be led into believing that such a view of the state might think of it as playing the crucial role of a vital coordinating mechanism that would be able to counteract the possibilities of conflict between the aims and functions of various groups and associations. It would then be *primus inter pares*, a first among equals, among associations, rather than enjoying the status of majestic over-lordship. Notice that the pluralist view of the state differs from the monist view on two different fronts, apart from and in addition to what has been differentiated as the severe sovereignty of the monist state and the soft sovereignty of the pluralist one. First, the monist view assumes the state flowing seamlessly out of the pursuit of individual self-interest sans conflict, while the pluralist view of the state factors in conflict by looking at the state as *possibly* playing a crucial coordinating role to counteract and mitigate the effects of conflicts and collisions among associations and groups. Second, the monist view predominantly factors in individuals and factors out groups and associations while the pluralist view gives a significant amount of attention to the plurality of groups.

In the interpretation of the pluralist state put forward here, a great deal of stress has been placed on the coordinating role that the state needs to make to counteract the effects of conflicts between different groups. On the basis of the crucial coordinating role, the state has been interpreted as *primus inter pares*, or first among equals, rather than as an excessively special majestic over-lordship. However, a prominent English pluralist, G.D.H. Cole, in his writings, denies the role of coordination to the state altogether.[31] One can speculate that this denial of a crucial coordinating function to the state could be on account of Cole's desire to rule out and prevent the state from taking recourse to a form of severe sovereignty. However, it is not just that. It also has to do with Cole's ideas on representative democracy, whereby he wants to eliminate the rather generalized forms of representation that pervade most representative democracies in the world and that, from his perspective, make quite a hash out of representation. He wants to connect representative democracy with the functions of associations. As a result Cole favours a form of functional representation, whereby the generalized and diffuse nature of territorial representation that has existed in most democracies can be replaced. He suggests:

> True representation, therefore, like true association, is always specific and functional, and never general and inclusive. What is represented is never man, the individual, but always certain purposes common to groups of individuals. That theory of representative government which is based upon the idea that individuals can be represented as wholes is a false theory, and destructive of personal rights and social well being.[32]

In fact, one notices that the crucial role of coordination that he vigorously wanted to deny to the state reappears at the level of functional representation. Cole critiques the Westminster Parliament, supposed to represent the kind of untainted severe sovereignty that he seems to be opposing:

> Thus, misrepresentation is seen at its worst to-day in that professedly omnicompetent 'representative' body – Parliament – and in the Cabinet which is supposed to depend upon it, Parliament professes to represent all the citizens in all things, and therefore as a rule represents none of them in anything.

However, in these times of the Johnson cabinet's outright berating of the Parliament and indeed the very insinuation that its intent is to frustrate the will of the people, this point made by Cole stands out: 'This is not the fault of the actual Members of Parliament, they muddle because they are set the impossible task of being good at everything, and representing, everybody in relation to every purpose'. Much of what he has said leads him to the conclusion that, 'real democracy is to be found, not in a single omnicompetent representative assembly, but in a system of co-ordinated functional representative bodies'.[33] Once again, in Cole's account, coordination is not done by the State, but occurs at the level of the multiplicity of functional representative bodies.

Cole's point about functional representation flows out of his idea of associations and functions that he has previously talked about before taking up a consideration

84 'Let's take back control'

of democracy and representation. Associations have a clear vision on their aims and objectives and are organized around the attainment of those purposes and functions. This is done more simply at lower and less complex levels of association and tends to get more difficult as one proceeds to more complex, larger and all-encompassing ones. By the time one reaches the complexity and expanse of the association that we know as the state, Cole notes: 'In the largest and most complex forms of association, such as the state, the ordinary member is reduced to a mere voter, and all the direction of actual affairs is done by representatives – or misrepresentatives'. All that Cole is doing is to connect the understanding of the purpose and functions of associations that he has already enunciated, to his ideas on democracy and the particular form of representation that it needs to be based on. The result of this connecting of the functions of associations to ideas on democracy is in fact quite dramatic. Not only does he clairvoyantly see beyond what he dismissively calls the 'general prejudice in favour of democracy' but tends to suggest a kind of multiple voting for the interested voter rather than the flat and superficially democratic principle of one person one vote, which he dismisses as 'the cant of a false democracy'. This may not be the best place to go into his radical reconsideration of representative democracy, but one is tempted to read these lines in the light of claims by critics of the Brexit referendum that many voters were ill-informed and wilfully misinformed about what they were getting themselves into:

> Many and keen voters are best of all; but few and keen voters are the next best. A vast and uninterested electorate voting on a general and undefined issue is the worst of all. Yet that is what we call democracy today.[34]

The actual reasons for Cole's denial of a coordinating role for the state is stated far more emphatically when he takes up the question of coercion, when he suggests that 'clearly co-ordination and coercion go hand in hand'. The claim for coordination by a sovereign state is ordinarily made on the assumption that the state includes all other associations within its territorial ambit, while all other associations include only a fraction of people. However, Cole suggests that the state:

> may include everybody, but it does not include the whole of everybody; it may represent some purposes common to everybody, but it does not represent all the purposes common to everybody. This being so, it can no longer lay claim to sovereignty on the ground that it represents and includes everybody; for the sovereign, if there is one, must represent and include, as far as possible, the whole of everybody.[35]

The forgotten tradition of English pluralism. The death of trade unionism and the return of sovereignty with a vengeance

One of the biggest targets that the English pluralists attacked was the idea of sovereignty, especially as it had been enunciated and developed from Bodin, through

Hobbes, right up to John Austin. In the opinion of most English pluralists, statism, strengthened and fortified by 'severe sovereignty', tends to especially crack down on the church, the trade guild and the trade union. Around the time that the English pluralists were writing, the momentous Taff Vale case of July 1901 was heard by the House of Lords, which, in those days, would still have been the highest court of appeal until the UK Supreme Court was created more than a century later in 2009. The Taff Vale case has had momentous consequences for the British trade union movement. While the Taff Vale case recognized trade unions as legal corporations, and as a result some who were sympathetic to the cause of trade unionism looked at this aspect of the judgement as favourable, it held that unions were liable to bear the financial costs and fallout of their decision to strike work. As a result of the case, the unions were liable to pay £23,000 to the Taff Vale Railway Company, where the industrial action had taken place. The reversal suffered by trade unions as a result of the Taff Vale ruling provided the impetus for the creation of the Labour Party, supported by subscriptions paid by members. The trade union movement and its recently created vehicle, the Labour Party, were to receive another blow, this time in the year 1909 in the form of the Osborne judgement, as a result of which unions could not contribute funds in support of a political party. The disadvantageous effects of this were to be reversed four years later in 1913, when legislation was passed to restore the unions' freedom to contribute funds for the running of the Labour Party.[36]

It is the implications of the state crackdown on trade unionism that has had severe consequences on politics in the UK and, for that matter, the rest of the world since the 1970s. From the end of the 1970s, there arose a general feeling that the trade unions were becoming too strong, especially the powerful mining unions, which were apparently holding the country to ransom. The 1974 snap general election was called by Conservative Prime Minister Edward Heath, almost in exasperation, when he posed the question to the electorate 'Who Governs?'[37] Heath of course lost, paving the way for the Labour government of Harold Wilson. This was just two years after the success enjoyed by Arthur Scargill and the NUM in the 1972 Saltley coke works industrial action, when the striking miners were able to prevent the transport of coke by assembling in large numbers at the gates of the plant. With the return of Harold Wilson to power in 1974, Labour encouraged a kind of corporatism, with the trade unions regularly coming down to 10 Downing Street and deciding issues in a convivial manner. This was to remain a feature of British politics throughout the decade. It remained intact, even with Wilson stepping down in March 1976 and the power centre within Labour moving distinctly to the right under the Prime Ministership of James Callaghan and his Chancellor of the Exchequer Denis Healey. The larger political pendulum globally was also very clearly swinging to the right, and the politics of trade unionism was to be massively wrong-footed. Nothing could reflect the general state of exasperation with the unions than the 1978 winter of discontent, when famously industrial action resulted in garbage remaining uncollected and piling up in London and the dead remaining unburied.[38] The rise to power of Margaret Thatcher in May 1979 has become the stuff of legends in British politics against the backdrop described

86 'Let's take back control'

previously. Thatcher, of course, started plotting the downfall of the NUM and struck the decisive hammer blow against trade unionism with the 1984–1985 Miners' Strike.

One of the best accounts of the Miners' Strike is David Peace's novel *GB 84*. In the author's note at the beginning of the book, Peace explains its character in the following manner: 'With the exception of those persons appearing as well-known personalities under their own names, albeit often in occult circumstance, all other characters are a fiction in a novel based upon a fact'.[39] Peace's book was published 20 years after the Miners' Strike and is a striking work of 'fiction based upon a fact'. The book is dark and intense, very much a part of the 'Yorkshire noir' that his work has been characterized as. It brings up the 'occult' in terms of the dark acts of the Thatcher government in terms of the employment of the British intelligence agency MI5 and the central role played by the head of MI5, Stella Rimington, to break up the strike action of the NUM led by Arthur Scargill. Peace's book facilitates a move to a more sinister, perhaps occult, notion of sovereignty as the chapter reaches its conclusion.

However, to revert briefly to the English pluralists, the point remains that their ire against the kind of severe sovereignty discussed earlier was not entirely misplaced. Severe sovereignty became the blunt instrumentality of the state that struck the decisive hammer blow against the NUM and by extension trade unionism itself. At the height of the 1984–1985 Miners' Strike, Mrs Thatcher's regime declared an almost outright war with the NUM, portraying it as the 'enemy within'. With her famous victory in the Falklands War very recently behind her, she drew a parallel with the Argentine junta as the enemy without and the NUM leadership, 'the enemy within, much more difficult to fight, [and] just as dangerous to liberty'. This was, in many ways, an extraordinary statement to make by a prime minister and was immediately rebuked by the opposition leader Neil Kinnock: 'Any prime minister of Britain who confuses a fascist dictator who invades British sovereign territory with British trade unions and with miners, I think is not fit to govern this country'.[40] In fact, to continue with the references to Latin American dictatorships, Arthur Scargill had complained about the severity of police actions against striking miners at the Orgreave coke works in May 1984, when he compared them to 'an actual police state tantamount to something you are used to seeing in Chile or Bolivia'.[41] The references to Latin America were not accidental, as Mrs Thatcher often expressed admiration at the brutal promotion of neoliberalism by Chilean dictator Augusto Pinochet. Pinochet's outrageous human rights violations in Chile and the flashes of brutality witnessed in Thatcher's Britain can perhaps give us the best clue about the supposed free markets of neoliberalism. When push comes to shove, as they certainly did at the 'Battle of Orgreave' in May 1984, the free market is enforced by the police baton or the military jackboot.[42] One can also get a clear sense of how far Thatcher's Conservatism had travelled from the *comparatively* more benign one-nation Toryism of an earlier generation such as Harold Macmillan from what he had to say in 1984:

> It breaks my heart to see what is happening in our country today. A terrible strike is being carried on by the best men in the world. They beat the Kaiser's

army and they beat Hitler's army. They never gave in. The strike is endless and pointless. We cannot afford action of this kind. . . . I can only describe as wicked the hatred that has been introduced.[43]

Policing tactics were transformed from being a general maintenance of law and order on the streets into a more intimidating paramilitary presence with police forces actually inflicting bodily harm. This was being perfected by the British state and was especially manifest at Orgreave in May 1984. The way in which police would ride horses into picketing miners and the effect of their creating a fearsome noise as they banged their special riot batons on their special shields is more in line with the situation of a war. An assessment of the neoliberal obsession with the rolling back of the frontiers of the state would always need to be done in the light of the simultaneous rolling out of the harsh repressive arm of the very same neoliberal state.[44]

More sinisterly, the identification and the declaration of the striking miners as the 'enemy within' by Mrs Thatcher is clearly an instance of the controversial political theorist Carl Schmitt's understanding of politics as the identification of friends and enemies. Matthew Hart, in his reading of David Peace's dark and disturbing book *GB84*, suggests: 'In its dissolution of the corporatist compromise of the 1970s and its instinctive hostility toward the politics of consensus, Thatcherism has an affinity with Schmitt's theorization of political power as indivisible and antagonistic'.[45] Such an understanding of politics raises the stakes extraordinarily high as the identification of friend and enemy makes the opponent a threat to one's very own existence. This would be the complete opposite of liberal and consensual politics. The unfolding of the Brexit phenomenon has revealed the sharply polarized divisions of British society, suggesting that Mrs Thatcher's 11-year rule could really be considered to be the prelude to Brexit itself. You are either Leave or Remain, you are with us or against us. If you are against, then you are a traitor to the cause, and Schmitt would suggest: 'Each participant is in a position to judge whether the adversary intends to negate his opponent's way of life and therefore must be repulsed or fought in order to preserve one's own form of existence'.[46] Brexit, understood in the frame of this kind of Schmittian politics, would then represent the very tragic, rather than strange, death of liberal politics, thereby recalling in more dire ways the title of George Dangerfield's book *The Strange Death of Liberal Britain*.[47]

But there is much more that needs to be teased out of Mrs Thatcher's identification of 'the enemy within'. Of course, it is a high point of the political when the enemy is clearly within sight and identified. However, the implications of this Schmittian identification extend to an invocation of a particular kind of sovereignty far severer and even tougher than the one that has so far been talked about in this chapter. Mrs Thatcher's politics celebrated the supposed sovereignty of the individual. There was no such thing as society, as she famously proclaimed. But let us see what is left of the individual in the Schmittian framework that we have adopted here to understand Mrs Thatcher's crushing of the Miners' Strike through the identification of the 'enemy within'. When the first miners started drifting

88 'Let's take back control'

back to work and were immediately labelled as 'scabs' by their fellow workers, who were still striking, this is what Mrs Thatcher had to say about them: '"Scabs" their former workmates call them. Scabs? They are lions!'[48] Such a lionization of the individual, who went against the threatening herd, would be ruled out by Schmitt himself.

As Tracy Strong explains in her foreword, Schmitt's concept of the political stands against his conception of 'political romanticism', which was the subject of one of his early books. Such political romanticism would celebrate, indeed lionize, the individual to create an endless discussion of individual and differing perspectives. This would be the complete opposite of the political in Schmitt, which is characterized by closure of endless perpetual points of view. This is where Schmitt's conception of sovereignty would come in to strike the decisive hammer blow against not just the trade union but the individual himself, for that matter. Tracy Strong notes how the conception of the political in Schmitt stands in consonance with his conception of sovereignty, which is the making of the authoritative decision concerned with the exception, sans any reference to anything but the decision itself. Here, we have the return of the splendid isolation of the sovereign in a form far severer than was the target of the English pluralists. This is what the supposed invocation of sovereignty in the slogan 'Let's take back control' would culminate in, whereby sovereignty would become the blunt instrumentality that created the grounds for, to borrow from the title of Hannah Arendt's book, the 'origins of totalitarianism'. It is no wonder that in true Schmittian sovereign manner, Boris Johnson just wants to 'get Brexit done'. Period.

Notes

1 Juliette Ringersen-Biardeaud, '"Let's take back control": Brexit and the debate on sovereignty', *French Journal of British Studies*, Vol. XXII, No. 2 (2017).
2 Suri Ratnapala, *Jurisprudence*, Cambridge University Press, Cambridge, 2009, pg. 42.
3 www.youtube.com/watch?v=q4GLeIS9Dtw; Accessed 1 February 2021. David Reid, 'Boris Johnson set for Brexit showdown in historic day for UK politics', *CNBC*, Friday 18 October 2019. www.cnbc.com/2019/10/19/brexit-boris-johnson-set-for-show down-in-historic-day-for-uk-politics.html. Accessed 1 February 2021.
    Perhaps Johnson would do well to heed the words written by Philip Stephens in his article 'Boris Johnson is wrong. Parliament has the ultimate authority' published by *The Financial Times* a few months before the 2016 referendum:
    'So to take back sovereignty can be to surrender control'. At the beginning of the article, Stephens notes how sovereignty has become the 'neuralgic word' in the British debate about the Europe. www.ft.com/content/26b6a12c-daf2-11e5-a72f-1e7744c66818. Accessed 1 February 2021.
4 See *The Sun* front page of 29 August 2019, which gushingly reported Boris Johnson's decision to prorogue parliament. Above the headline 'Hey Big Suspender', it announced with its characteristic bawdiness: 'Ballsy Boris comes out fighting'. www.theguardian. com/politics/2019/aug/29/day-democracy-died-what-the-papers-say-about-prorogu ing-parliament. Accessed 1 February 2021.
5 Hannah Arendt, *The Origins of Totalitarianism*, Penguin Modern Classics, London, 2017, Arendt suggests that the view of giving an undue deference to the voice of the people extends 'back to the same fundamental error of regarding the mob as identical with

rather than as a caricature of the people'. The following lines from Arendt's book in the section on anti-Semitism, where she is discussing the Dreyfus Affair, can be considered especially relevant for Boris Johnson's Brexit Britain. This is actually quite ironical given the fact that every time a charge of Islamophobia is made against him, rather than responding to it, Johnson engages in a kind of 'whataboutery' regarding the anti-Semitism that is prevalent in the British Labour Party, which, by available accounts, has reached quite problematic levels under the leadership of Jeremy Corbyn. But consider these lines from Arendt:

> The mob is primarily a group in which the residue of all classes are represented. This makes it so easy to mistake the mob for the people, which also comprises all strata of society. While the people in all great revolutions fight for true representation, the mob always will shout for the 'strong man,' the 'great leader'. For the mob hates society from which it is excluded, as well as Parliament where it is not represented. Plebiscites, therefore, with which the modern mob leaders have obtained such excellent results, are an old concept of politicians who rely upon the mob.
>
> (pg. 138)

6 Harold Laski, 'The pluralist state', in Paul Q. Hirst (ed.) *The Pluralist Theory of the State: Selected Writings of G.D.H. Cole, J.N. Figgis, and H.J. Laski*, Routledge, London and New York, 1989, pg. 184. In terms of the articulation of the monistic theory of the state and a centralization of power, Laski notes:

> We must ceaselessly remember that the monistic theory of the state was born in an age of crisis and that each period of its revivification has synchronized with some momentous event which has signalized a change in the distribution of political power. Bodin, as is well-known, was of that party which, in an age of religious warfare, asserted, lest it perish in an alien battle, the supremacy of the state. Hobbes sought the means of order in a period when King and Parliament battled for the balance of power. Bentham published his Fragment on the eve of the Declaration of Independence; and Adam Smith, in the same year, was outlining the programme of another and profounder revolution. Hegel's philosophy was the outcome of a vision of German multiplicity destroyed by the unity of France. Austin's book was conceived when the middle classes of France and England had, in their various ways, achieved the conquest of a state hitherto but partly open to their ambition.
>
> (pg. 184)

7 Harold Laski, 'The pluralist state', pg. 185.
8 See Paul Mason, 'Are we living through another 1930s?', *The Guardian*, Monday 1 August 2016. www.theguardian.com/commentisfree/2016/aug/01/are-we-living-through-another-1930s-paul-mason. Accessed 1 February 2021.
9 Hannah Arendt, *The Origins of Totalitarianism*, pg. 180.
10 Otto Gierke, *Political Writings of the Middle Age*, Translated with an introduction by Frederic William Maitland, Cambridge University Press, Cambridge, 1987.
11 www.youtube.com/watch?v=v0u-pBzKbAU. Accessed 1 February 2021.
12 Simon Bulmer, Martin Burch, Patricia Hogwood and Andrew Scott, 'UK devolution and the European Union: a tale of cooperative asymmetry?', *Publius*, Vol. 36, No. 1 (Winter 2006), pgs. 75–93. https://www.jstor.com/stable/20184943. Accessed 7 August 2020.
13 Michael White, 'Boris, the EU and Hitler: bad taste, bad judgment', *The Guardian*, Sunday 15 May 2016. www.theguardian.com/politics/2016/may/15/boris-johnson-eu-hitler-bad-taste-bad-judgment. Accessed 1 February 2021.
14 The lines from the opening of the Eighteenth Brumaire deserve being quoted in full: Hegel remarks somewhere that all great world-historic facts and personages appear, so to speak, twice. He forgot to add: the first time as tragedy, the second time as farce. Caussidiere for Danton, Louis Blanc for Robespierre, the Montagne of 1848 to 1851 for the

90 'Let's take back control'

Montagne of 1793 to 1795, the nephew for the uncle. And the same caricature occurs in the circumstances of the second edition of the Eighteenth Brumaire. www.marxists.org/archive/marx/works/1852/18th-brumaire/ch01.htm. Accessed 30 January 2021.

15 Richard Hoggart, *The Uses of Literacy: Aspects of Working-Class Life*, Penguin Classics, London, 2009.

16 Julia Stapleton, 'English pluralism as cultural definition: the social and political thought of George Unwin', *Journal of the History of Ideas*, Vol. 52, No. 4 (October–December 1991), pgs. 665–684. https://www.jstor.org/stable/2709971. Accessed 5 April 2021.

17 Paul Q. Hirst, *The Pluralist Theory of the State: Selected Writings of G.D.H. Cole, J.N. Figgis, and H.J. Laski*, Routledge, London and New York, 1989, pg. 23.

18 '"Gina Miller" Who is campaigner behind Brexit court cases', *BBC News*, 25 September 2019. www.bbc.com/news/uk-politics-37861888. Accessed 7 August 2020.

19 Jonathan Freedland, 'A disgrace? Not at all: we'll miss this House of Commons', *The Guardian*, Friday 1 November 2019. Freedland notes:

> Yet in truth, far from waving off the outgoing Commons with jeers and condemnation, we should thank them for their service. The very fact that Boris Johnson itched to see them gone is testament to their achievement. They have done their job – of acting as a restraint on the executive – with unusual ingenuity and even, whisper it, bravery.

Freedland also pays tribute to the Speaker John Bercow, who, he notes, was 'hardly shy of public attention, knew his duty was to defend parliament against the power-grabbing instincts of the executive'. www.theguardian.com/commentisfree/2019/nov/01/house-of-commons-mps-women-abuse. Accessed 1 February 2021.

20 Owen Bowcott, Ben Quinn and Severin Carrell, 'Johnson's suspension of parliament unlawful, supreme court rules', *The Guardian*, Tuesday 24 September 2019. https://www.theguardian.com/law/2019/sep/24/boris-johnsons-suspension-of-parliament-unlawful-supreme-court-rules-prorogue. Accessed 1 February 2021.

21 'What was the Benn Act?' The UK in a changing Europe.

> If the Article 50 process were extended, which it was, the Act also created further obligations for the Government to lay reports on the status of negotiations with the EU, which could be voted on by the House of Commons. The Act was introduced as a Private Members' Bill by the Labour MP Hilary Benn. It passed Third Reading in the House of Commons with a majority of 28 (327 votes to 299) and gained Royal Assent on 9 September 2019.
>
> *(www.ukandeu.ac.uk/fact-figures/the-benn-act/.*
> *Accessed 8 August 2020)*

22 'Operation Yellowhammer'. The Institute for Government. www.instituteforgovernment.org.uk/explainers/operation-yellowhammer. Accessed 8 August 2020.

23 Kate Proctor and Peter Walker, 'Boris Johnson: I'd rather be dead in ditch than agree Brexit extension', *The Guardian*, Thursday 5 September 2019. www.theguardian.com/politics/2019/sep/05/boris-johnson-rather-be-dead-in-ditch-than-agree-brexit-extension. Accessed 8 August 2020.

24 Ellen Berry, 'From "no problem" to no deal: how Brexit supporters embraced the Cliff Edge', *The New York Times*, 23 March 2019. www.nytimes.com/2019/03/23/world/europe/brexit-no-deal-may.html. Accessed 8 August 2020.

25 'Boris Johnson: the boy who wanted to be world king', *BBC News*, 24 July 2019. www.bbc.com/news/av/uk-politics-49088773/boris-johnson-the-boy-who-wanted-to-be-world-king. Accessed 8 August 2020.

26 Zamira Rahim, 'Labour MP Jess Phillips receives death threat "quoting Boris Johnson"', *The Independent*, Thursday 26 September 2019. www.independent.co.uk/news/uk/politics/jess-philips-death-threat-boris-johnson-brexit-speech-labour-parliament-a9121231.html. Accessed 1 February 2021.

27 www.youtube.com/watch?v=u8FAhyQEJRI. Accessed 1 February 2021.

28 Tom Caygill, 'The withdrawal agreement bill in the commons: a good outcome for parliamentary scrutiny', *British Politics and Policy at LSE*, 23 October 2019. https://blogs.lse.ac.uk/politicsandpolicy/wab-scrutiny. Accessed 12 August 2020.

29 Frances Perraudin, Ben Quinn and Kevin Rawlinson, 'Brexit legislation "paused" after MPs reject Boris Johnson's timetable – as it happened', *The Guardian*, Tuesday 22 October 2019. www.theguardian.com/politics/blog/live/2019/oct/22/brexit-boris-johnson-deal-leave-eu-live-news?page=with%3Ablock-5daf44c98f0859498cfb27a3. Accessed 12 August 2020.

30 Joe Murphy and Nicholas Cecil, 'Turkeys vote for Christmas: labour caves and backs December vote – but some Tories fears going to polls without delivering Brexit', *London Evening Standard*, Tuesday 29 October 2019. www.standard.co.uk/news/politics/boris-johnson-offers-december-11-election-as-labour-vows-to-back-prechristmas-poll-a4273136.html. Accessed 12 August 2020.

31 This is what G.D.H Cole, 'Democracy and representation', in Paul Q. Hirst (ed.) *The Pluralist Theory of the State: Selected Writings of G.D.H. Cole, J.N. Figgis, and H.J. Laski*, Routledge, London and New York, 1989, has to say:

> This is a conclusion of far-reaching and fundamental importance; for if the state is not the coordinating authority within the community, neither is it, in the sense usually attached to the term, 'sovereign'. But the claim to 'sovereignty' is that on which the most exalted pretensions of the state are based. Almost all modern theories of the state attribute to it not merely a superiority to all other forms of association, but an absolute difference in kind, by virtue of which it is supposed to possess, in theory at least, an unlimited authority over every other association and every other individual in the community.
>
> *(pg. 80)*

32 G.D.H. Cole, 'Democracy and representation', pg. 84.

33 G.D.H. Cole, 'Democracy and representation', pg. 85.

34 G.D.H. Cole, 'Democracy and representation', pg. 90.

35 G.D.H. Cole, 'Democracy and representation', pg. 100.

36 I have relied on Henry Pelling's *A History of British Trade Unionism*, Penguin Books, Harmondsworth, 1965, chapter 7 'From Taff Vale to Triple Alliance, 1900–14'.

37 Lewis Baston, 'Elections past: who governs?', *The Guardian*, 4 April 2005. www.theguardian.com/politics/2005/apr/04/electionspast.past9. Accessed 27 January 2021.

38 For a highly readable account of the decade of the 1970s in Britain, see Andy Beckett, *When the Lights went out: Britain in the 1970s*, Faber & Faber, London, 2009.

39 David Peace, *GB84*, Faber & Faber, London, 2004. See Matthew Hart, 'The third English Civil War: David Peace's "occult history" of Thatcherism', *Contemporary Literature*, Vol. 49, No. 4, Contemporary Literature and the State (Winter 2008), pgs. 573–596. https://www.jstor.org/stable/20616402. Accessed 19 November 2019.

40 Quoted in Graham Stewart, *Bang: A History of Britain in the 1980s*, Atlantic Books, London, 2013, pg. 353.

41 Quoted in Graham Stewart, *Bang: A History of Britain in the 1980s*, pg. 348.

42 For a sense of Thatcher's warmth towards Pinochet when he was arrested in the UK by Tony Blair's Labour government in the late 1990s, see Mat Youkee, 'Thatcher sent Pinochet finest scotch during former dictator's UK house arrest', *The Guardian*, Friday October 4th 2019. www.theguardian.com/world/2019/oct/04/margaret-thatcher-pinochet-chile-scotch-malt-whisky. Accessed 1 February 2021.

43 Quoted in Graham Stewart, *Bang! A History of Britain in the 1980s*, Atlantic Books, London, 2013, pg. 354. Stewart notes that Macmillan's 'perspective was a world – or at least a couple of generations – away from that of Thatcher'.

44 See Tony Bunyan, 'From Saltley to Orgreave via Brixton', *Journal of Law and Society*, Vol. 12, No. 3, The State v. the People: Lessons from the Coal Dispute (Winter 1985), pgs. 293–303. https://www.jstor.org/stable/1410123. Accessed 19 November 2019.

45 See Matthew Hart, 'The third English Civil War: David Peace's "occult history" of Thatcherism', pg. 591.
46 quoted in Tracy B. Strong, 'Foreword: dimensions of the new debate Around Carl Schmitt', in Carl Schmitt (ed.) *The Concept of the Political*, Expanded Edition, Translated and with an Introduction by George Schwab. With a Foreword by Tracy B. Strong and Notes by Leo Strauss, The University of Chicago Press, Chicago, IL and London, 2007, pg. xvi.
47 George Dangerfield, *The Strange Death of Liberal England*, Capricorn Books, New York, 1961.
48 Quoted in Graham Stewart, *Bang! A History of Britain in the 1980s*, pg. 353.

5

BREXIT AND THE WORSENING CLIMATE OF DEMOCRACY

This chapter will look at the Brexit process as an instance of a worsening climate of democracy. The result of the June 2016 referendum, which went in the direction of a narrow 52 per cent majority of those in favour of leaving the EU, came as something of a seismic shock to many. This was followed very closely in November of the same year by the Trump presidential victory in the US, which seemed to be a confirmation of matters in the state of democracy getting worse. The same year, in 2016, the rather bombastic and foul-mouthed Rodrigo Duterte was elected as the President of the Philippines.

Events of the kind described earlier have prompted several observers and theorists of democracy, in a prophecy of doom sort of way, to suggest that this represents an incipient end or death of democracy. Mark Chou, for instance, suggests that democracy is an unsustainable idea and that it tends to sow the seeds of its own destruction.[1] The regularity with which electorates are returning powerful leaders of a populist stripe to power has given rise to an almost apocalyptic sense of democracies across the world standing at the edge of a precipice. The sense of foreboding is captured well by Yascha Mounk at the beginning of his book *The People vs. Democracy*:

> There are long decades in which history seems to slow to a crawl. Elections are won and lost, laws adopted and repealed, new stars born and legends carried to their graves. But for all the ordinary business of time passing, the lodestars of culture, society, and politics remain the same.
>
> Then there are those short years in which everything changes all at once. Political newcomers storm the stage. Voters clamor for policies that were unthinkable until yesterday. Social tensions that had long simmered under the surface erupt into terrifying explosions. A system of government that had seemed immutable looks as though it might come apart.

94 Brexit and worsening democracy

This is the kind of moment in which we find ourselves.[2]

In the light of the outbreak of the Coronavirus pandemic in early 2020, it almost seems as if a health crisis of this apocalyptic scale is on the verge of completely shaking up politics and democracy. The Pandora's box that democracy seems to have become across the world has been reinforced in successive elections by ever-higher concentrations and doses of the same formula. This is the rise to power of the angry, nationalistic strongman. It almost seems as if elections are like a loaded dice that, with every electoral roll, ensure victory for right-wing authoritarian populists.

As this chapter was being written, reports came flooding in of a leaked internal Labour Party report that, on the basis of internal communications of Labour members, talked about how many of them, quite often in key positions, worked to destroy the possibility of their own party forming a government under leader Jeremy Corbyn in the 2017 UK elections.[3] The odds have seemed so definitely stacked against most centre-left political parties that they have been fearful of going too far to the left, citing the example of the catastrophic performance of Jeremy Corbyn's Labour Party in the UK Parliamentary elections in December 2019. This was perhaps the warning signal for the Democrats in the US and the reason why Bernie Sanders's nomination for the party was effectively scuttled after Joe Biden's surge in the primaries in early March 2020.[4] Remarkably, as left-wing parties were wary of going too far left, parties of the right have been breaking all barriers in their move to the right. Effectively, they have obliterated all distinctions between the lunatic fringe on the right and the respectability traditionally attached to a mainstream right-wing political party. Boris Johnson's Conservatives have moved so far to the right that they have occupied the far-right terrain of UKIP and the Brexit party, accomplishing the impossible manoeuvre of 'out-Faraging' Nigel Farage.[5] In the US, Trump's Republicans were never so cravenly beholden to the eccentricities of a man whose behaviour has been extraordinary in terms of its lack of political maturity and outright churlishness. In comparison, the Reagan presidency and the Bush Junior presidency seem almost statesmanlike and gentlemanly in their restraint and forbearance. The series of election results of the recent past are indicative of a crisis so deep-seated in politics and democracy that the ordinary cycle of elections and democracies are unlikely to ever provide a solution.

Just before he died, the German Nobel Laureate and writer Gunter Grass gave an interview to the Spanish newspaper *El Pais*, in which he suggested that the world was sleep-walking into World War III.[6] Perhaps the Coronavirus pandemic is the crisis that will serve as the equivalent of World War III for democracies that had been traipsing to the tune of Pied Pipers such as Trump, Johnson and all the other strongman figures who have been catapulted to positions of power in their respective countries over the last few years. The Coronavirus pandemic, in the immediate short run, certainly reinforces the authoritarian hands of these right-wing populists. If one were to analyse the tunes of these pied pipers, there is to be found a remarkable uniformity, as if the music had been pirated from one master copy. It would contain enthusiastic strains of making their countries great again, determinedly putting their countries first, effectively ditching humanity and relegating it to the last; there would be nasty, menacing strains aimed at all minorities and migrants. Needless to add that there would have to be profuse strains of very pretentious patriotism. Notice that the tune of these demagogic pied pipers, especially Trump and, in diminishing order, the others, misses very conspicuously the note of public health. If there is one element that the Coronavirus pandemic brings back to the political agenda, it is the idea of public health. This may well be the undoing in the long run of the demagogic pied pipers who have so thoroughly infantilized their electorates traipsing merrily behind them like the children in Robert Browning's poem *The Pied Piper of Hamelin*.

One of the most significant manifestations of the worsening climate of democracy is the coarsening of the democratic discourse and a plunging of this discourse to abysmally low depths. Think of the rhetoric of Donald Trump, the bile of Rodrigo Duterte and the rather disappointing kind of anti-intellectualism manifested especially, but not exclusively, by the Leave side of the Brexit divide, and one gets a sense of what is meant by the worsening climate of democracy. As a concrete example of the false and unintelligent nature of the debate that preceded the actual referendum, take the example of the Leave side's red campaign bus that was painted with the slogan that claimed Britain would be able to save £350 million pounds a week that it could then spend on the beleaguered, but respected and much-loved NHS. The slogan went like this: 'We send the EU £350 million a week, let's fund our NHS instead'.[7] Not only was the figure patently false, but it seemed to work very effectively in the Leave side's victory. The message painted on the side of the bus certainly travelled much in the way that a lie is able to travel halfway around the world even as the truth starts to put its shoes on. Take an even more serious instance of debased democratic discourse. It is often suggested that words have consequences. This became painfully obvious when the Labour MP from Batley and Spen, Jo Cox, was killed by a man shouting Britain First, just a few days before the date of the referendum.[8]

The debasement of the democratic surround

Debased democratic discourse of the kind mentioned in the previous paragraph tends to harm what in the analysis here is referred to as the 'democratic surround'. By invoking the idea of a democratic surround, a distinction is made here between the core kernel of democracy, which is the idea itself, and the democratic surround, which consists of a set of enabling circumstances that allow the ideal of democracy to achieve some form of coherence and fruition. The notion of the 'democratic surround' can be considered analogous to the protective atmospheric blanket that swaddles the earth. In a continuation of this atmospheric analogy, the worsening climate of democracy, variously understood as a spiral of falsehood, fake news, outright lies, innuendo and hate-speech, is understood as contributing to the pestilence of the democratic surround that then threatens to stifle, strangle and kill

96 Brexit and worsening democracy

off the democratic core. As a parallel to the pestilence of the democratic surround, consider these words of Joseph Schumpeter in his 1948 book *Capitalism, Socialism & Democracy*, where Schumpeter considers the prioritizing of socialism over democracy, which, in Marx's view, is required as 'in order to bring true democracy to life it is necessary to remove the poisonous fumes of capitalism that asphyxiate it'.[9] By making a distinction between democratic core and democratic surround, the analysis in this chapter, perhaps in a hopelessly optimistic sort of way, suggests that democracy's fate does not necessarily have to be the 'chronicle of a death foretold', to borrow from the title of Gabriel Garcia Marquez's novel.[10] There may be ways of protecting and perpetuating the idea of democracy from the inevitable death that many observers and theorists have increasingly talked about. Steven Levitsky and Daniel Ziblatt, in their much discussed book *How Democracies Die: What History Reveals About Our Future*, suggest that usually when people think about the death of democracy they think of coups and military generals bringing about such an eventuality. However, they suggest that there are other less dramatic and equally destructive ways to break democracy.

> Democracies may die at the hands not of generals but of elected leaders – presidents or prime ministers who subvert the very process that brought them to power. Some of these leaders dismantle democracy quickly as Hitler did in the wake of the 1933 Reichstag fire in Germany. More often, though, democracies erode slowly, in barely visible steps.[11]

If one were to do a quick global survey of democracy as the decade of the 2010s closed, it would be hard not to miss a pattern in which in many countries of the world, electoral results regularly returned right-wing authoritarian populist leaders. They are supposedly powerful and strong men who were considered good and reliable enough to get things right by sufficiently large numbers in their respective countries. Many Americans felt that Donald Trump was the right man to 'make America great again', intriguing if one contrasts the notion of greatness to the pettiness of the man himself. Narendra Modi's strongman image in India, with his self-proclaimed, rather boastful and spirited 56-inch chest, was further swelled with an even larger majority in the 2019 parliamentary election than the one in 2014. In Turkey, Recep Tayyip Erdogan's grip over power continued to consolidate and strengthen itself throughout the decade. The same can be said about Viktor Orban and his dominance in Hungary. In Brazil, the victory of Jair Bolsonaro can only be further confirmation of the same trend. In the December 2019 elections in the UK, the electorate was sufficiently convinced that 'ballsy Boris', as he was once referred to on the front page of the bawdy Rupert Murdoch-owned tabloid *The Sun*, was the right man to 'Get Brexit Done'.[12] There certainly were other countries and elections which did not confirm this trend and where the centre did hold the ground against a resurgent right. The victory of Emmanuel Macron in France would be an instance in which the populist right was kept at bay. The same can be said about Mark Rutte's victory in the Dutch election in 2017. In Germany, the centre held ground even as the right-wing AfD made electoral gains. In Mexico, a centre-left politician, Andres Manuel Lopez Obrador (AMLO), was elected in 2018.

It is hard not to miss the pattern of the strongmen authoritarian rulers controlling some of the major countries of the world. Many of them successfully presented themselves as rank outsiders to the political Establishment. This implied that they were on the side of the common people against cunning and conning political Establishments that had been taking people for a ride. In the UK, Boris Johnson may be an exception to this as he is very much part of the British Establishment with his privileged Eton and Oxford background. Even then, Johnson's campaign pointed to the supposed Islingtonian elitism of his rival, Jeremy Corbyn. This was a reference to the North London constituency that Corbyn has represented as Member of Parliament for well over three decades. This alleged Islingtonian elitism seemed to draw attention away from Boris Johnson's own far more established Etonian elitism, and can only be called a proverbial instance of the pot calling the kettle black.

There have been lies, deception and dishonesty that many of these strongmen have taken recourse to. That has not prevented a critical mass of their electorates from reposing a strange kind of trust in them that is, at most times, difficult to fathom. Most of these strongmen have sworn by a hard-line nationalism. They have generally professed a belief in economic reforms and free-market capitalism, albeit many a times taking protectionist stances in the face of international trade competition. They have all expressed a resolve to fight with determination the scourge of international terrorism. Connected to this zeal in the fight against terrorism has been an unmistakable rise of Islamophobia, except for Mr Erdogan for obvious reasons. The rising levels of Islamophobia have been especially pronounced with Mr Trump in the US, Mr Johnson in the UK, Mr Orban in Hungary and Mr Modi in India. They have, in line with Samuel Johnson's adage, frequently taken recourse to that famous 'last refuge of the scoundrel', which is a rather over-the-top-patriotism. All these strongmen have engaged in rhetoric and action that has been harsh and detrimental to vulnerable minorities in their countries.

Some of the most outrageous decisions taken by such democratically elected leaders are justified with the sanctimonious invocation of 'the people'. In other words, populist leaders seek to justify their decisions by suggesting that it is somehow sanctioned by 'the people'. Those who attempt to take exception to this manner of the people speaking are admonished that for far too long degenerate elites have stifled the genuine voice of the people. Now that they have finally spoken, it is time for everyone to listen, almost in reverential silence. The effect is a chilling silencing of dissent.

It is certainly true that for far too long the concerns of people have generally not been allowed to be voiced effectively in democracies. However, it is difficult to accept uncritically the way the people are supposedly speaking in strains of unreserved endorsement of strongmen leaders. There is present a strange combination of anger and bombast that threatens to hack away at the procedures, intricacies and subtleties of constitutional and democratic provisions. Any attempt to question decisions backed by 'the people' is dismissed as elitist, anti-democratic, unpatriotic or anti-national. Such reckless acts of democratic bravado are done by the leader in the name of 'the people'. The leader acts almost as a ventriloquist to the people, telling it like it is in a plain, unsophisticated and unvarnished sort of way that is shorn of the sophistry and spin doctoring of the conventional politician. They are words that 'the people' have felt and uttered, perhaps to themselves or among the like-minded. There is a strange kind of empowerment felt when those same words are spoken by the leader.

Clearly, 'the people' is not actually a faithful representation. It is in the words and analysis of Hannah Arendt in her 1951 work *The Origins of Totalitarianism* a 'caricature' of the people. A caricature, as we all know, is an exaggerated depiction of an individual or a political personality. The exaggeration is usually done by playing up a particular aspect of the depiction, usually the head. In the case of the populist invocation of the people, it is the angry excitability or the hot-headedness of the people that is accentuated, suggesting that they have waited far too long and can be easily fomented and worked up into an angry mob. The angry mob can be notoriously directionless, and this would represent the headless character of 'the people', a strangely ironical sort of decapitation, after the initial caricatured representation. The decapitation would perhaps also represent the transformation of 'the people' into a mob that is then compensated by the mob now being headed by the wisdom of the 'strongman' and the 'great leader' who speaks in the name of the voiceless, perhaps even headless mob.[13] In the context of this idea of 'the people' becoming transformed into the mob, it may be relevant to quote the American poet Carl Sandburg and this poem:

> I am the people – the mob – the crowd – the mass.
> . . . The Napoleons come from me and the Lincolns.
> They die. And then I send forth more Napoleons and
> Lincolns.
> . . . Sometimes I growl, shake myself and spatter a few red
> drops for history to remember. Then – I forget.
> When I, the people, learn to remember, when I, the
> people, use the lessons of yesterday and no longer
> forget who robbed me last year, who played me for a
> fool – then there will be no speaker in all the world say
> the name: "The People," with any fleck of a sneer in
> his voice of any far-off smile of derision.
> The mob – the crowd – the mass – will arrive then.[14]

Democracy in the times of neoliberalism

The question that obviously needs asking is what has made democracy reach such a sorry situation. The answer provided in the analysis here is that democracy has been thoroughly and completely re-configured by neoliberal politics and more specifically what lies at the centrepiece of such politics, which is the conceptual device of the market. A more detailed analysis of the neoliberal market is attempted in the next section of the chapter, after this section tries to evoke the manner in which democracy has been re-crafted and re-configured by neoliberalism.

Neoliberalism has endorsed a bare-bones and highly formalistic version of democracy that is confined to the regular and often ritualistic holding of elections. There is furthermore the mere presence of a rather attenuated set of rights for individuals. Individual citizens are themselves understood more in the nature of consumers with the set of rights mentioned earlier matching such consumer citizen bearers. The character of the citizenry itself is best captured by the term civic privatism, where individuals remain confined to constricted silos of self-interest that militate against any possibility of more capacious conceptions of the common good. There is the merely formal presence of constitutional safeguards for free speech with not too much thought given to the corrosion of these safeguards as a result of the omnipresence of a small number of media conglomerates controlling most of the media space. There is again the mere semblance of the possibility of an independent judiciary. If we quickly revert to the distinction made at the very beginning of this chapter between the core kernel of democracy and the larger 'democratic surround', the conception of democracy in neoliberalism is confined to the core kernel of democracy. It is aggressively against the presence of what has been earlier referred to as the democratic surround. It can be understood as a democracy sans democratization. It could even be suggestive of a 'hatred' of the democratic surround being overly and unduly suffused with too much democracy.[15]

Even more intriguingly, democracy in the times of neoliberalism is a kind of tick-box one that resembles those numerous forms made contemptuously familiar by neoliberal regulatory regimes, where a series of boxes must be checked. Are elections regularly held? Do citizens have certain formulaic rights often associated with a kind of consumer citizenship? Is there some semblance of an independent judiciary? Are there signs of an independent press? This thin attenuated nature of democracy is sketchy enough to be contained in a power point presentation.[16]

One way of analysing what has happened to democracy, especially in the over four decades of neoliberal dominance and to some extent in the preceding three decades of Keynesian dominance, is to go back to Joseph Schumpeter's 1948 book *Capitalism, Socialism & Democracy*. A reading of Schumpeter's book in the roughly seven decades since it was published reveals how democracy has so completely moved away from socialism and so completely aligned with capitalism that it has become almost congruent with and coterminous to capitalism. An interesting staging post of this movement of democracy's complete congruence with capitalism would be the years between 1989 and 1991, when, with the end of many socialist command economies of Eastern Europe, the fall of the Berlin Wall and the collapse of the Soviet Union, markets were understood to be the best guarantor of freedoms so cherished by democracy. This gave us another of those familiar hyphenated terms in politics, market-democracy.

What the hyphenated term market-democracy conveys is how democracy, which clearly comes after the market in the hyphenated order, has reflected and replicated within itself the structure of the capitalist free market. As a result, democracy today has increasingly become a form of revealed preference, where voters use their franchise to reveal a preference for a particular brand of leader. The flavour of the season in terms of the trendiest leaders is the strong one who can take quick, effective and efficient decisions. This often-ruthless decisiveness and efficiency is considered superior to the rigmarole of traditional politics that meanders and works its way endlessly and languidly through institutional procedures. In other words, the market for democracy is much akin to advertising. Election campaigns themselves have become, over the decades, very much like advertising campaigns. Schumpeter captured the point presciently in 1948 before the 1950s boom in the advertising industry:

> The ways in which issues and the popular will on any issue are being manufactured is exactly analogous to the ways of commercial advertising. We find the same attempts to contact the subconscious. We find the same technique of creating favorable and unfavorable associations which are the more effective the less rational they are. We find the same evasions and reticences and the same trick of producing opinion by reiterated assertion that is successful precisely to the extent to which it avoids rational argument and the danger of awakening the critical faculties of the people.[17]

The economist Paul Baran, commenting on the sustained manner in which advertising targeted people in the United States, suggested that it made them want 'what they don't need and not want what they do'.[18] The power of advertising in politics would suggest the ability to crucially set the agenda for the electorate and significantly put many things out of the agenda, thereby pushing beyond the political pale many issues that may be of crucial significance. One of the earlier and most talked about instances of an advertising agency and its successful foray into the field of the political is the period immediately preceding the 1979 election in the UK, when the Labour Party was voted out of power, leading to the rise of Margaret Thatcher. The Saatchi and Saatchi advertising campaign that suggested 'Labour isn't working' is widely perceived to have played a decisive role in Labour's defeat in 1979. One of the stories is that the poster with the slogan 'Labour isn't working' would have ordinarily fallen into oblivion, had it not been for the Labour Chancellor of the Exchequer, Denis Healey, petulantly complaining in the House of Commons that the poster represented a new low as the Conservatives were now 'selling politics as if it was soap powder'. This comment was supposedly enough to put a forgotten poster back into circulation. The rest, as we are often prone to saying, is history.[19]

Democracy and public goods

In addition to this point about advertising markets and the more general conception of the market that is expanded upon in a subsequent section, the argument here is that the damage to democracy wrought by neoliberalism has been even more decisive in terms of the evisceration and ultimate discrediting of the very idea of public goods. Public goods are understood as goods that are provisioned through the public exchequer. In other words, their very provisioning involves full-blown political issues of taxation and representation, unlike the trivialization of advertising markets. The major and more obvious examples of public goods are housing, healthcare and education. Public goods are not only facilitated by progressive taxation that has a redistributive effect but, perhaps more decisively for our purposes here, create the possibility of a positive externality.[20] In the case of a public good such as education, while the immediate and primary recipient may be an individual, the benefits tend in the manner of a beneficial overspill to flow to others around, creating the possibility of an enlightened, educated and better society. This could act as a breakwater against the ever-present possibility and continuous threat of the dumbing-down of society. More significantly, public goods, through the creation of positive externalities, contribute favourably to the democratic surround and thereby contribute to the sustenance of democracy.

To reiterate the importance of public goods: the positive externalities created by public goods contribute to the democratic surround that, in turn, contributes to the sustenance of the core kernel of democracy. A measure of how far higher education has moved from being able to help sustain and strengthen democracy can be had by considering some of the ideas of American philosopher John Dewey. Dewey hints at the immense possibilities that breaking social barriers such as class boundaries and the resultant class mixing can have on societies and how democracy and education can partake of this process and contribute to its furtherance. While the great enriching element in schools and higher education has emerged from their being class-mixing institutions, recent developments such as the privatization of higher education and the rise in university tuition fees have meant that education will remain the exclusive preserve of the well-to-do, who can continue to buy themselves the university degrees that provide desirable career routes. The resultant lack of diversity in the university experience would tend to rob university life of the crucial diversity and multiplicity of perspectives, which can make education truly transformative. What one notices in Dewey is how he tends to merge the famed diversity of democracy with the provisioning of numerous stimuli and perspectives through education. Dewey suggests:

> Obviously a society to which stratification into separate classes would be fatal, must see to it that intellectual opportunities (sic) accessible to all on equable and easy terms. A society marked off into classes need be specially attentive only to the education of its ruling elements.[21]

This tendency to eviscerate and hollow-out existing and established public goods is generally preceded by an excoriation of those very goods and a general railing against the inefficiency and waste of resources that the provisioning of public goods creates. One of the earliest happy hunting grounds of neoliberalism in the

102 Brexit and worsening democracy

UK under Mrs Thatcher's flagship 'right to buy' policy involved the sale of council houses and the consequent privatization of housing in the early 1980s.[22] The move made the country into a nation of obsessive and compulsive homeowners. Neo-liberalism paves the ground for the extension of and creation of markets in areas where such an existence may not exactly be desirable. It has the tendency to create markets in addition to housing in areas such as healthcare, education and transportation. There could be a market for everything. The obsession to create markets itself stems from a perverse preoccupation with efficiency and accountability.

In the sphere of higher education, the tendency to create markets has resulted in a narrowing of the concerns of academia and an almost mindless obsession with recording the way in which the academic utilizes his/her time. It has given rise to the culture of churning out publications for the sake of demonstrating and proving, often in a vacuous and over-zealous sort of way, to the relevant regulatory authority, that work is being continually engaged in. This situation itself arises from a deep suspicion in the neoliberal mindset that academics, especially the ones in the humanities and social sciences, do not do any actual work. It is very evident that in the kind of environment nurtured by markets, there is little room for the notion of trust. What has ensued in academia has often been referred to in countries like the UK as a 'tick-box culture', the reference to that ubiquitously familiar form, where an individual's responses must be mechanically slotted into a set of available response options. In a country like India, it has created a kind of pointless point scoring. Every single activity such as publishing a paper or giving a lecture is assigned a certain weightage in terms of points that are then totted up in an assessment of overall performance. The effect is the emergence of a kind of academic Phariseeism, where, in the obsession with following the minutiae and details of regulations, the larger spirit of academic pursuits is lost. A large part of this, to reiterate, has to do with the suspicion and mistrust that one of the founding figures of neoliberalism, the former British Prime Minister Margaret Thatcher, held towards academics, especially in the humanities and social sciences. In the crass, philistine world inhabited by Mrs Thatcher, work was confined to earning a living and contributing to the economy. It was typical, austere, stern and forbidding Conservatism with admonishments of the kind that there must be 'an honest day's pay for an honest day's work'. The point about the futility of academic markets is captured well by Jan-Muller Werner:

> Is the success of the Trumps, Bolsonaros and Johnsons of this world proof that the people can always be seduced by demagogues – and simply don't know what's good for them? Distrust of professionalism does not come out of nowhere. Neoliberalism paved the way for these attitudes. Margaret Thatcher memorably held that academics didn't really do any work; in fact, they all – with the possible exception of scientists – seemed to be lefties wasting taxpayers' money. Tories introduced the imperative constantly to audit and assess (and discipline and punish those not measuring up); only what could be counted, counted. Governments that praised "free markets" – the

spontaneous emergence of economic order – actually ended up constructing entirely artificial "markets" in academia and healthcare.[23]

One can, in the manner of staunch neoliberals who are wont to suggest that governments have no business to be in business, turn the phrase around and really give it back by suggesting that there are zones that markets really have no business being in. In addition to this expansion and proliferation of the market into every sphere of life, neoliberalism has, through its taxation regimes, resulted in a systemic increase in inequality.[24] The levels of inequality created by neoliberalism and its ideas of taxation being a severe disincentive to the flourishing of human creativity and enterprise add up to the perpetuation of this inequality that is in turn connected to the worsening climate of democracy. The general tendency of neoliberal tax regimes seems to have been a very rapid decline in the top rate of income taxation, and it goes without saying that this makes it significantly less progressive. There has been a rise in indirect taxes such as the valued added tax (VAT). A continuous decline in rates of corporation tax has been set in motion to lure businesses into countries and persuade them to continue to operate in those jurisdictions. The lingering effects of the Laffer curve are obvious in the direction that neoliberal tax regimes have taken, the most absurd of these directions being the suggestion of a flat rate of income tax. Much of the emphasis has been to simplify the alleged complexity of tax regimes.[25] Rather ironically, this emphasis on simplicity has given rise to some of the most complex and mind-boggling of tax evasion schemes that include offshore tax havens, sending many people scurrying to find where on earth exotic places such as the British Virgin Islands are.

Democracy during the Keynesian consensus

The analysis here by no means suggests that the state of democracy before the advent of neoliberalism was in perfect shape. It was, however, especially in many advanced capitalist economies, in a far better shape than what neoliberalism was to render. In the years from 1945, which is the end of Second World War, to 1973, which was the year of the Yom Kippur War and the decision by the Organization of Petroleum Exporting Countries (OPEC) to significantly hike oil prices, lay some of the 'golden years' of capitalism. With it came a period of stability for Western democracies that contrast to the severe democratic ructions that we have become so familiar with in the last few years of the 2010s. In all these years, the staid stability of Western democracies was to contrast with the often-bewildering gyrations of non-Western democracies. The American-led West continued to send and supply 'carbon copies' of democracy to parts of the world, where it was felt democracy was wanting and therefore wanted. In a strange irony, Brexit and the Trump presidential victory might represent, in the words of Partha Chatterjee, how 'various features that are characteristic of democracies in Africa or Asia are now being seen in Europe and the United States because of underlying structural

104 Brexit and worsening democracy

relations that have long tied metropolitan centers to their colonial and postcolonial peripheries'.[26] This would clearly be a case of the chickens coming home to roost.

The viability of many western democracies in these decades was maintained by secular growth rates in the economy and the prospects of full employment for the population remaining within sight and striking distance. These were the years of the Rawlsian–Keynesian consensus, which collapsed in the decade of the 1970s owing to the phenomenon of 'stagflation', the simultaneous presence of stagnation in the economy combined with inflation, which tended to render Keynesian fiscal measures redundant.[27] The reasons for the relative stability in many democracies had to do with the economy humming along like an efficient engine, creating the necessary economic growth that led to rising standards of living and higher levels of employment. This crisis of the 1970s led to the consensus created by the overlapping ideas of a philosopher and an economist, John Rawls and John Maynard Keynes (Rawlsian–Keynesian) being broken. This was to be replaced by another consensus, a neoliberal one, created by the coming together, especially, of the ideas of Friedrich August von Hayek and Milton Friedman. Daniel Stedman Jones, in his book *Masters of the Universe: Hayek, Friedman and the Birth of Neoliberal Politics*, explains how in 1947 Hayek and Friedman brought a disparate group of intellectuals together in Switzerland to discuss how liberalism could face the challenges of the then dominant 'collectivism', a term that quite remarkably encompassed Nazi and Soviet totalitarianism, American New Deal liberalism and British social-democracy. This meeting would create the Mont Pelerin society, named after the place in Switzerland where they first met.[28] The Mont Pelerin society and the ideas on markets, deregulation and privatization that it would come to be associated with, itself had a number of branches and components. One component was centred at the London School of Economics, where Hayek taught and where he was able to facilitate the appointment of Karl Popper after the publication of the latter's well-known book *The Open Society and its Enemies*. There was the group of German ordoliberals based at the University of Freiburg. A crucial component was the set of economists at the University of Vienna, headed notably by August von Mises. Across the Atlantic, there was the University of Chicago, where Milton Friedman was based, and there was also a set of economists such as James Buchanan and Gordon Tullock focusing on public choice at Virginia.

To stay with the condition of democracy and politics in the years immediately after the Second World War just a little longer, Timothy Mitchell, in his book *Carbon Democracy*, has noted the influence of Cambridge economist John Maynard Keynes on the creation of the new world order even as the Second World War was ending. Keynes did not live long enough to see the ways in which his ideas continued to influence politics and society for at least three decades after his death, well until the 1970s, if not much beyond. Mitchell suggests that under Keynes's influence the concept of the economy was prefixed with a definitive article to make it into 'the economy', marking a transition from it being a process to now becoming a thing. This new entity was now to be placed at the centre of politics and was to be put beyond the pale of democratic contestation and into the hands of the technical and professional competence of economists who would play an increasingly influential role in key advisory and decision-making structures of government. This is how Mitchell describes the process:

> The shaping of Western democratic politics from the 1930s onwards was carried out in part through the application of new kinds of economic expertise: the development and deployment of Keynesian economic knowledge; its expansion into different areas of policy and debate, including colonial administration; its increasingly technical nature; and the efforts to claim an increasing variety of topics as subject to determination not by democratic debate but by economic planning and knowledge. The Keynesian and New Deal elaboration of economic knowledge was a response to the threat of populist politics, especially in the wake of the 1929 financial crisis and the labour militancy that accompanied it and that re-emerged a decade later. Economics provided a method of setting limits to democratic practice, and maintaining them.[29]

Placing the economy at the centre has had the effect of making politics subordinate to and having necessarily to tail the economy, wherever that has led. Especially since the Second World War, politicians have been voted into power in the hope that they will get the economy right. A sense of the centrality of the economy to politics can be had from a consideration of the 1992 US presidential election, when Bill Clinton's successful election campaign was guided by the slogan, 'It's the economy stupid'. By this time, Keynesian ideas had generally fallen out of favour in most economic policy- and decision-making circles. It can, however, with a touch of irony, be suggested that the idea of the economy being central to politics has had a generally free run and been offered many 'free meals' in the era of neoliberal dominance, despite Milton Friedman suggesting that the idea of a free lunch does not exist.

A further twist of irony of the political tailing the economic cannot be lost. Keynes himself was an avid reader of Aristotle's *Nicomachean Ethics*. Despite the centrality that Keynes's legacy has given to the economy, Keynes, in some early papers on ethics, makes a distinction between practical ethics and speculative ethics. The matters that concern the economy would fall into practical ethics and thereby lay the preparatory material grounds for larger concerns of final ends and what constitutes the good life that would fall in the domain of speculative ethics. Here, there is a clear ranking of the material concerns of the economic in the more mundane domain of practical ethics. Unlike the high levels of consideration and esteem that modern politics and government tend to give to the professional economist, the problem of the economy for Keynes is no more than a transient one, and the economist should be a bit like a humble dentist.[30] The reduction of the economist to the level of a dentist would be quite the comedown. From the centrality that Keynes's ideas gave to the economy and the sense that the economy was merely material preparatory ground for higher forms of speculative ethics, there seems to emerge in Keynes something akin to a double life. There is, on the one hand, the public one linked to his activities as an economist and political adviser. There is, on the other, the private and artistic dimension that can be associated with his membership of the Bloomsbury group.[31] Clearly, the idea of the economic being a preparation for the higher purposes of speculative ethics would constitute part of the private and the artistic.

However, let us revert to the head of the ethical tradition that Keynes harkened back to, Aristotle himself. Aristotle would certainly be turning over in his grave at the thought of the political being subordinated to the economic in modern times as he famously considered politics an authoritative master science. In Book I of the *Nicomachean Ethics*, he suggested that the activity of politics is supreme as its ends circumscribe and set limits to the ends of lesser activities such as the household or the *oikos*.[32] The *oikos* is the supposedly lesser realm of the private, and it is from the term *oikos* that we get the modern term economics. Closer to modern times has emerged the realm of the social, which, Hannah Arendt observes in her book *The Human Condition*, has not only blurred the distinction between the public and the private but has hosted the emergence of the economy as a kind of collective national housekeeping, giving economics a newfound prestige from its earlier obscurity.[33] The current relationship of the economic and the political might, in Aristotle's view, be one of the tail of the economic wagging the dog of the political.

The market for degenerate democratic discourse

There is a remarkable and an almost unthinking endorsement of the market in neoliberal thought. Remarkably, in neoliberal theory, the solution to the possibilities of the failure of markets is, well, more markets. In fact, neoliberalism would go the extent of ruling out any possibility of market failure, reposing its trust in the inherent ability of markets to self-correct. Philip Mirowski, in his interestingly titled book *Never Let a Serious Crisis Go To Waste: How Neoliberalism Survived the Financial Meltdown*, suggests that neoliberals, especially for the purposes of sloganeering and public understanding, treat the market as a 'natural' and 'inexorable' state of mankind.[34]

Mirowski suggests that there are a number of possible ways in which the market is understood in neoliberalism. First, there is the conception of the market straight out of the textbooks of nineteenth-century neoclassical economics and which would be imported straight into neoliberal politics and is largely associated with the Chicago school component of the Mont Pelerin Society. The second one is associated with the Austrian school of economics offshoot of the Mont Pelerin Society and suggests the vital role played by entrepreneurs in being able to discover and supply to consumers what they themselves may be unaware of on account of the uncertainty of the future. A further third conception is one that comes from the ideas of Friedrich August von Hayek, which suggests the vast superiority of the market as a signalling and information processing mechanism, a superiority unmatched by any human endeavour such as states and the meticulous planning and organization that such state-led human efforts entail. There is a further fourth understanding that comes from German ordoliberals, another component of the Neoliberal Thought Collective, where emphasis is placed on the state directly organizing the competitive functioning of markets and involving other social institutions. Mirowski suggests that it is the Hayekian idea of the market as an efficient signalling mechanism that is the most pronounced strain of the market to be found in neoliberal political thought, and further observes: 'Hence, contrary to much that has been written on the beliefs of our protagonists, neoliberals do not speak with one voice on the key concept of the market'.[35]

The trust in the market that is especially found in a thinker such as Hayek is further combined with a centrality that is given by him to 'ignorance'. This combination of trust in markets and reliance on 'ignorance' results in the complete undermining of any notion or possibility of the truth. In fact, this would give us a key to understanding the degenerate and debased discourse that democracy under the auspices of neoliberalism can give rise to. Usually, ignorance is understood as something to be dispelled through the light of education, for instance, or some similar edifying idea. Mirowski suggests that ignorance plays such an important role in Hayek as it combines with the know-all character of the market. Given the omniscient, omnipresent and omnipotent character of the market in neoliberal thought, which gives us this day our daily bread and upon whose workings individuals and governments must never trespass, it is a wonder that the Lord's prayer has not been rewritten under neoliberal auspices.[36]

Connected to this would be how Hayek and neoliberalism seem to have a suspiciously disparaging role of intellectuals, especially ones that are employed by universities or public intellectuals located on the left of the political spectrum. In neoliberalism, the role of the intellectual is usually understood as a huckster of ideas, pushing the agenda that s/he has been paid to push, rather than a disinterested pursuit of the truth *a la* Socrates speaking truth to power. Hayek's neoliberal market is then a far cry from the Athenian agora that was the theatre of operation of Socrates and his method of the elenchus, where definitions bandied about by Socrates' loquacious interlocutors were dissected for their inconsistencies in a search for the truth.

The attitude of suspicion towards intellectuals and the tendency to see them as hucksters and pen-pushers of ideas in the direction they are paid to write are further manifest in the kind of disdain of intellectualism and expertise that one finds in populist outbursts across the world and, very specifically for our purposes, in the Brexit (non)-debates, where there has been a lot of shouting and talking past each other. While neoliberalism is dismissive of universities as ivory towers and further dismissive of intellectuals supposedly spinning yarns of theoretical daydreams as they sit in those ivory towers, it does tend to promote an even more secretive and reclusive kind of intellectual in an even darker sort of den, the think tank. Think tanks have been the most important vectors and purveyors of neoliberal ideas. The Mont Pelerin Society, the original thought collective that birthed twentieth-century neoliberalism, would be an excellent example of such lack of transparency in its workings.[37] There are numerous think tanks such as the AEI and the Heritage Foundation on the American side of the Atlantic and the Legatum institute and the Institute for Economic Affairs (IEA) on the British side. Many of these think tanks are members of the Atlas network, which has its headquarters in Atlanta, Georgia. Their funding is often linked with the tobacco industry and such other commercial interests. With continuous access to many members of the Boris Johnson cabinet, these think-tanks exerted their influence to bring about a 'hard Brexit' to thereby pull the UK away from a closer relationship with the EU and effect a trade deal with the US that would significantly undermine existing health and safety regulation standards.[38] Such a trade deal with the US would, in all probability, demand greater access for US pharmaceutical companies in the UK health market and inevitably push the UK's NHS further down the road of privatization.

The best example of the kind of shadowy intellectualism that neoliberalism favours is the dark genius behind much of Brexit, Dominic Cummings himself. Cummings is known for his long blogs, many of them unreadable but highly influential, nevertheless. Stefan Collini has done the yeoman's service of trawling through these writings.[39] One gets a sense that Cummings's intellectualism is characterized by a dangerous and condescending superciliousness to those he thinks are less clever than himself, which might be everyone else, by his own estimation. This kind of condescension would in fact be far worse than the contempt that 'the people' are held in by Remainers. Ardent Brexiteers never fail to remind everyone of the contempt those opposed to Brexit hold for those who voted to leave, in other words 'the people'. Cummings himself has suggested, with his usual know-all demeanour, that many journalists should step out of London and stop talking to 'rich Remainers'.[40]

The issue here is that a manifestation of populism such as Brexit and the electoral victory of Boris Johnson represent the paradoxical coalescence of, on the one hand, an uninformed and often dangerously debased democratic discourse and, on the other, a haughty hyper-intellectualism. This dichotomy reflects what Mirowski refers to as the 'double truth doctrine'[41] of neoliberalism, an exoteric truth for the ignorant masses and an esoteric truth for the smart select super-intellectuals of the Dominic Cummings variety. What we have then is a democratic discourse that is deliberately dumbed-down by neoliberalism. One of the ways in which the democratic discourse can be dumbed down in the long term is by education no longer remaining a public good. With the commoditization of education, especially higher education, what one has is an unimaginably steep rise in its cost with a consequent escalation of student debt that many individuals start incurring.

But the more immediate cause of the drastic fall in the democratic discourse is 'the media', especially the exponential proliferation of private media groups, often at the expense of public broadcasters such as the BBC. Despite its many limitations, one of the significant things about public broadcasting is that is sets a certain benchmark off which the media discourse can be read. The BBC has always been a thorn in the sides of most British governments, and the Conservatives seem to have had a particular problem. British television culture was at one time widely respected across the world as a result of the emphasis on learning and improvement that it sought to inculcate in the wider public under the influence and inspiration of Lord Reith, one of the more celebrated Directors-General.[42] This changed dramatically with the rise of reality television and the obsession with achieving celebrity status. Nick Clarke, in an aptly titled book *The Shadow of a Nation: How Celebrity Destroyed Britain*, quotes the Director-General Sir William Haley in his introduction to the 1952 BBC Yearbook:

> The essence of Broadcasting is that it is a means of communication capable of conveying intelligence into every home simultaneously. In British Broadcasting it has been consistently sought to ensure that intelligence shall be made up of information, entertainment and education.[43]

It is no wonder that Dominic Cummings wants to cancel the BBC's license fee, which is the major source of funding for the organization and which allows it to commission programmes that do not necessarily have to cater to the whimsicality of the market.

The connection and similarities between notoriously dumbed-down reality television shows and neoliberalism is especially striking. The emphasis on viewer participation through voting on mobile phones and messaging systems tends to give the illusion of control, a very remote one at that, very much in the manner of neoliberal democracy. The enthusiasm with which reality television programmes such as *Strictly Come Dancing* and *Get me out of here I'm a celebrity* are lapped up by viewers becomes all the more interesting when one notes that many times British politicians are enthusiastic participants. As the vacuity of the Blair years rolled on, nothing could be more representative of the broken nature of Britain than a controversy that broke out at the very end of Blair's premiership. In early 2007, on the sets of the British reality television show *Big Brother*, one of the participants, the prominent Indian film actress Shilpa Shetty, was reduced to tears after she was racially abused by the British television celebrity Jade Goody. The controversy gave rise to something of a diplomatic row between India and the UK. The issue was raised in the British parliament, and much was said on the matter in the British and Indian media. While the details of the episode need not detain us, what is important is how the episode reflected the extensive preponderance of a particular kind of media culture in larger British society, which itself was widely seen as broken.[44]

A strange case of democratic outbreak after the 2007 financial crisis

The analysis of democracy thus far in this chapter has been in terms of the confined way democracy has been configured by the dominance of neoliberalism. This has resulted in a constricted check-box sort of democracy. This constricted nature of democracy has been captured and evoked far more effectively by Sheldon Wolin in his book *Democracy Incorporated: Managed Democracy and the Specter of*

Inverted Totalitarianism.[45] This book came out around the time that the 2007–2008 global financial crisis was unfolding. The idea of 'managed democracy' effectively conveyed the almost bottled-up manner of democracy and that this managing of democracy was done by Wall Street financial interests.

Around three years after the global financial crisis, there was a strange case of a democratic outbreak that flared up for a brief while and then, just as quickly, receded. This brief flare-up and quick withdrawal have given us a series of right-wing authoritarian regimes across the world that have the real possibility of putting democracy to death. The emergence of right-wing authoritarian populist regimes across the world, it is suggested here, is linked to the strange case of democratic outbreak that has been mentioned.

One of the more spectacular aspects of the democratic outbreak was the way indignant citizens flowed out onto the streets and seemed to reclaim, for a while, some well-known and some other not-so-well-known public squares, as images of these places were beamed across the world. In the early part of the 2010s, the news cycle familiarized many people across the world with Tahrir Square in Egypt, Zuccotti Park in New York, Gezi Park in Istanbul, Syntagma Square in Athens and the Ramlila Maidan in Delhi. In all these public squares, defiant citizens sang songs, waved flags, lit candles and did what citizens are supposed to do: reclaim from unscrupulous elites what was rightfully theirs. More remarkable was the fact that very often these democratic outbreaks took decidedly right-wing authoritarian turns rather than a left-wing one that some had hoped for.[46]

One of the first instances of the dramatic democratic outbreak was the Arab Spring, which took many people across the world by surprise, just as the decade of the 2010s was opening.[47] Very soon after, in 2011, there was the series of Occupy Wall Street movements across the world with their defiant protest against the micro-elites running their respective countries. The movement's aims and intentions were very effectively conveyed by the slogan 'We are the 99%'. In India, in the same year as the Occupy movements, just as the North Indian summer was beginning to scorch the land, there emerged rather suddenly a protest movement against corruption that had a 'holier than thou attitude' in terms of affixing all the blame for corruption on the country's notorious political class. It quickly conceived and gave birth to a political party that was christened the Aam Aadmi Party (AAP) or common man's party, which, in its local-level consultative strategies, seemed deeply enamoured of some form of direct democracy. The common man's party, in the years since its birth and as a completely new political entity, has done remarkably well electorally, winning spectacularly each time in three successive provincial assembly elections in the small state of Delhi, which is also the national capital. In Brazil, there was similar outrage against the corruption of the left-wing government of Dilma Rousseff and her predecessor Lula de Silva, with the launching of the federal investigation Operation Car Wash by the prominent judge Sergio Moro. As a result of the investigation and the media-driven interest that it created, Dilma Rousseff was impeached and Lula de Silva was arrested.[48] In the case of both India and Brazil, the outrage against corruption culminated in the coming to power of two powerful right-wing populists, Narendra Modi and Jair Bolsonaro. In fact, parallels can be made between the roles played by the Comptroller and Auditor General in India, Vinod Rai, and judge Sergio Moro in Brazil in terms of their roles in discrediting and consequently pulling down incumbent governments in their countries.

The curious case of democratic outbreak after the global financial crisis would also include the Brexit referendum of 2016. There was obviously something missing and terribly wrong in all these upsurges. In addition to the vital missing element, there was a surfeit of political energy that they had that was powered along by a media gone overboard in terms of its reportage and the omnipresence of its 24/7 cycle. There was further the support and accompaniment of the strange workings of social media, whose full implications for democracy we are only now beginning to fathom.

Almost all the instances of the democratic outbreak, Brexit included, had a surfeit of the supposedly democratic in them, most prominently the sanctimonious appeal to 'the people'. As much as there was a surge to reclaim the public sphere, what was missing was what Hannah Arendt in *The Human Condition* called the *vita activa*. As Arendt explains, with the term *vita activa*, she proposes 'to designate three human activities: labor, work and action'. It is the third action that will be of specific interest as this chapter draws to a close. Arendt's ideas help us identify the missing commitment among the actors, leading these movements to *reconfigure* the public sphere anew rather than merely *reclaim* the public square. In other words, most of the actors in these movements made a foray into the public square with a surfeit of political energy in the hope that things could be made better and tolerable and then one could get back to living the lives that they were used to living. Arendt's concept of the *vita activa* has been invoked because it emphasizes the need for political actors to construct anew in line with the emphasis in her ideas on the renewed possibilities that birth and natality give rise to. The coronavirus pandemic has underlined the futility of getting back to any normal that we were all too familiar with like revivals and Keynesian kick-starts of economic growth that would be accompanied by the regular pattern of election cycles. There can be no going back to the familiar, however comforting that may be for many. Politics will have to, of necessity, craft the public sphere anew, to signify a birth and natality after the inevitability of death and mortality that the coronavirus pandemic has made only too clear. As Arendt explains:

> However, of the three (labour, work and action), action has the closest connection with the human condition of natality; the new beginning inherent in birth can make itself felt in the world only because the newcomer possesses the capacity to begin something anew, that is, of acting. In this sense of initiative, an element of action, and therefore of natality, is inherent in all human activities. Moreover, since action is the political activity par excellence, natality, and not mortality, may be the central category of political, as distinguished from metaphysical, thought.[49]

It seems surreally strange to think of the outbreak of democratic energy described earlier as the final flaring-up of the flame of democracy before the fatal flickering out. One would hope that the reports of the death of democracy are 'greatly exaggerated' as the American humourist and writer Mark Twain said upon hearing news of his own death. Can we, in the manner of the continuity of the British monarchy, shout 'Democracy is dead! Long live democracy!' The future is up for grabs and there may be more than a mere world to win.

Notes

1 Mark Chou, *Democracy Against Itself: Sustaining an Unsustainable Idea*, Edinburgh University Press, Edinburgh, 2014, pg. 2.
2 Yascha Mounk, *The People vs. Democracy: Why Our Freedom Is in Danger and How to Save It*, Harvard University Press, Cambridge, MA and London, 2018, pg. 1
3 David Child, 'UK labour party orders probe into leaked anti-Semitism report', *Al Jazeera*, 13 April, 2020. www.aljazeera.com/news/2020/4/13/uk-labour-party-orders-probe-into-leaked-anti-semitism-report. Accessed 19 August 2020.
4 Molly Ball, 'Joe Biden's super Tuesday surge reshapes the democratic race', *Time*, 4 March 2020. https://time.com/5795288/joe-biden-bernie-sanders-super-tuesday/. Accessed 19 August 2020.
5 The warning about not trying to 'out-Farage Farage' was from Labour leader Ed Miliband aimed at Prime Minister David Cameron back in 2013, when the latter seemed to be making a series of compromises to win back Conservative voters who had moved to Nigel Farage's UKIP. In January 2013, Cameron had already announced the fateful in-out referendum that would result in Brexit. This is what Miliband said:

> The lesson for the prime minister is you can't out-Farage Farage. Banging on about Europe won't convince the public, and the people behind him will keep coming back for more. A Europe referendum tomorrow, drop same-sex marriage, the demands go on. They will never be satisfied.
> *(Nicholas Watt, 'Queen's speech: Ed Miliband accuses David Cameron of joining Ukip "circus"', The Guardian, Wednesday, 8 May 2013. www.theguardian.com/politics/2013/may/08/queens-speech-miliband-cameron-ukip. Accessed 18 August 2020.)*

6 'Gunter Grass: final interview reveals author's fears of another world war', *The Guardian*, Tuesday 14 April 2015. www.theguardian.com/books/2015/apr/14/gunter-grass-final-interview-authors-fears-of-another-world-war. Accessed 18 August 2020.
7 Andrew Reid, 'Buses and breaking point: freedom of expression and the "Brexit" campaign', *Ethical Theory and Moral Practice*, Vol. 22 (2019), pgs. 623–637. https://doi.org/10.1007/s10677-019-09999-1. Accessed 10 April 2020.
8 Ian Cobain, Nazia Parveen and Matthew Taylor, 'The slow-burning hatred that led Thomas Mair to murder Jo Cox', *The Guardian*, Wednesday 23 November 2016. www.theguardian.com/uk-news/2016/nov/23/thomas-mair-slow-burning-hatred-led-to-jo-cox-murder. Accessed 16 August 2020.
9 Joseph Schumpeter, *Capitalism, Socialism & Democracy*, Adarsh Books, New Delhi, 2011, pg. 236.
10 Nayantara Sehgal, 'In the 2019 Lok Sabha polls, story-telling took precedence over reality', *The Indian Express*, 19 June 2019. https://indianexpress.com/article/opinion/columns/2019-election-outcome-once-upon-a-time-a-nation-5787244/. Accessed 28 April 2020.
11 Steven Levitsky and Daniel Ziblatt, *How Democracies Die: What History Reveals About Our Future*, Penguin Random House, New York, 2018, pg. 3.

12 Steve Hawkes, Matt Dathan and Nick Gutteridge, 'Hey big suspender: Boris Johnson leaves Remainers reeling with masterstroke to close Parliament to push through Brexit', *The Sun*, 29 August 2019. www.thesun.co.uk/news/brexit/9816936/boris-johnson-remainers-suspend-parliament/. Accessed 1 February 2021.

13 Hannah Arendt, *The Origins of Totalitarianism*, Penguin Modern Classics, London, 2017, pg. 138.

14 Quoted in Partha Chatterjee, *I Am the People: Reflections on Popular Sovereignty Today*, Permanent Black, Ranikhet, 2020, pg. 122.

15 The 'hatred' here is obviously a reference to Jacques Rancier's provocative little book *The Hatred of Democracy*, Verso, London and New York, 2005. Ranciere does an interesting contrast, a kind of mirror-image lateral inversion of what democracy, at a minimum, is supposed to be and what it actually turns out to be:

> With this in mind, we can specify the rules that lay down the minimal conditions under which a representative system can be declared democratic: short and non-renewable electoral mandates that cannot be held concurrently; a monopoly of people's representatives over the formulation of laws; a ban on State functionaries becoming the representatives of the people; a bare minimum of campaigns and campaign costs; and the monitoring of possible interference by economic powers in the electoral process.
>
> *(pg. 72)*

Having enumerated the minimal conditions, Ranciere suggests the following in terms of what is almost akin to a mirror image, lateral inversion:

> All one has to do provoke hilarity today is list them. With good reason – for what we call democracy is a statist and governmental functioning that is exactly the contrary: eternally elected members holding concurrent or alternating municipal, regional, legislative and/or ministerial functions and whose essential link to the people is that of the representation of regional interests; governments which make laws themselves; representatives of the people that largely come from one administrative school; ministers or their collaborators who are also given posts in public or semi-public companies; fraudulent financing of parties through public works contracts; businesspeople who invest sums in trying to win electoral mandates; owners of private media empires that use their public functions to monopolize the empire of the public media. In a word: the monopolizing of *la chose publique* by a sold alliance of State oligarchy and economic oligarchy.
>
> *(pgs. 72–73)*

16 The idea of democracy contained on a power point presentation is taken from Timothy Mitchell's book *Carbon Democracy: Political Power in the Age of Oil*, Verso, London and New York, 2011:

> This is the conception shared by an American expert on democracy sent to southern Iraq, nine months after the US invasion of 2003, to discuss 'capacity building' with the members of the provincial council: 'Welcome to your new democracy,' he said as he began displaying PowerPoint slides of the administrative structure the Americans had designed. 'I have met you before. I have met you in Cambodia. I have met you in Russia. I have met you in Nigeria.' At which point, we are told, two members of the council walked out. For an expert on democracy, democratic politics is fundamentally the same everywhere. It consists of a set of procedures and political forms that are to be reproduced in every successful instance of democratisation, in one variant or another, as though democracy occurs only as a carbon copy of itself. Democracy is based on a model, an original idea, that can be copied from one place to the next. If it fails, as it seems to in many oil states, the reason must be that some part of the model is missing or malfunctioning.
>
> *(pg. 2)*

114 Brexit and worsening democracy

17 Joseph Schumpeter, *Capitalism, Socialism & Democracy*, pg. 263.
18 Quoted in Douglas Dowd, *Capitalism and its Economics: A Critical History*, Pluto Press, London and Ann Arbor, MI, 2004, pg. 156. Dowd's book is an irreverent take down of many of the most well-known economists.
19 Denis Healey is quoted in Graham Stewart's book *Bang! A History of Britain in the 1980s*, Atlantic Books, London, 2013, pgs. 29–30. Stewart also notes that the Saatchi and Saatchi poster was voted 'poster of the century', by *Campaign*, the advertising industry's leading magazine. He suggests: 'Its success supposedly showed that advertising companies had come of age. They were not just about marketing cold beer to men and refrigerators to women. They could sell a political party too'.
20 See Partha Dasgupta, *Economics: A Very Short Introduction,* Oxford University Press, Oxford, 2007, pgs. 52–54.
21 John Dewey, *Democracy and Education: An Introduction to the Philosophy of Education*, Foreword by Krishna Kumar, Aakar Books Classics, New Delhi, 2019, pgs. 93–94.
22 See Daniel Stedman Jones, *Masters of the Universe: Hayek, Friedman and the Birth of Neoliberal Politics*, Princeton University Press, Princeton, 2012, chapter 7, 'Neoliberalism Applied? The Transformation of Affordable Housing and Urban Policy in the United States and Britain, 1945–2000'. The writings of John Lanchester are a very insightful source for understanding the effects of the housing market, homeownership and gentrification. See John Lanchester's novel, *Capital*, Faber & Faber, London, 2012.
23 Jan-Werner Muller, 'Why do rightwing populist leaders oppose experts?', *The Guardian*, 26 March 2020. www.theguardian.com/commentisfree/2020/mar/26/rightwing-populist-leaders-oppose-experts-not-elites. Accessed 24 April 2020.
24 Joseph Stiglitz, *The Price of Inequality*, Penguin Books, London, 2013.
25 Stephen Smith, *Taxation: A Very Short Introduction*, Oxford University Press, Oxford, 2015, pgs. 106–108.
26 Partha Chatterjee, *I Am the People: Reflections on Popular Sovereignty Today*, pg. x.
27 David Harvey, *The Condition of Postmodernity, An Inquiry into the Origins of Cultural Change*, Blackwell, Oxford, 1989.
28 Daniel Stedman Jones, *Masters of the Universe: Hayek, Friedman, and the Birth of Neoliberal Politics*, Princeton University Press, Princeton, 2013, pg. 4.
29 Timothy Mitchell, *Carbon Democracy: Political Power in the Age of Oil*, pg. 124.
30 See Anna Carabelli, 'Keynes's Aristotelian eudaimonic conception of happiness and the requirement of material and institutional preconditions: the scope for economics and economic policy', *Annals of the Fondazione Luigi Einaudi*, Vol. LIII (December 2019), pgs. 213–226.

> What is the 'economic problem' for Keynes? A transient problem, solvable. Economics supplies the material preconditions for a happy and good life. The solutions of economic problems is only a precondition to facing 'the real problems of man' (that is the "speculative ethics"). Economics is a means, a material precondition to secure speculative ethics, so to supply material means to spiritual ends, an Aristotelian precondition for speculative ethics. Economists are, as we will see, no more than dentists.
>
> *(pg. 223)*

31 Michel Beaud and Gilles Dostaler, *Economic Thought Since Keynes: A History and Dictionary of Major Economists*, Translated from French by Valerie Cauchemez with the participation of Eric Litwack, Edward Elgar, Aldershot, pg. 19. The book further notes that Keynes followed a tradition dating back to Aristotle and the Scholastics and which was further reaffirmed by Sidgwick, Marshall and his own father John Neville Keynes as a result of which he considered economics as a moral science. Rather than being a mathematical science closed unto itself, economics had to open itself out to other disciplines. Strangely, contemporary economics has developed in a direction different from the one envisaged by Keynes himself (pg. 25).

Brexit and worsening democracy **115**

32 Aristotle, *Nicomachean Ethics*, Cambridge Texts in the History of Philosophy, Translated and Edited by Roger Crisp, Cambridge University Press, Cambridge, 2004, Book I.

33 Hannah Arendt, *The Human Condition*, Introduction by Margaret Canovan, The University of Chicago Press, Chicago, IL and London, 1998. Arendt's eloquence deserves nothing less than to be quoted in full rather than merely being paraphrased:

> The emergence of society – the rise of housekeeping, its activities, problems, and organizational devices – from the shadowy interior of the household into the light of the public sphere, has not only blurred the old borderline between private and political, it has also changed almost beyond recognition the meaning of the two terms and their significance for the life of the individual and the citizen.
>
> *(pg. 38)*

34 Philip Mirowski, *Never Let a Serious Crisis Go to Waste: How Neoliberalism Survived the Financial Meltdown* Verso, London and New York pg. 56.

35 Philip Mirowski, *Never Let a Serious Crisis Go to Waste*, pg. 54–55.

36 An instance of the Lord's prayer being parodied can be found in E.P. Thompson's much renowned book *The Making of the English Working Class*, Vintage Books, New York, 1966:

> Our Lord who art in the Treasury, whatsoever be thy name, thy power be prolonged, thy will be done throughout the empire, as it is in each session. Give us our usual sops, and forgive us our occasional absences on divisions; as we promise not to forgive those that divide against thee. Turn us not out of our places; but keep us in the House of Commons, the land of Pensions and Plenty; and deliver us from the people. Amen.
>
> *(pg. 721)*

37 Daniel Stedman Jones, *Masters of the Universe: Hayek, Friedman and the Birth of Neoliberal Politics*, chapter 4, 'A Transatlantic Network: Think Tanks and the Ideological Entrepreneurs'. On pgs. 134–135, Jones notes:

> A transatlantic network of sympathetic businessmen and fundraisers, journalists and politicians, policy experts and academics grew and spread neoliberal ideas between the 1940s and 1970s. These individuals were successful at ideas through a new type of political organization, the think tank. The first wave of neoliberal think tanks were set up in the 1940s and 1950s and included the American Enterprise Institute (AEI) and the Foundation for Economic Education (FEE) in the United States, and the Institute of Economic Affairs (IEA) in Britain. A second wave of neoliberal think tanks were established in the 1970s, including the Centre for Policy Studies (CPS) and the Adam Smith Institute (ASI) in Britain and the Heritage Foundation and the Cato Institute in the United States. These organizations would later directly influence the policies of the Thatcher and Reagan administrations in the 1980s. But in the immediate postwar decades, neoliberal thought might have been confined to academic circles were it not for the growth of a network to spread its message of individual liberty, free markets, low taxes, deregulation, and limited government on both sides of the Atlantic.

38 Felicity Lawrence, Rob Evans, David Pegg, Caelainn Barr and Pamela Duncan, 'How the right's radical thinkers reshaped the conservative party', *The Guardian*, The Long Read, Friday 29 November 2019. www.theguardian.com/politics/2019/nov/29/rightwing-thinktank-conservative-boris-johnson-brexit-atlas-network. Accessed 26 February 2020.

39 Stefan Collini, 'Inside the mind of Dominic Cummings', *The Guardian*, The Long Read, Thursday, 6 February 2020. www.theguardian.com/politics/2020/feb/06/inside-the-mind-of-dominic-cummings-brexit-boris-johnson-conservative. Accessed 27 February 2020.

116 Brexit and worsening democracy

40 'Cummings: stop talking to "rich Remainers"', *BBC News*. www.bbc.com/news/av/uk-politics-49649631/dominic-cummings-stop-talking-to-rich-remainers. Accessed 21 August 2020.

41 See Philip Mirowski, *Never Let A Serious Crisis go to Waste*, pg. 68. Mirowski argues:

> What I shall refer to here is the proposition that an intellectual thought collective might actually concede that, as a corollary of its developed understanding of politics, it would be necessary to maintain an exoteric version of its doctrine for the masses – because that would be safer for the world and more beneficial for ordinary society – but simultaneously hold fast to an esoteric for a small closed elite, envisioned as the keepers of the flame of the collective's wisdom.

42 See the Al Jazeera documentary *Battle for the BBC* for the troubled relationship between the broadcaster and the British government and especially on the more problematic aspects of Lord Reith's decision making during the 1926 General Strike. https://www.aljazeera.com/program/the-listening-post/2020/11/21/battle-for-the-bbc.

43 Nick Clarke, *The Shadow of a Nation: How Celebrity Destroyed Britain*, Phoenix Paperback, London, 2003, pg. 28.

44 See Kirsty Hughes, 'Of chicken stock cubes, an international race row and British society today', *Economic and Political Weekly*, Vol. 42, No. 5 (3–9 February 2007), pgs. 348–349.

45 Sheldon Wolin, *Inverted Totalitarianism: Managed Democracy and the Specter of Inverted Totalitarianism*, Princeton University Press, Princeton and Oxford, 2010.

46 Marina Sitrin and Dario Azzellini capture the enthusiasm and left-wing hopes well in their book *They Can't Represent Us! Reinventing Democracy from Greece to Occupy*, Verso, London and New York, 2014, pg. 5:

> Something new is happening – something new in content, depth, breadth and global consistency. Societies around the world are in movement. Since the end of 2010 millions of people have been taking to the streets in cities, towns and villages – assembling in plazas, occupying parks, buildings, homes, and schools. There is a growing global movement of refusal – and simultaneously, in that refusal, a movement of creation. Millions are shouting 'No!' as they manifest alternatives to what is being refused. People from below are rising up, but rather than going toward the top, they are moving, as the Zapatistas suggested, 'from below and to the left, where the heart resides'.
>
> *(pg. 5)*

47 Hamid Dabashi, *The Arab Spring: The End of Postcolonialism*, Zed Books, London, 2012.

48 I have relied on the 2019 documentary *The Edge of Democracy* directed by Petra Costa for some of the points made about democracy in Brazil and the manner in which the left-wing government of Dilma Roussef was brought down by a zealous media campaign and how judge Sergio Moro played an important role in the arrest of former President Lula da Silva. With Lula in jail, the path to power for Jair Bolsonaro was smoothened. Sergio Moro was given the position of justice minister in Bolsonaro's government. In mid-2019, there was a series of doubts raised about Segio Moro's impartiality and conduct as a judge in Operation Car Wash, a federal investigation that was meant to root out corruption in Brazilian political life. See Vanessa Barbara, 'Where do you turn when the anti-corruption crusaders are dirty?', *The New York Times*, 5 July 2019. Just as the writing of this chapter was being completed in April 2020, news started pouring in of Sergio Moro's resignation as justice minister, creating a massive political crisis for Jair Bolsonaro. Tom Phillips, 'Brazil's star justice minister Sergio Moro resigns in blow to Jair Bolsonaro', *The Guardian*, Friday 24 April 2020. www.theguardian.com/world/2020/apr/24/brazil-justice-minister-sergio-moro-resigns-jair-bolsonaro. Accessed 25 April 2020.

49 Hannah Arendt, *The Human Condition*, pg. 9.

6

BREXIT, AND THE SUM OF ALL FEARS

Racism, Islamophobia and anti-Semitism

This chapter looks at Brexit as the culmination of the sum of many British fears. Many of these have to do with the fear of the foreigner. Brexit could be considered as the concatenation of many of those elements that sully the supposed purity of Englishness. It bears reiterating, as has been said several times in these pages, that the great tragedy behind Brexit is how the genuineness of the grievance that underlay it has been so decisively transformed into a general, very vehement and a largely unreasonable anger against immigration.

What Brexit also reveals is the tenuous nature of Britain's multiculturalism that rather superficially celebrated and showcased the country's diversity, and the apogee of which was Tony Blair's 'Cool Britannia' branding exercise of the late 1990s.[1] While Brexit represents a decisive defeat of British multiculturalism, the unleashing of various forms of racism in the wake of Brexit also reflects the dismal failure on the part of British multiculturalism in the face of such a resurgence. In fact, British multiculturalism could never counter racism, but merely contained it in a bottle that had Blair's 'Cool Britannia' label affixed to it. Brexit has certainly let the genie of racism out of the multicultural bottle that contained it. Like all genies, it seems that this one offered three wishes to be fulfilled. The one that topped the Brexit Britain wish list seemed to be to get the country out of Europe. An ominous warning, which the British should perhaps have heeded, is to be careful what they wished for.

Brexit, Johnson and Islamophobia

Boris Johnson has Muslim ancestors from Turkey. His great grandfather Ali Kemal was the last interior minister of the Ottoman Empire, the political entity that, at the height of its power, was one of the biggest sources of unease and wariness of the power of Islam in Christian Europe. When Johnson ascended to the Prime

118 Brexit, and the sum of all fears

Ministership, there were celebrations in the village of Kalfat, north of Ankara, where his ancestors came from.[2] In the seventeenth century, when the Ottoman Empire was at the peak of its political ascendance, allegations would often be made of Englishmen 'Turning Turk', if they were perceived to be too favourably inclined towards that political power or were on the verge of conversion to Islam.[3] Johnson's intense Islamophobia almost seems to stem from his very determinedly turning away from his Turkish roots. After his remarkable and unexpected electoral landslide, there were more celebrations in the Turkish village his great grandfather came from.

The unfolding of the Brexit process has led to tremendous levels of hatred being let loose, quite often on British streets, resulting in attacks on people perceived to be on the wrong side. Even before the June 2016 referendum, the Labour MP from the Yorkshire constituency of Batley and Spen, Jo Cox, was fatally stabbed by a man shouting 'Britain first'.[4] Levels of hatred have risen significantly as the Brexit process has unfolded. The unalloyed English nationalism that has been the carrier and purveyor of Brexit seems to have diminished the relevance of multicultural refinements and niceties. Brexit has enhanced levels and depths of hatred and suspicion of the 'other'. The 'other' here really is a straw man that has been filled with sentiments of anti-immigration and Islamophobia. As far as anti-immigrant sentiments are concerned, Johnson's predecessor, Prime Minister Theresa May, stoked them considerably, especially when she was Home Secretary in David Cameron's government. May was responsible for creating a 'hostile environment' against immigrants. She notably sent a bus around telling illegal immigrants to go home.[5] This would constitute another instance of a bus carrying a toxic message, the other one being Johnson's famous red bus with its claim of saving money to the tune of £350 million per week from the EU, which could then be used to fund the NHS. The extent of the horrors from the hostile environment policy on immigration was revealed in the Windrush scandal, when many people who had arrived in Britain from the Caribbean as far back as the 1950s and 1960s were wrongly deported, causing much distress and upheaval. Immigration policy has been one of the most significant levers used by the British state to define a sense of Britishness, by excluding, rejecting and ejecting by deportation, undesirable others. Robin Cohen summarizes the point most pithily: ' "We know who we are by who we reject". Or – to be more pertinent to my current argument – "we know who we are by who we eject" '.[6]

When it comes to the other sentiment stuffed in the straw man of the Brexit 'other', Islamophobia, Prime Minister Boris Johnson's contribution has been truly peerless. His *Daily Telegraph* column, for which, notably, he is paid £275,000 a year, suggested that Muslim women wearing *burqas* looked like 'letter boxes' and 'bank robbers'.[7] Comments such as these could quite easily be characterized as hate speech. They most certainly contributed to rising levels of Islamophobia that have manifested themselves in greater levels of attacks and harassment of Muslims on British streets, as often recorded by the organization 'Tell MAMA'. Time and again, Johnson's strategy, whenever he has been called out for these rather appalling remarks, has been to deflect attention away from his own party's Islamophobia by talking about the anti-Semitism of the Labour Party. When the Sikh Labour MP Tanmanjeet Singh Dhesi eloquently and passionately asked Johnson to apologize in the House of Commons in late 2019, for his remarks on Muslim women, not only did Johnson engage in a classic instance of 'whataboutery', by raising the issue of the Labour Party's anti-Semitism, but he justified his comments by calling them a 'strong liberal defense' of womens' rights to wear what they want.[8] On other occasions, Johnson has doggedly refused to apologize by invoking the familiar principle of the finest expressions of free speech.

At a late stage of the 2019 election campaign, Johnson seemed to apologize in a vague sort of way to those his comments may have caused hurt and offence. This was more likely to have been a crass electoral strategy for which Johnson, given his reputation, could even sell that itself, or much else for that matter.[9] Johnson's 'apology', if it can be called that, followed very close on the heels of Corbyn's refusal to apologize for anti-Semitism in Labour ranks. Once Johnson had said sorry, Corbyn was also quick to issue an apology, one that almost seemed to be wrangled out of him in an interview.[10] The British are of course known for saying sorry all too frequently.

Johnson's repeated Islamophobic statements cannot be seen in isolation, and the ground for them has been prepared, so to say, in numerous comments unduly and prejudicially critical of Islam that have come from his predecessors, both Conservative and Labour Prime Ministers and politicians. David Cameron, in his February 2011 speech at the 47th Munich Security Conference, bewailed the failures of 'state multiculturalism', as he called it, and attempted to point towards problematic strains of Islam.[11] Cameron's views were not as toxically presented as they tend to be in someone like Boris Johnson, but the Munich speech does indicate the manner in which the possibilities for Johnson's later, far more bombastic remarks were created.

If one stepped back further into the late 1990s and early 2000s, similar sentiments were expressed by Tony Blair as Prime Minister, sentiments that were remarkably echoed and reinforced by several of his cabinet colleagues such as Jack Straw, Harriet Harman and David Blunkett, just to name three of the more prominent ones in a long list. There was, in many of these comments, an attempt to make a division between Islam as a religion of peace and harmony on the one hand and misguided interpretations of the religion that especially young Muslim men were influenced by, on the other. The remarks were numerous, but let us confine ourselves to the one on Muslim women and the *hijab*. In 2006, Jack Straw described the face veil as a 'visible mark of separation and difference'. Harriet Harman again spoke rather patronizingly of wanting women to be fully included and how the veil was an obstacle to their fuller participation in society on equal terms.[12]

The general trend of many of these speeches and statements made by New Labour ministers, 111 of which were analysed in a paper by Leon Moosavi, was to vaguely define a set of British values undergirded by tolerance, free speech, the rule of law, fair play, democracy and liberty. Islam and Muslims, it was then suggested,

120 Brexit, and the sum of all fears

fell out of the pale, some a little tantalizingly out of it, and others so extremely outside that they were perhaps, irredeemable. Conflicting signals, at times endorsing British multiculturalism and at other times suggesting that it had created separate and parallel enclaves, cut-off from British values, were sent. This has prompted Moosavi to note that most of these speeches were Islamophobic and that they often adhered to a 'Party line, meaning that they were not speaking as individuals but had been briefed centrally with what to say. That was evident because so many of the statements were almost identical even when made by different ministers on different occasions.'[13]

Anti-Semitism and Islamophobia conjoined

Anti-Semitism and Islamophobia have become so thoroughly conjoined in the recent Brexit debate that a discussion of one would necessarily involve a discussion of the other. Both are forms of racism, which as a form of discrimination has itself become transmuted into what has often been called a 'new racism'. Recent accusations of Islamophobia levelled at the Conservatives and accusations of anti-Semitism made against the Labour Party would then necessarily have to be looked at together at a conceptual level. The All Party Parliamentary Group (APPG) on British Muslims published a 'Report on the inquiry into a working definition of Islamophobia/anti-Muslim hatred'. Islamophobia has only recently entered the policy discourse in the past two decades and, on account of this, 'it does not enjoy the longer history and popular acceptance of terms such as racism or anti-Semitism'. The report considered the Runnymede Trust's efforts since 1997 to come up with a definition of Islamophobia. It also noted that in 2017 the Runnymede Trust produced another report where it put forward a short and a long definition of Islamophobia. The APPG noted that the long definition put forward in this more recent report by the Runnymede Trust takes further steps to 'embed Islamophobia in anti-racism paradigms and incorporates features of the UN's definition of racism within its longer definition to signify the structural and other impediments anti-Muslim racism presents to the pursuit of equality for Muslims'. The APPG also noted that, in the same year, in 2017, Dr Chris Allen suggested that the definition of anti-Semitism should also be used as a template for a definition of Islamophobia.[14]

Corbyn, Brexit and anti-Semitism

Jeremy Corbyn has always seemed rather bewildered at the accusations of anti-Semitism levelled against him. He cannot be associated with any outrageously anti-Semitic remark. Corbyn did chide in a 2013 video, British Zionists for not getting English irony, despite having lived in the country for long periods of time.[15] This might be considered one of the more problematic remarks that he personally made. It would, however, pale into insignificance in comparison to the depths that Johnson is capable of plumbing. One further reason why Corbyn seems to be completely bewildered by accusations of anti-Semitism has to do with the fact that he considers himself a consistent campaigner against all forms of racism. Anti-Semitism is one form of racism, and Corbyn would naturally consider himself against such a form. The accusations of anti-Semitism in the Labour Party have surfaced and snowballed quite recently with Corbyn's assumption of party leadership. They can be linked to the rise of the Momentum faction within Labour that facilitated Corbyn's dominance in the party.

Similar claims about anti-Semitism were completely missing when Ed Miliband, himself Jewish, was leader of the Labour Party. Consider the much talked about photograph of him eating a bacon sandwich in early 2014.[16] The notorious Rupert Murdoch-owned tabloid, *The Sun*, splashed the picture on its front page to suggest that Miliband could not even handle eating a bacon sandwich. Running the country as prime minister would be too tall an order. There was clearly an anti-Semitic element here with Miliband's Jewish identity and the bacon sandwich acting as a subtext. Remarkably, this never got called out for the anti-Semitism that it obviously was.

Perhaps in the run-up to the December 2019 elections, Jeremy Corbyn became the most unpopular person in the UK. Not that Boris Johnson was very popular for that matter. The election almost became a contest of which person would prove to be less popular. The electoral contest, in terms of the disastrous performance of Corbyn's Labour party and the surprisingly good performance of Johnson's Conservatives, could almost be summed up as a case of the British 'not hating Johnson less, but hating Corbyn more'. The rise of Corbyn to Labour leadership in 2015, the way he led a Labour surge in the May 2017 elections to deprive Theresa May of any possibility of a parliamentary majority, to the very disappointing performance in the 2019 elections is strange. His rise to Labour leadership in 2015 to succeed Ed Miliband could be a natural movement of the Labour party leadership to the left after the Blairite interlude from 1994 all the way to 2007. The fact that Ed and not his brother, David Miliband, won the party leadership in 2010 was again a confirmation that the Labour party could not continue on the Blairite centrist grounds, where it was thought that the party had discovered the magic third way that could keep winning them elections.

However, the question needs to be asked, what accounts for Corbyn's near-disastrous performance? What made him so unpopular in the northern Labour heartlands that the Labour red wall was breached and someone like Boris Johnson, of all people, could rampage around in these bastions? Was it to do with allegations of anti-Semitism against Corbyn? Was it to do with Corbyn's North London 'Islingtonian elitism' that the northern heartlands could just not accept? Why on earth would Boris Johnson, with his established Etonian elitism, be so successful where Corbyn failed so miserably? Again, Corbyn's unpopularity becomes even more intriguing given the fact that many aspects of the Labour Party manifesto and the policies contained in it were exceedingly popular. Was it because of his stand on terrorism? Was this then linked to questions of loyalty to the nation? Or was it owing to his lack of deference to the monarchy? Was it, to use the words of Owen

Hatherley in an article in the *Guardian*, a case of Corbyn being an 'intellectual pacifist who didn't genuflect enough to patriotism'?[17] Was Corbyn hopelessly locked in the socialist politics of the 1970s? If that really was the case, how does one account for Corbyn and Labour's forward-looking arguments on climate change through support for a Green New Deal and a green industrial revolution? By those standards Johnson's politics would still be frozen in time also back in the 1970s, when climate change was almost an unnoticeable blip on the horizon.

These questions became further compounded by the leaking of an 860-page document in the first week of April 2020, just as Keir Starmer took over the leadership of the Labour Party. The document was compiled by Corbyn sympathizers and blamed individuals from the right-wing of the Labour Party of working to prevent a Labour victory. The document was also dismissive of the BBC Panorama investigation broadcast in early July 2019, which interviewed whistle-blowers from within the Labour Party who levelled serious allegations of anti-Semitism. Many Corbyn sympathizers took the document as suggestive of an orchestrated campaign to undermine and jeopardize Corbyn's leadership.[18] This was a view that was reinforced by a four-part *Al Jazeera* investigation that suggested the working of a deep-seated lobby in the UK, active on university campuses and also in both mainstream parties, Labour and Conservative.[19]

In late October 2020, the Equality and Human Rights Commission (EHRC) published its findings into complaints of anti-Semitism in the Labour party. The report was damning in terms of its criticism of Labour's handling of the issue. The response to the report by Labour leader Keir Starmer and his predecessor Jeremy Corbyn could almost be called a study in contrast. Starmer readily accepted the report's findings and pledged to do his best to eliminate the problem from within Labour party ranks. Corbyn, while acknowledging the presence of the problem, also rather problematically suggested that instances had been exaggerated to discredit the party's prospects.[20]

The labour left and anti-Semitism

The allegations of anti-Semitism against Corbyn need to be understood in a deeper sort of way. One historical parallel that is available are charges of anti-Semitism that were made against Labour politician Ernest Bevin, who was the British Foreign Secretary between 1945 and 1951, the crucial period just after the Second World War when the British Mandate in Palestine expired, and the state of Israel was created. Raphael Langham notes a 'common view' about him being anti-Semitic and how this influenced his foreign policy. Langham further notes that the 'accusations of antisemitism only arose after he became Foreign Secretary, but they were so strong and widely held that they have been subsequently addressed by many historians and all his biographers, as well as in memoirs of his contemporaries'.

Langham takes up a number of views on Bevin and remarkably notes how one view suggests that Bevin was anti-Semitic, while the other view seems to be almost completely the opposite. Consider the two tallest Jewish leaders, Chaim Weizmann and David Ben-Gurion. Weizmann felt that Bevin was blinded by his hatred of the Jews, while David Ben-Gurion made the distinction between anti-Semitism and anti-Zionism, to suggest that he was the latter, rather than the former. More recently, the historian Avi Shlaim considered Bevin to be the 'guardian angel of the infant state' (Israel), while another historian, Efraim Karsh, responded that Shlaim's comments on Israel were the exact opposite of the truth. Based on a set of at least three almost contrasting opinions on the British Foreign Secretary, Langham suggests that Bevin was something of an enigma when it came to the question of his attitude towards Jews.[21] Langham peers into the early circumstances of Bevin's birth and childhood and suggests that there is no possibility of his imbibing any anti-Semitic influences. In fact, Langham notes that in 1920, Bevin and his wife moved to Golders Green in London, associated with a significant Jewish presence. Where Bevin lived was not far from the site that would become Dunstan Road synagogue, two years after Bevin's move to the area. Langham notes that one of Bevin's biographers have suggested that a move such as this could hardly be considered to come from someone filled with hatred for Jews.[22]

Bevin's record in terms of his views on Jews is a mixed bag, but he is hardly someone who can be called an incorrigible anti-Semite. Langham notes that Bevin certainly did express prejudice towards Jews, but he suggests that he cannot be considered someone with a deep-seated prejudice or hatred.[23]

As far as the anti-Semitism of which Jeremy Corbyn has been criticized, this has quite often been understood as one emanating from the far left of the British political spectrum. From the perspective of those sympathetic to Israel, the suggestion is that the far left in Britain tends to view Israel as a form of settler colonialism and sides with varying forms of Arab nationalism, especially Palestinian nationalism. This kind of anti-Semitism of the far left, it is further suggested, has flared up especially since the second intifada of September 2000.[24] Allegations of anti-Semitism levelled against the left also get entangled with the question of legitimate criticism of the actions of the state of Israel. Even supporters of Israel tend to agree that not all criticism of Israel can be called anti-Semitic, but it is very often difficult to decide the point where legitimate criticism becomes anti-Semitic and expands into a larger demonization of Israel.[25]

In September 2018, there was controversy at the Labour party conference over the full and complete acceptance of the International Holocaust Remembrance Alliance's (IHRA) definition of anti-Semitism. The Labour party had already been through one round of sustained criticism over allegations of anti-Semitism during the summer months preceding the party conference. While the full definition was finally adopted, Jeremy Corbyn seemed to resist a full acceptance of the IHRA definition, bringing up the question of legitimate criticism of Israel and submitting a one-and-a-half-page statement that was rejected by the party's National Executive Committee (NEC). In hindsight, it seems that an attitude of the kind that Corbyn displayed back in 2018 only added fuel to raging flames of anti-Semitism allegations that did much to sink his leadership of Labour.[26]

Anti-Semitism from the late nineteenth century

While there has been a more general hatred of Jews that has prevailed for as long as the faith has been in existence, it is the more modern manifestation of the phenomenon that needs to be considered.[27] In considering this modern manifestation of anti-Semitism as a stigmatization and hatred of Jews, there is a tendency to focus on that most gruesome manifestation of anti-Semitism in the twentieth century in the form of the Holocaust and to view the advancing levels of anti-Semitism throughout the nineteenth century and early part of the twentieth century, as almost inexorably moving towards this most tragic of denouements.

For the purposes of this chapter, the focus on anti-Semitism will be confined to understanding it as arising from the late nineteenth century in a predominantly Central European setting and is further linked to the problem of a supposed lack of Jewish assimilation when it came to the question of the nation-state. The nation-state is here the central analytical focus in order to understand the phenomenon, which will then lead onto a further consideration of Islamophobia, where again the nation-state remains the rubric through which this other form of hatred can be understood.

The nation-state is a remarkably homogenizing and assimilationist entity by its very nature, especially when one contrasts it with preceding empires that encompassed and often encouraged diversity. There is a connection between the assimilationist tendency of the nation-state and the status of Jews in nineteenth-century Europe with their perceived cosmopolitanism and supposed access to powerful political Establishments attained through the financial and banking channels they controlled, and which were used to support European governments.[28] Anti-Semitism in the nineteenth century was very much about Jews and their awkward relationship, or rather anomalous non-relationship, with the nation-state. Hannah Arendt, in her analysis of anti-Semitism, links the rise of the modern variant of the phenomenon to the rise and decline of the nation-state.[29] In fact Arendt even dismisses the 'hasty explanations' that have identified anti-Semitism with 'rampant nationalism and xenophobic outbursts'. She goes on to suggest:

> Unfortunately, the fact is that modern antisemitism grew in proportion as traditional nationalism declined, and reached its climax at the exact moment when the European system of nation-states and its precarious balance of power crashed.[30]

The most famous episode connected to the spread of anti-Semitism was, of course, the Dreyfus Affair, which happened at the end of the year 1894 in France. This controversy was very much about the supposed extra-territorial loyalty of Alfred Dreyfus, a Jewish officer of the French General Staff who was accused of spying for the Germans. The case brings up the unflinching loyalty that nation-states expect from individuals and citizens within their borders. Hannah Arendt, in her long consideration of the Dreyfus affair, notes how it actually originated at the very end of the nineteenth century, had a significantly long resonance in the twentieth century that was just about to unfold, and was one of the most far-reaching and consequential developments of the French Third Republic. It reveals how the nation-state can become very readily a rallying cry for a vague and dangerous idea of the people. Arendt notes very insightfully that such dangerous invocations are actually a 'caricature of the people'. This acute observation is immediately followed by a paragraph that is worth quoting in full as it so fulsomely resonates with Boris Johnson's Brexit Britain:

> The mob is primarily a group in which the residue of all classes are represented. This makes it so easy to mistake the mob for the people, which also comprises all strata of society. While the people in all great revolutions fight for true representation, the mob always will shout for the 'strong man,' the 'great leader,'. For the mob hates society from which it is excluded, as well as Parliament where it is not represented. Plebiscites, therefore, with which modern mob leaders have obtained such excellent results, are an old concept of politicians who rely upon the mob. One of the more intelligent leaders of the Anti-Dreyfusards, Deroulede, clamoured for a 'Republic through plebiscite'.[31]

Brexit and the reassertion of the nation-state

Brexit, in the analysis of this book, is understood as a rallying around and reinforcement of the nation-state in the face of the supranational EU. The vehemence with which supporters of Brexit are also supporters of the nation-state, which is further reinforced by strong notions of sovereignty, could represent one of the more powerful flickers of the nation-state as it proceeds to be snuffed out by political, economic and technological forces unleashed by globalization. The nation-state is viewed here as an entity whose time is up. Arendt talked about the decline of the nation-state in her book *The Origins of Totalitarianism* published in 1950. The decline of the nation-state is, however, taking a tremendously long time to work itself out and could signal, if not its ultimate obsolescence as a political entity, at least a significant undermining. A phenomenon such as Brexit vociferously advocates the continued and lively persistence and even rebirth of the nation-state.

A discerning observer can, however, see the redundant and vacuous nature of the nation-state in the face of an almost existential crisis such as climate change. Individual nation-states simply lack the ability to handle climate crises on their own. As climate change and global pollution are unaffected by the narrow confines of nation-states, a politics that is increasingly forced to respond to issues of the climate will tend to overlook the nation-state. In fact, one can almost suggest an inverse relation between nationalist politics and climate change. The issue of climate change was literally absent from Boris Johnson's election campaign and his politics more generally. The same can be said of the politics of Trump and his

Republican party in the US. The Labour manifesto did pledge itself to the Green New Deal. The issue of climate change simply does not seem to exist in the sunny uplands that hard Brexiteers inhabit.

The writing of this chapter was completed a little before the outbreak of the Coronavirus pandemic, which initially seemed to reinforce the significance of nation-states as borders were closed and societies went into lockdown. However, the bankruptcy of nation-state responses became increasingly obvious as a global pandemic does not respect borders. What we witnessed across the world was a remarkable flare-up of vaccine nationalism, in which different nations, and especially the richer ones, clamoured to get their populations vaccinated, forgetting that the persistence of the virus anywhere in the world would still be a threat. Pope Francis was able to capture the problem when he pointed out in his traditional 'Urbi et Orbi' (to the City and the World) address on Christmas day that the 'walls of nationalism' would be unable to keep the vaccine away. He suggested, 'At this moment in history, marked by ecological crisis and grave economic and social imbalances only worsened by the coronavirus pandemic, it is all the more important for us to acknowledge one another as brothers and sisters'.[32] The South African epidemiologist Salim Abdool Karim, in an interview, pointed out 'None of us is safe from Covid if one us is not. We have mutual interdependence.'[33]

The Coronavirus pandemic and the irony of nationalistic responses that it has given rise to are a reminder of the enduring relevance of Stoic philosophy. Stoicism is very often understood as transcending the nation-state and its confined sense of belonging. The Stoic philosopher of the first and second centuries CE, Hierocles, suggested that all individuals are at the centre of a series of concentric circles, the inner circles of which comprise close family relations and friends. Moving outwards are circles encompassing more extended collectives and groupings, and the outermost circle represents humanity itself to which we are connected indissolubly. It may be wise to draw that outermost circle inwards and towards us every once and again as the Coronavirus pandemic so poignantly reminds us. A Stoic like Hierocles would suggest that there are moral obligations that each individual has to the outermost circle of humanity.[34]

The futile nature of nationalistic assertions in the face of the global Coronavirus pandemic prompted the World Health Organization (WHO) to warn countries of the perils of engaging in vaccine nationalism. Stephen Buranyi, writing in *The Guardian* suggested,

> To call this vaccine nationalism seems unnecessary since every stage of the coronavirus crisis has been marked by resurgent nationalism; and by the states previously most invested in the idea of an interconnected world recoiling from it, thrashing about in anger when the system no longer seemed to serve their interests.[35]

Much in the same manner that Hannah Arendt linked anti-Semitism to the vicissitudes of the nation-state, the racism emanating from the Brexit process in the form of Islamophobia and anti-Semitism needs to be linked to the inane hyperactivity of the nation-state, thrashing about and flagellating in the face of global crises such as environmental ones or health crises such as the Coronavirus pandemic. Jews became the subject of anti-Semitic hatred owing to their awkwardly anomalous and consequently unassimilable situation *between* various European nation-states in Hannah Arendt's analysis.[36] Islamophobia seems to arise from the threat that Muslims pose as potential fifth columnists lodged securely *within* the nation-state. This distinction that has just been made in the conjoint analysis of anti-Semitism and Islamophobia is then, in terms of problematic positioning, *between* and *within* nation-states, respectively. Further, the problematic positioning of Muslims within the nation-state as potential fifth columnists is connected to a larger pan-national Islamic presence.

The *European Islamophobia Report 2018* notes that, in addition to the implementation of anti-Muslim legislation that threatens religious freedom, many countries have attempted to create versions of 'national Islam' by severing the ties that bind Muslim population presences with larger global transnational connections.[37] Here again there is a contrast between Islamophobia and anti-Semitism. The common point of reference so far in the conjoined analysis of these two phenomena has been, to reiterate, the nation-state. The difference arises in terms of Islamophobia arising from the Muslim presence deep within the nation-state, a bit like a sleeper cell lodged within and waiting to be detonated by a larger pan-national Islamic presence. In contrast, anti-Semitism, when it arose in the late nineteenth century, stemmed from a problematic positioning of Jews between nation-states. Furthermore, anti-Semitism was reinforced by pan-European appeals transcending the nation-state. Again, Arendt suggests that Nazism and the anti-Semitism associated with it were not restricted to the narrow confines of the nation-state but had a wider internationalist appeal.[38]

New racism and the nation-state

The 'new racism' that has become a feature since the last quarter of the twentieth century has tended to align itself much more closely with the nation-state. Paul Gilroy, in his much-celebrated book *There Ain't No Black in the Union Jack*, has noted that the novelty of this new racism lies in its ability to bring together themes such as patriotism, nationalism, xenophobia, Englishness, Britishness, militarism and gender difference. This new racism, with its far greater cultural connotations, manifests itself in certain ways in family life so that, as Gilroy notes, families become the 'nation in microcosm'.[39] It is perhaps no accident that the divisiveness of Brexit has reportedly riven many families.

Racism contributes to the configuration of the nation-state in a way that most political tendencies do not even want to seem to notice, prompting Gilroy to observe: 'The possibility of politically significant connections between nationalism and contemporary racism is either unseen or felt to be unworthy of detailed discussion'. Gilroy makes these observations in the light of developments in

Britain during and immediately after the Falklands War of 1982. He seems to be appalled by the British Left's response to the Falklands crisis, which could only seem to mirror and reflect the patriotism that the ruling Conservative Party was displaying so brazenly. As he suggests, in times such as the Falklands crisis, 'few arguments are made which justify the need to make the nation-state a primary focus of radical political consciousness'.[40] With regard to many figures on the British left who found no alternative but to almost literally wear their patriotism on their sleeves, Gilroy has the following sharp observation to make: 'When it comes to their patriotism, it would appear that England's left intellectuals become so many radical rabbits transfixed and immobile in the path of an onrushing populist nationalism'.[41]

The patterns of discrimination that racism gives rise to are sutured and segued very thoroughly into the very structures, seams and integuments of the nation-state. Any attempt to address the patterns of discriminations arising from racism is likely to be perceived as an attempt to undo and tear apart the very fabric of the nation-state itself. Thus, racism in the UK is an integral part of the very configuration of the nation-state. Any attempt to call for a redressal of problems of racism is likely to be met with accusations of wanting to tear apart the fabric of the nation itself. In fact, assertions of bonding within and protecting the nation-state from without are likely to be made vociferously at precisely such moments by the hyper-patriotic right to quell the possibility of redressing racism. This was made plain in the report of the Commission on Race and Ethnic Disparities or the Sewell Commission released in late March 2021. The report denied the existence of institutional racism. It also implied that those activists who continued to vociferously point to the existence of such racism were not merely mistaken but tended to disparage the nation itself. The *Guardian* columnist Nesrine Malik complained that the report seemed to frame those who were complaining about racism as the problem, as the ones who were 'doing Britain down'.[42] The report was commissioned by the Conservative Government after the ripple effects of the Black Lives Matter movement in the US, arising from the killing of George Floyd in the summer of 2020, were felt in the UK.

Five macro levels from which Islamophobia is reinforced

It would be important to contrast the newness of the phenomenon of Islamophobia with modern anti-Semitism, which has been around since at least the late nineteenth century. There are broadly five macro levels from which the phenomenon of Islamophobia receives reinforcement.

Orientalism

First, a historically pre-existing Orientalist world view that has been locked into place by virtue of European colonial expansion and practice. This point will not be elaborated upon in too much detail here and will only be used to connect to the next point.

Islamophobia expands with the discrediting of multiculturalism

Second, Islamophobia is likely to be given a significant boost with the discrediting of multiculturalism. Multiculturalism policies, especially the British variant, are a legacy of the extensive presence of the British Empire. Such policies arose from a reverse movement of populations from the erstwhile colonial peripheries into the metropolitan centre as the British Empire declined and contracted. The initial enthusiasm for multiculturalism policies has given way to a clearly discernible rejection of multiculturalism as the first two decades of the twenty-first century have played out.

There is a correlation between the decline of multiculturalism and the rise of Islamophobia. One of the ways of gauging the rise in academic interest in Islamophobia is to take note of the All Parliamentary Party Group on British Muslims report that has already been mentioned. Based on oral evidence from Bertie Vidgen, PhD student at the University of Oxford, the report suggested that before the 1990s there were only six scholarly papers on Islamophobia. This number increased to 33 in the decade of the 1990s. This changed with the turn of the century, with 310 papers released in the 2000s and a 'staggering' 1632 in the 2010s with the decade not even over when the report was written.[43]

One of the most significant manifestations of the disillusionment, indeed outright dislike of multiculturalism was the tragic shooting of many youngsters in Norway by Anders Behring Breivik in July 2011. In the eyes of the right, multiculturalism is viewed as a kind of cover and excuse for the more unapologetic public presence of Islam. This antipathy towards multiculturalism as an idea could have interesting parallels to the way secularism, as a political idea, is demonized by right-wing Hindutva nationalist supporters as a prop that provides an unnecessary and undeserved 'appeasement' of Muslims in India. Vociferous denunciation of multiculturalism, though by no means all criticism of it, can be a carrier and purveyor of Islamophobia.

Islam and liberal-democracy

The third and next macro level at which Islamophobia can be encouraged is the idea that Islam is simply not compatible with liberal-democracy. This is more in the manner of a prejudicial disposition and an obstinately held view. It looks at liberal-democracy as a finished, final project that can never be accommodative of the Muslim presence in various European lands. It breaks down into national variants such as the idea that Islam is incompatible with Danish society, or German society or British society. Such a sentiment is contained in the figures that suggest

130 Brexit, and the sum of all fears

that nearly half of the voters of the governing Conservative Party in the UK believe that Islam is incompatible with the 'British way of life'.[44] Note that this kind of view would have little by way of explaining the near collapse of liberal-democracy in a country such as Hungary and the championing of an illiberal democracy by the Hungarian leader Viktor Orban.

Global war on terrorism

Fourth, the war on terrorism prosecuted by Western powers, notably the US with the UK acting as largely an accompanying sidekick, has greatly contributed to the expansion of Islamophobia. The wholesale equating of Islam with terrorism is not just a factually incorrect proposition but seems to have been maliciously spread by vast sections of the right-wing media. Not just the equating of Islam with terrorism, but even the suggestion that terrorism is such a huge problem, is itself part of this game of exaggeration that large sections of the right-wing media seem to dilate upon without any sense of proportion. The issue of terrorism in merely statistical terms, as a terrible occurrence that can happen to an innocent non-combatant and bystander, is quite low. Contrast such low possibilities to the kind of massive investment in foreign and public policy made by many governments across the world when it comes to the issue of terrorism. This is then likely to be multiplied exponentially by media coverage, which generally does not ask for accountability from governments in their measures taken to counter terrorism.

To reiterate, the preoccupation among large numbers of nation-states with terrorism is a significant contributor to the phenomenon of Islamophobia, especially when that terrorism is associated almost exclusively with Islam. For instance, the authors of the *European Islamophobia Report 2018* complain that they:

> received criticism and sarcasm from European right-wing circles for including the section "Terrorist Attacks against Muslims" in the introduction to the 2017 *European Islamophobia Report*. According to these circles, "Islamophobic terror" was an oxymoron as Muslims are supposed to be the only people responsible for terror attacks in the world and are certainly not the targeted victims of such violence.

The report goes on to note that this is far from an isolated view, citing researchers from Georgia State University and the University of Alabama who, in a study published in *Justice Quarterly* in March 2017, found that attacks perpetrated by Muslims were likely to receive on average 357 per cent more coverage than other attacks in the US.[45] What this predominantly right-wing perspective suggests is the complete and total equating of terrorism with Islam, which can be contained in a simple but highly misleading aphorism such as the following: 'all Muslims may not be terrorists, but all terrorists are Muslims'.

This suggests that Islamophobia has been mainstreamed and normalized in European society. This mainstreaming and normalization of Islamophobia indicate a process by which this form of hatred arises from the far-right of the political spectrum but then spreads to the rest of society, affecting assumptions on the centre and even the left of the political spectrum. This normalization and mainstreaming of Islamophobia are buttressed by what the compilers of the *European Islamophobia Report 2018* refer to as the phenomenon of 'legalizing Islamophobia', which is the practice of European societies to validate Islamophobic ideas by enacting legislation such as banning headscarves in France, banning fasting in schools in Austria and the controversial anti-ghetto laws in Denmark passed in early 2018. These are forms of legislation that tend to affect Muslim religious practices particularly adversely.[46] This has continued, even as far-right-inspired terror against Muslims has been coming under the scanner.

The Internet and the media

The fifth and final macro structure that gives rise to widespread Islamophobia is the pervasiveness of the Internet and the influence of the media. This would not just be confined to web pages that are Islamophobic and spread hatred against Islam and Muslims, but social media platforms such as Facebook, WhatsApp and Twitter. Facebook's role in the Rohingya genocide in Myanmar was widely talked about, as there was an inability to detect and expunge hateful comments made against the Rohingya, which fuelled violence against them. The influential role of Facebook in democratic processes, specifically its role in the 23 June 2016 referendum in the UK that resulted in Brexit, is of course well-known.[47]

In addition to these five macro levels at which the phenomenon of Islamophobia is strengthened, it can manifest itself at very local levels. Individuals in interaction with agencies of the state, people standing in queues at shopping markets, waiting at the petrol pump, all these would be the various sites at which one is likely to encounter Islamophobic behaviour and abuse. The phenomenon is especially acutely manifested in response to the veils of Muslim women. Organizations such as Tell MAMA frequently report incidents of Muslim women having their veils and *hijabs* pulled off in aggressive Islamophobic attacks. However, to connect the grand levels at which Islamophobia is reinforced to actual manifestation, one would need to highlight the idea of an institutional presence of Islamophobia. In other words, the term institutional conveys the heavy entrenchment of Islamophobia that is deployed not merely in casual everyday situations but lodges itself in the processes and workings of institutions, thereby creating significant difficulties for Muslims.

Before a consideration of Brexit and how it has accelerated rates of Islamophobia that are experienced in British society, it may be worthwhile pointing out that levels of Islamophobia were on the rise much before Brexit. Significant landmark occurrences in British society such as the Rushdie affair, the impact of the two gulf wars and the ramifications of the war on terror, in which the UK has been an active participant, can be connected with enhanced levels of Islamophobia. Two years before the 2016 referendum, there was the much talked about Trojan horse affair in 2014 that rocked many schools in Birmingham. The right-wing press, in extremely exaggerated coverage, suggested that there was a widespread conspiracy to 'Islamize' these schools. This was an exaggerated manner of coverage that was uncritically taken up by David Cameron's Conservative government. It was later discovered that there was certainly an attempt in some schools to push Islamic religious ideas, but to call it an organized conspiracy was taking things too far. Regarding the Trojan horse affair, Aristotle Kallis writes:

> The handing of the investigation by the Department of Education and the education regulator Ofsted was widely criticized for giving in to a sensationalist approach to the matter that did lasting damage to community relations and added fuel to an Islamophobic climate in British society.[48]

Brexit and Islamophobia

Brexit has given rise to much higher levels of Islamophobia for the simple reason that, rather tragically, Brexit has become reduced to a general fear and hatred of immigration. One of the most undesirable components of this immigrant tide happens to be Muslims and Islam. The kind of hard Brexit commandeered by Boris Johnson could only further advance already high levels of Islamophobia. Aristotle Kallis, in his country report on the UK in the *European Islamophobia Report 2018*, notes the transformation of the UKIP, one of the most powerful political vehicles making the case for Britain to leave the EU, into an openly Islamophobic party, especially when, in 2018, it elected a new leader, Gerard Batten. It then went on to appoint the English Defence League leader Tommy Robinson as party advisor.

The denial of Islamophobia in the UK

One of the problems with the question of Islamophobia in the UK is the tendency to deny its very existence. An instance of this denial would be the influential right-wing philosopher and public intellectual Roger Scruton, who died just as this chapter was being written in January 2020. The Conservative government was forced to sack Scruton from a government advisory position when he suggested that Islamophobia was a 'propaganda word'.[49] He was later to be reinstated. Baroness Warsi, a Muslim cabinet member in David Cameron's government, has consistently talked about the widespread presence of Islamophobia among the ranks of the Conservatives. She had to resign in frustration and has often raised the lack of concerned response in the Conservative Party. It was found in the way the Conservative Party, under Theresa May, refused to accept the working definition on Islamophobia that was prepared and presented by the APPG on British Muslims. Many suggested that the problem of Islamophobia within the Conservative Party was likely to be aggravated with Boris Johnson's landslide victory in the December 2019 elections. Suhaiymah Manzoor Khan, writing in *The Guardian*, argued: 'If this election was the "second Brexit referendum", this should come as no surprise. The first was won by stoking racism and Islamophobia'.[50]

Brexit, and the sum of all fears **133**

As far as denial of Islamophobia is concerned, it comes right from the very top, the Conservative government of the UK, and is evident in the way it has dealt with the APPG report and its definition of Islamophobia. It has consistently refused to accept the working definition that has been offered. Boris Johnson, just a few days after his 12 December 2019 election victory, backtracked on the previously promised commitment to conduct an inquiry into the prevalence of Islamophobia and replaced it with a rather more anodyne, broad-brush inquiry into how the Conservative Party deals with complaints of discrimination. The Muslim Council of Britain accused the Conservatives of 'denial, dismissal and deceit' over the problem and also suggested that the party had a 'blind spot' for Islamophobia within its own ranks and that it allowed the problem to 'fester in society'.[51] Intriguingly, the person chosen to chair the committee, Swaran Singh of Warwick University and a former equality and human rights commissioner, contributed to an online publication *Spiked*, whose editor Brendan O'Neill has been known to dismiss the concept of Islamophobia.[52] The role of Brendan O'Neill and the publication *Spiked* in the unfolding of Brexit, when he actually advocated mob violence on the streets, has also been commented upon in another part of this book in Chapter 3.

The chorus of denial about the very existence of Islamophobia is taken up by right-wing think tanks such as Policy Exchange, which refuted the APPG report on Islamophobia in its own 24-page report authored by Sir John Jenkins. Trevor Phillips, the former Chairman of the Equality and Human Rights Commission, wrote a preface to the report that suggested an equating of Islamophobia with racism would be detrimental to integration. This is furthered by the Quilliam Foundation, which also criticized the APPG definition of Islamophobia. This persistent denial of Islamophobia could be easily read as a clear affirmation of the existence of the beastly phenomenon in British society. What we have then is an ecosystem of definition denial that facilitates the sustenance and proliferation of the phenomenon. This depiction of what has been called an ecosystem of Islamophobia and denial of a definition has been summed up by Aristotle Kallis as follows:

> It therefore seems that the Islamophobia 'sceptics' within the broader British Muslim community have swiftly joined forces with like-minded mainstream sceptics from the press and from certain think tanks in a coordinated defence of the government's refusal to accept the APPG's proposed definition of 'Islamophobia'.[53]

Brexit itself does not have any positive agenda for the future of Britain apart from a series of dislikes that begins with the dislike of the EU. Like any political phenomenon fired by a recrudescent nationalism that targets a detested other, Brexit is directed by a hatred of immigrants and more specifically Muslim ones. Back in 2006, when the controversy around the Danish newspaper *Jyllands-Posten* and its cartoon depicting the Prophet Muhammad was still raging, the British publication *The Spectator* had to pull down one of the controversial cartoons portraying the Prophet with a bomb in his turban. Until then, no British news organization had

134 Brexit, and the sum of all fears

chosen to reproduce the *Jyllands-Posten* cartoons. *Spectator* eventually had to do a U-turn when acting editor Stuart Reid felt that the depiction was not appropriate. Reid claimed that he did not have responsibility for the *Spectator* website, where 'the guy who has overall responsibility' was a certain Dominic Cummings. When he was contacted, Cummings, with his usual tight-lipped and cold-stare demeanour said, 'I have zero comment'.[54]

Notes

1 Richard Power Sayeed, 'How cool Britannia helped fuel Brexit', *Vice*, 24 October 2017. www.vice.com/en_uk/article/d3dvdw/how-cool-britannia-led-to-brexit. Accessed 18 August 2020.
2 Alice Tidey, 'Residents in Boris Johnson's ancestral Turkish village "proud" of his election as UK PM', *Euronews*, 26 July 2019. www.euronews.com/2019/07/26/residents-in-boris-johnson-s-ancestral-turkish-village-proud-of-his-election-as-uk-pm. Accessed 2 January 2020.
3 Humberto Garcia, *Islam and the English Enlightenment, 1670–1840*, Johns Hopkins University Press, Baltimore, MD, 2012.
4 Holly Christodoulou and Jon Lockett in their article 'MP's killer: who killed Jo Cox and where is Thomas Mair now?', *The Sun*, 27 September 2019, referred to Thomas Mair, as 'a white supremacist'. The article further informs us that he carried out searches on a far-right Internet publication, the Klu Klux Klan. A Third Reich golden eagle featuring a swastika was found on top of a bookcase at Mair's house. The search also unearthed press cuttings on the Norwegian mass killer Anders Behring Breivik. www.thesun.co.uk/news/2022683/jo-cox-killer-thomas-mair-now/. Accessed 18 August 2020.
5 Sonya Sceats, 'Theresa May's legacy is the hostile environment – how can she evoke Nicholas Winton in her resignation speech?', *The Independent*, 25 May 2019. www.independent.co.uk/voices/theresa-may-resigns-hostile-environment-nicholas-winton-immigration-windrush-scandal-a8929966.html. Accessed 18 August 2020. Sir Nicholas Winton referred to in the title of the article is known as the British Oscar Schindler as he saved hundreds of child refugees from the Nazis.
6 Robin Cohen, *Migration and its Enemies: Global Capital, Migrant Labour and the Nation-State*, Ashgate, Aldershot, 2008, pgs. 65–66.
7 Zamira Rahim, 'Boris Johnson's Daily Telegraph salary is £275,000 a year', *The Independent*, 2 October 2018. Rahim suggests 'Mr. Johnson spends 10 hours a month writing his column, for which he earns £22, 916.66 a month, equivalent to a rate of £2,291 an hour'. www.independent.co.uk/news/uk/politics/boris-johnson-daily-telegraph-salary-wage-column-parliamentary-register-interests-a8567351.html. Accessed 2 February 2021.
8 Kate Proctor, 'Boris Johnson urged to apologise for "derogatory and racist" letterboxes article', *The Guardian*, Wednesday 4 September 2019. www.theguardian.com/politics/2019/sep/04/boris-johnson-urged-to-apologise-for-muslim-women-letterboxes-article. Accessed 18 August 2020.
9 'Boris Johnson refuses to apologise for racist "burka" comments', *Al Jazeera*, 29 November 2019. www.aljazeera.com/news/2019/11/boris-johnson-refuses-apologise-racist-burka-comments-191129101017762.html. Accessed 18 August 2020.
10 Kate Proctor, 'Corbyn apologises for anti-Semitism in labour party', *The Guardian*, Tuesday 3 December 2019. www.theguardian.com/politics/2019/dec/03/corbyn-apologises-for-antisemitism-in-labour-party. Accessed 18 August 2020.
11 John F. Burns, 'Cameron criticizes "multiculturalism" in Britain', *The New York Times*, 5 February 2011. www.nytimes.com/2011/02/06/world/europe/06britain.html. Accessed 2 February 2021.

Brexit, and the sum of all fears **135**

12 Leon Moosavi, 'Orientalism at home: Islamophobia in the representations of Islam and Muslims by the New Labour government', *Ethnicities*, Vol. 15, No. 5 (October 2015), pgs. 652–674. https://www.jstor.org/stable/24811014. Accessed 21 January 2020. The Jack Straw quote is on pg. 655, and Harriet Harman's observations are on pgs. 665–666. Referring to both these ministers, Moosavi suggests that they 'not only encouraged a removal of some aspect of clothing that some Muslims hold precious, but also demanded that Muslim women join the workforce in greater numbers'.

13 Leon Moosavi, 'Orientalism at home: Islamophobia in the representations of Islam and Muslims by the New Labour government', pgs. 652–674, 669.

14 The All Party Parliamentary Group on British Muslims, *Islamophobia Defined: Report on the Inquiry into a Working Definition of Islamophobia*, London, 2018, pgs. 23–25.

15 Rebecca Mead, 'Jeremy Corbyn and the fetishization of English irony', *The New Yorker*, 27 August 2018. www.newyorker.com/culture/cultural-comment/the-english-fetishi zation-of-irony. Accessed 2 February 2021.

16 James McCandless, 'How a bacon sandwich derailed Ed Miliband's UK political career', *HuffPost*, 12 October 2018. www.huffpost.com/entry/ed-miliband-bacon-sandwich_n_ 5bbe27b0e4b01470d0580898. Accessed 2 February 2021.

17 Owen Hatherley, 'If you must compare Corbyn to a past Labour leader, it isn't Michael Foot', *The Guardian*, Friday 27 December 2019. www.theguardian.com/ commentisfree/2019/dec/27/compare-corbyn-labour-michael-foot-neil-kinnock. Accessed 2 February 2021.

18 Rowena Mason, ' "Hostility to Corbyn" curbed Labour efforts to tackle antisemitism, says leaked report', *The Guardian*, Sunday 12 April 2020, https://www.theguardian. com/politics/2020/apr/12/hostility-to-corbyn-curbed-labour-efforts-to-tackle-anti semitism-says-leaked-report?CMP=Share_AndroidApp_Other. Accessed 5 April 2021.

19 Robert Fisk, 'Al Jazeera did a hard-hitting investigation into US and Israeli lobbying – so why won't they air it?', *The Independent*, Thursday 15 March 2018. www. independent.co.uk/voices/al-jazeera-investigation-us-israel-lobbying-not-published- why-qatar-a8257191.html. Accessed 19 August 2020.

20 Jennifer Scott, 'What does the Labour anti-Semitism report say?', *BBC News*, 29 October 2020. www.bbc.com/news/uk-politics-54731222. Accessed 1 February 2021.

21 Raphael Langham, 'The Bevin Enigma: what motivated Ernest Bevin's opposition to the establishment of a Jewish state in Palestine', *Jewish Historical Studies*, Vol. 44 (2012), pgs. 165–166. https://www.jstor.org/stable/41806170. Accessed 5 April 2021.

22 Raphael Langham, 'The Bevin Enigma: what motivated Ernest Bevin's opposition to the establishment of a Jewish state in Palestine', pg. 167.

23 Langham notes:

> Thus in the course of the 1930s Bevin expressed a few prejudices but he became aware of the plight of Jewish refugees and gained knowledge of Jewish political aspirations in Palestine. He appeared sympathetic on all these issues, thus hardly someone harbouring deep antisemitic prejudices.
>
> *(pg. 170)*

24 Ben Cohen, 'The persistence of anti-Semitism on the British left', *Jewish Political Studies Review*, Vol. 16, No. 3/4 "Emerging Anti-Semitic Themes" (Fall 2004), pgs. 157–169. https://www.jstor.org/stable/25834610. Accessed 21 January 2020.

25 Efraim Sicher, 'The image of Israel and postcolonial discourse in the early 21st century: a view from Britain', *Israel Studies*, Vol. 16, No. 1 (Spring 2011), pgs. 1–25. https:// www.jstor.org/stable/10.2979/isr.2011.16.1.1. Accessed 21 January 2020.

26 Dan Sabbagh, 'Labour adopts IHRA antisemitism definition in full', *The Guardian*, Tuesday 4 September 2018. www.theguardian.com/politics/2018/sep/04/labour- adopts-ihra-antisemitism-definition-in-full. Accessed 2 February 2021. The most controversial passage in Corbyn's statement was this one:

> It cannot be considered racist to treat Israel like any other state or assess its conduct against the standards of international law. Nor should it be regarded as antisemitic

136 Brexit, and the sum of all fears

to describe Israel, its policies or the circumstances around its foundation as racist because of their discriminatory impact, or to support another settlement of the Israel-Palestine conflict.

27 Steven Beller, *Anti-Semitism: A Very Short Introduction*, Oxford University Press, Oxford, 2015, pg. 1.
28 On the novelist Marcel Proust as a witness to the assimilationism of the French Third Republic, especially in the backdrop of the Dreyfuss Affair, see Yolande Jansen, 'Proust as a Witness of assimilation in 19th century France', in his book Secularism, Assimilation and the Crisis of Multiculturalism: French Modernist Legacies, Amsterdam University Press, 2013. https://www.jstor.org/stable/j.ctt6wp7qd.7. Accessed 5 April 2021. One of the interesting lines in which Jansen's arguments progress is in terms of a broad historical comparison between Jewish oppression and its attendant anti-Semitism with loathing of Muslims and the rise in Islamophobia.
29 Hannah Arendt, *The Origins of Totalitarianism*, Penguin Modern Classics, London, 2017. Consider these lines:

> The simultaneous decline of the European nation-state and growth of antisemitic movements, the coincident downfall of nationally organized Europe and the extermination of Jews, which was prepared for by the victory of antisemitism over all competing isms in the preceding struggle for persuasion of public opinion, have to be taken as a serious indication of the source of anti-semitism. Modern antisemitism must be seen in the more general framework of the development of the nation-state, and at the same time its source must be found in certain aspects of Jewish history and specifically Jewish functions during the last centuries.
>
> *(pg. 11–12)*

30 Hannah Arendt, *The Origins of Totalitarianism*, pg. 3.
31 Hannah Arendt, *The Origins of Totalitarianism* pg. 138.
32 "Pope Francis calls for Covid-19 vaccines to be shared', *Deutsche Welle News,* 25 December 2020. www.dw.com/en/pope-francis-calls-for-covid-19-vaccines-to-be-shared/a-56058396. Accessed 2 February 2021.
33 Zoe Corbyn, 'Interview. Salim Abdool Karim: "None of us are safe from Covid if one of us is not. We have mutual interdependence"', *The Guardian*, Saturday 10 January 2021. www.theguardian.com/world/2021/jan/10/salim-abdool-karim-none-of-us-are-safe-from-covid-if-one-of-us-is-not-we-have-mutual-interdependence. Accessed 2 February 2021.
34 Martha Nussbaum, *The Therapy of Desire: Theory and Practice in Hellenistic Ethics*, Princeton University Press, Princeton, 2013, pgs. 342–343.
35 Stephen Buranyi, '"Vaccine nationalism" stands in the way of an end to the Covid-19 crisis', *The Guardian*, Friday 14 August 2020. www.theguardian.com/commentisfree/2020/aug/14/vaccine-nationalism-stands-in-the-of-an-end-to-the-covid-19-crisis. Accessed 20 August 2020.
36 Hannah Arendt, *The Origins of Totalitarianism* notes:

> Without territory and without a government of their own, the Jews had always been an inter-European element; this international status the nation-state necessarily preserved because the Jews' financial services rested on it. But even when their economic usefulness had exhausted itself, the inter-European status of the Jews remained of great national importance in times of national conflicts and wars.
>
> *(pgs. 23–24)*

37 Enes Bayrakli and Farid Hafez (eds.) *European Islamophobia Report 2018*, SETA, Istanbul, 2019:

> Beyond the implementation of anti-Muslim legislation that threatens religious freedom, many countries are also following a policy of creating a national Islam,

disconnecting the global nature of religion, and, thus, cutting transnational cooperation, when it comes to financial and organizational support. On the other hand, Christian churches and other religious communities are not facing similar restrictions.

(pg. 27)

38 Hannah Arendt, The Origins of Totalitarianism argues:

It has already been noticed that the Nazis were not simple nationalists. Their nationalist propaganda was directed towards their fellow-travelers and not their convinced members; the latter, on the contrary, were never allowed to lose sight of a consistently supranational approach to politics. Nazi 'nationalism' had more than one aspect in common with the recent nationalistic propaganda in the Soviet Union, which is also used only to feed the prejudices of the masses. The Nazis had a genuine and never revoked contempt for the narrowness of nationalism, the provincialism of the nation-state, and they repeated time and again that their 'movement', international in scope like Bolshevik movement, was more important to them than any state, which would necessarily be bound to a specific territory. And not only the Nazis, but fifty years of antisemitic history, stand as evidence against the identification of antisemitism with nationalism. The first antisemitic parties in the last decades of the nineteenth century were also among the first that banded together internationally. From the very beginning, they called international congresses and were concerned with a co-ordination of international, or at least inter-European, activities.

(pg. 4)

39 Paul Gilroy, *There Aint No Black in the Union Jack*, Routledge Classic, London and New York, 2002, pg. 42.
40 Paul Gilroy, *There Aint No Black in the Union Jack,* pg. 56.
41 Paul Gilroy, *There Aint No Black in the Union Jack,* pg. 58.
42 Nesrine Malik, 'The race report was a cynical trap – but if I point that out, I'm "doing Britain down"', *The Guardian*, Monday 5 April 2021. https://www.theguardian.com/commentisfree/2021/apr/05/race-report-trap-britain-government-institutional-racism?CMP=Share_AndroidApp_Other. Accessed 5 April 2021.
43 The All Party Parliamentary Group on British Muslims, *Islamophobia Defined: Report on the Inquiry into a Working Definition of Islamophobia*, 2018, pg. 27.
44 *European Islamophobia Report 2018*, pg. 33.
45 *European Islamophobia Report 2018*, pg. 20–21.
46 *European Islamophobia Report 2018*, pgs. 18–19.
47 Hannah-Ellis Petersen, 'Facebook admits failings over incitement to violence in Myanmar', *The Guardian*, Tuesday 6 November 2018. www.theguardian.com/technology/2018/nov/06/facebook-admits-it-has-not-done-enough-to-quell-hate-in-myanmar. Accessed 20 August 2020. Petersen's article talks about a report by San Francisco-based nonprofit Business for Social Responsibility (BSR), which found that 'Facebook has become a means for those seeking to spread hate and cause harm, and posts have been linked to offline violence'. The article also talks about a 'UN fact-finding mission to Myanmar, which concluded a genocide had taken place against the Rohingya in Rakhine, specifically singled out the role of Facebook in fanning the flames of anti-Muslim sentiment and violence'. The role of Facebook in elections and specifically the Brexit referendum has already been talked about extensively. See Carol Cadwalladr, 'My Ted talk: how I took in the tech titans in their lair', *The Guardian*, Sunday 21 April 2019. www.theguardian.com/uk-news/2019/apr/21/carole-cadwalladr-ted-tech-google-facebook-zuckerberg-silicon-valley. Accessed 20 August 2020.
48 Aristotle Kallis 'Islamophobia in the United Kingdom: national report 2018', in Enes Bayrakli and Farid Hafez (eds.) *European Islamophobia Report, 2018*, SETA, Istanbul, 2019, pg. 809.

49 Afzal Khan, 'The conservative party owes Britain's Muslim community an apology', *The Guardian*, Monday 15 April 2019. www.theguardian.com/commentisfree/2019/apr/15/roger-scruton-conservative-party-islamophobia. Accessed 20 August 2020. Khan suggests in his article:

> The Scruton story really goes to the heart of the Conservative party's problem with Islamophobia. It exposes the depressing reality that they don't really think there's anything wrong with it. They are not abhorred by it the way we all should be by all hatreds and prejudices.

50 Suhaiymah Manzoor-Khan, 'Under Boris Johnson, Islamophobia will reach a sinister new level', *The Guardian*, 5 January, 2020. www.theguardian.com/commentisfree/2020/jan/05/boris-johnson-islamophobia-sinister-level-muslims. Accessed 20 August 2020.
51 Laura Hughes, 'Conservatives launch review after Islamophobia accusations', *Financial Times*, 17 December 2019. www.ft.com/content/b35e6fb4-20f9-11ea-92da-f0c92e957a96. Accessed 20 August 2020.
52 Samira Shackle, 'It's shameful that Johnson has reneged on the inquiry into Tory Islamophobia', *The Guardian*, Monday 23 December 2019. www.theguardian.com/commentisfree/2019/dec/23/boris-johnson-reneged-inquiry-islamophobia-british-muslims. Accessed 20 August 2020.
53 Aristotle Kallis, 'Islamophobia in the United Kingdom: national report 2018', pg. 822.
54 Chris Tryhorn, 'Spectator makes cartoon U-turn', *The Guardian*, Thursday 2 February 2006. www.theguardian.com/media/2006/feb/02/newmedia.race. Accessed 20 August 2020.

CONCLUSION

Brexit: conclusively inconclusive?

> 'What we call the beginning is often the end/And to make an end is to make a new beginning'.
>
> T.S. Eliot

After months and years of agonizing over whether there would be a deal or the UK would leave the EU without a deal, one was struck on the day before Christmas Eve, a week before the 31 January 2020 deadline. The deal was announced with much fanfare on the British side with Prime Minister Boris Johnson photographed, both arms outstretched on either side and thumbs upturned on both ends. There was more circumspection from the European side, with EU Commissioner Ursula Von der Leyen turning to literature as she seemed unable to suppress the twinge of sorrow she felt at the conclusion of the Brexit negotiations, which did not give her joy but brought relief. She suggested that 'parting is such sweet sorrow' and quoted T.S. Eliot: 'What we call the beginning is often the end/And to make an end is to make a new beginning'.[1] Von der Leyen had earlier in the year quoted George Eliot when the Brexit Withdrawal Bill was passed by the British Parliament and was up for approval by the European one: 'Only in the agony of parting do we look into the depths of love'. She went on to say to the UK, 'We will always love you and we will never be far'.[2]

Quite remarkably, the EU and many of its officials like Von der Leyen have never stopped short of displaying their Anglophilia. This has been met by continuing hostility towards Europe from Brexiteers. Many Brexit Party Members of the European Parliament turned their backs when the EU anthem *Ode to Joy* was played in July 2019.[3] Some months later in the EU Parliament, MEPs emotionally sang the Scottish poet Robert Burns's *Auld Lang Syne* when the Withdrawal Agreement Bill was being debated.[4] A lot of Brexit Britain has been about a rather

140 Conclusion

excessive patriotism, wrapped up in the Union Jack, with fulsome displays of love for country. It is strange to behold how love for country can be so acutely premised upon hostility and, often, outright hatred for European neighbours. The obsession with flag-waving patriotism was also much in evidence when the British government wanted to print them on the Oxford/AstraZeneca vaccines.[5] The profusion of patriotism seems to have convinced the Labour Party under Keir Starmer that the only way it can make its way back to power is by packaging itself proudly and pretentiously in the flag.[6]

As the Brexit process tails on into the uncertain future, it has also become strangely entwined with the difficulties that the Coronavirus pandemic has brought about. These were further compounded by the emergence of a more virulent UK strain of the virus. From the beginning, the Johnson government was characterized by its ham-handedness in responding to the Covid crisis, beginning with the delay in going into lockdown in the early part of the year and then the controversy over the tier system introduced by the government as the year drew to a close. Britain also became the first country off the blocks to start the vaccination process. One of the ministers in Johnson's very Brexit-obsessed cabinet, Gavin Williamson, perhaps amplifying the almost juvenile character of the PM and by extension his cabinet, suggested that this was on account of the UK being just a much 'better country'.[7] The UK constantly harped on its relative speed and success in vaccinating its population, and this would have served as a useful distraction from the less desirable fact that the UK had one of the highest fatalities from the virus, crossing the 100,000 mark in late January 2021.[8]

Nationalism as the ruination of nations

> There is a great deal of ruin in a nation.
> Adam Smith[9]

Once again nations across the world have succumbed to the seductive charms of nationalism. This time it has taken the form of 'vaccine nationalism'. Countries, especially the richer ones, have clamoured to buy up and hoard vaccines to the detriment of poorer countries in Africa and Asia. The thinking behind vaccine nationalism is rather thin in terms of intelligence. The point that has been repeatedly made is that populations will remain vulnerable if the virus is out there anywhere in the world.

In the squabble over vaccines, it was the EU side which took a more immature stand and, as result of which, it had to quickly backdown. The row began when the British-Swedish company AstraZeneca, which had manufactured one of the early vaccines in collaboration with researchers from Oxford University, announced a shortfall in its supply to the EU. EU officials rather petulantly complained of unfair treatment by the pharmaceutical company in comparison to the UK. The worst part of the spat was the invocation of Article 16 of the Northern Ireland Protocol by the EU, which stops supplies of goods flowing into Britain from the Republic of Ireland via Northern Ireland. There was a great deal of outrage expressed by the Irish Taoiseach Micheal Martin, the Archbishop of Canterbury Justin Welby and, not to mention, by the British government. The move on the part of the EU involved the most contentious issue of the Brexit process, the delicate matter of the border between the UK's Northern Ireland and the Republic of Ireland on the EU side. The embarrassed EU decided to beat a hasty retreat. The controversy over vaccines between the EU and the UK is just one of the early indicators of what friction between the two sides is likely to look like, 'the new normal' as academic and keen Brexit observer Anand Menon, writing in *The Guardian*, called it.[10]

Earlier in July 2020, the UK had opted out of the EU vaccine programme, a decision that had been criticized at the time by many as a refusal to cooperate with the EU. The UK's opting out was done in the light of perceived delays in the EU process.[11] With the benefit of hindsight, that can now be called a good decision as the UK raced ahead like a 'speedboat' with the EU lumbering behind like a 'tanker'.[12] This was obviously used by Brexiteers to talk up the wisdom in the Brexit decision.

The reality of Brexit is likely to be messier. The British side will want to use every opportunity to paint Brexit as a great success, one early case being its vaccination programme, which certainly got off to a much better start than the EU's. The portrayal of Brexit as a success story would add to the discomfiture of the EU. The case for Brexit was never a sensible one and the hard form that it took, involving the decision to leave the single market and the customs union, is likely to hit the UK hard economically. Export figures to the EU going through British ports for January 2021 revealed a 68 per cent drop from the previous January, largely on account of Brexit.[13] One of the constant reminders of the difficulties that Brexit introduced was the suggestion made by British government trade advisors that UK companies should set up separate companies inside the EU in order to circumvent the difficult paperwork now involved.[14]

The Brexit vision of looking to the Commonwealth group of nations, of which the UK still considers itself the centrepiece, as a kind of replacement of the EU as a major trading partner is a vision bereft of hard-nosed economic rationale. It is yet more sepia-tinted nostalgia that pulls the wool over the eyes of the Brexit constituency back home, still inspired by the fading memory of the British Empire. Denis Macshane suggests, 'Invoking the Commonwealth against Europe is very old hat for anti-Europeans. In 1963 Labour leader, Hugh Gaitskell cited the sacrifice of New Zealand soldiers in the First World War as a reason to reject joining the European Economic Community'.[15]

The election victory of Joe Biden in the US has massively wrong-footed the British politicians supportive of Brexit. Brexit would have looked more plausible in tandem with Donald Trump continuing in the White House. Brexit politicians such as Boris Johnson, Michael Gove and Nigel Farage never made any secret of their love for Donald Trump. The Biden administration, in its early days, gave clear indications that a US–UK trade deal was not high on its list of priorities.[16] This

142 Conclusion

should have served as a huge reality check for the so-called 'special relationship', on which so much of the self-perception of the UK has come to rest since the Second World War and the loss of the Empire.[17] The former West German chancellor Helmut Schmidt witheringly commented on the special relationship, that it is one 'so special that only one side knows that it exists'.[18] Brexit Britain can claim a victory in the form of the trade deal with Japan that was endorsed in December 2020.[19] A further statement of intent on the part of Brexit Britain was the application to join the Comprehensive and Progressive Agreement for Trans-Pacific Partnership (CPTPP), an 11-country trade group in the Pacific, at the end of January 2021.[20]

The contradiction of Brexit Britain will always remain a fascination with being world beating and looking far beyond the confined corners of Europe to other distant prospects of the world, while at the same time obsessing over the exceptionality of little England. It would be foolhardy for Brexit Britain to have too many illusions about the future role that it can play. Robin Niblett, director of Chatham House, in a paper published in January 2021, suggested that it would be wise for Britain not to 'reincarnate itself as a miniature power', and that it would be best to 'marshal its resources to be the broker of solutions to global challenges'. According to Niblett, this can 'emerge only from the competence and impact of Britain's diplomacy, from trust in its word, and from a return to the power of understatement for which the country was so widely respected in the past'.[21] There was clearly no element of understatement in the Brexit project with all its bluff and bluster.

What now?

The idea that Brexit has been 'done' is the stuff of hollow claims made by politicians such as Boris Johnson and Nigel Farage. Brexit and the thorny issues that it has thrown up will remain unresolved. The driving force behind Brexit was the idea of an assertive sovereignty that needed to be won back from the EU. What will the UK do with the sovereignty that has been restored? It may just look like a worthless piece of ornamentation that no one knows what to do with or a stash of currency whose value rapidly depletes, rendering it largely worthless.

The Europhile element of Britain seems to be grieving inconsolably for the loss of Europe, staring ever so hard at the Brexit door that has been slammed so tightly shut in the face of the EU. Such disconsolate grieving has resulted in a failure to appreciate the many flaws in the EU project, which contributed, to some degree, in fuelling the Brexit fire at home in Britain. Pro-Europe Remainers may fail to realize other doors and windows opening every time a door is shut in the manner of Brexit.[22] One way is to focus on the economic neoliberalism, not just on the British side that the left has long complained about, but also the neoliberal variant that dominates EU thinking in the form of German ordoliberalism. The Anglo-Saxon, Thatcherite version of neoliberalism has always favoured small states, low taxes and minimal regulation. It envisions Brexit Britain as an opportunity to get rid of environmental constraints, health and safety standards and protective provisions for workers. By slashing regulations and taxes, it aims at the creation of a

Conclusion **143**

Singapore-on-the-Thames, at the very doorsteps of Europe. German ordoliberalism, in contrast to the Anglo-Saxon variant, advocates a greater role for the state, is more regulation-friendly and has a mechanical, almost adamantine adherence to its own economic orthodoxy. It is difficult to visualize the continuing prevalence of such economic thinking in the years ahead. Brexit is likely to have a far-reaching impact on both the UK and the EU, especially through the largely unforeseeable law of unintended consequences.

If the left in the UK can make and mark Brexit as the inflexion point that brought about the demise of neoliberalism, then it may prove to be a worthy and historically significant staging post in the continuing story of Britain in Europe and the world.

Notes

1 www.theguardian.com/politics/video/2020/dec/24/time-to-leave-brexit-behind-says-ursula-von-der-leyen-after-deal-agreed-video. Accessed 7 February 2021.
2 'Speech by President Von der Leyen in the plenary of the European Parliament at the debate on the withdrawal agreement', European Union Website, 29 January 2020. https://ec.europa.eu/commission/presscorner/detail/en/speech_20_140. Accessed 7 February 2021.
3 'Brexit party MEPs turn backs in EU parliament', *BBC News*, 2 July 2019. www.bbc.com/news/uk-politics-48839829. Accessed 7 February 2021.
4 '"Auld Lang Syne": members of European parliament break into song after UK's Brexit', *News 18*, 31 January 2020. www.news18.com/news/buzz/auld-lang-syne-members-of-european-parliament-break-into-song-after-uks-brexit-2480565.html. Accessed 7 February 2021.
5 Kate Duffy, 'A UK government unit is said to have demanded that the British flag be printed on Oxford vaccine doses', *Business Insider*, November 27 2020. www.businessinsider.in/science/health/news/a-uk-government-unit-has-reportedly-demanded-the-british-flag-should-be-printed-on-oxford-vaccine-doses/articleshow/79450116.cms. Accessed 7 February 2021.
6 Jessica Elgot, 'Labour defends new strategy to focus on patriotism and union flag', *The Guardian*, Wednesday 3 February 2021. www.theguardian.com/politics/2021/feb/03/labour-defends-new-strategy-to-focus-on-patriotism-and-union-flag. Accessed 7 February 2021.
7 Thomas Penny and Alberto Nardelli, 'U.K. says it won vaccine race by being a "better country"', *Bloomberg Politics*, 3 December 2020. www.bloomberg.com/news/articles/2020-12-03/u-k-says-it-won-vaccine-race-because-it-s-a-better-country. Accessed 7 February 2021.
8 'Covid deaths: "Hard to compute the sorrow of 100 000 milestone" – PM', *BBC News*, 26 January 2021. www.bbc.com/news/uk-55814751. Accessed 8 February 2021.
9 Roger Bootle, *Making a Success of Brexit and Reforming the EU*, Nicholas Brealey Publishing, London and Boston, 2017, pg. 283.
10 Anand Menon, 'The vaccine rows are just the first of many spats between the EU and the UK', *The Guardian,* Tuesday 2 February 2021. www.theguardian.com/commentisfree/2021/feb/02/vaccine-rows-spats-eu-uk-competitor. Accessed 4 February 2021.
11 Nadeem Badshah, 'UK has opted out of EU Coronavirus programme', *The Guardian*, Friday 10 July 2020. www.theguardian.com/world/2020/jul/10/uk-has-opted-out-of-eu-coronavirus-vaccine-programme-sources-say. Accessed 7 July 2021.
12 April Roach, 'Ursula von der Leyen: UK Covid vaccine rollout is a "speedboat" compared to EU "tanker"', *Evening Standard*, Saturday 6 February 2021. www.standard.co.uk/

144 Conclusion

news/uk/ursula-von-der-leyen-uk-covid-vaccine-speadboat-eu-tanker-b918797.html. Accessed 7 February 2021.

13 Toby Helm, 'Fury at Gove as exports to EU slashed by 68% since Brexit', *The Guardian*, Saturday 6 February 2021. www.theguardian.com/politics/2021/feb/06/fury-at-gove-as-exports-to-eu-slashed-by-68-since-brexit. Accessed 7 February 2021.

14 Toby Helm, 'Move to EU to avoid Brexit costs', *The Guardian*, Saturday 23 January 2021. www.theguardian.com/politics/2021/jan/23/brexit-hit-firms-advised-government-officials-set-up-shop-in-eu. Accessed 8 February 2021.

15 Denis Macshane, *Brexiternity: The Uncertain Fate of Britain*, I.B. Tauris, London, 2019, pg. 134.

16 'Johnson presses Biden for new trade deal in post-Brexit era', *Mint*, 24 January 2021. www.livemint.com/news/world/johnson-presses-biden-for-new-trade-deal-in-post-brexit-era-11611447061062.html. Accessed 8 February 2021.

17 Max Hastings, 'Biden transition tests the U.S.-U.K. "special relationship"', *Bloomberg Quint*, 6 December 2020. www.bloombergquint.com/business/biden-transition-tests-the-u-s-u-k-special-relationship. Accessed 8 February 2021.

18 Lloyd Evans, '"Forget the special relationship. America is just not that into us": a Spectator debate', *The Spectator*, 27 November 2010. www.spectator.co.uk/article/-forget-the-special-relationship-america-is-just-not-that-into-us-a-spectator-debate-. Accessed 8 February 2021.

19 Takako Gakuto and Masaya Kato, 'Japan ratifies UK trade deal to take effect Jan 1', *Nikkei Asia*, 5 December 2020. https://asia.nikkei.com/Economy/Trade/Japan-ratifies-UK-trade-deal-to-take-effect-Jan.-1. Accessed 8 February 2021.

20 George Parker and Aime Williams, 'UK applies to join trans-Pacific trade group', *The Financial Times*, 1 February 2021. www.ft.com/content/000afd84-8c12-4cf2-8639-5b0f8e4092b7. Accessed 8 February 2021.

21 Robin Niblett, 'Global Britain, global broker: a blueprint for the UK's future international role', Research Paper, Chatham House. ISBN: 978 1 78413 440 2, 11 January 2021. www.chathamhouse.org/2021/01/global-britain-global-broker. Accessed 8 February 2021.

22 Larry Elliot, 'The left must stop mourning Brexit – and start seeing its huge potential', *The Guardian*, 31 December 2020. www.theguardian.com/commentisfree/2020/dec/31/the-left-brexit-economic-uk. Accessed 8 February 2021.

INDEX

anti-Semitism 6, 13–14, 17, 62, 89n5, 112n3, 128; Islamophobia conjoined 119–122; Labour left 122–123; late 19th century 124; nation-state 126–127

Arendt, Hannah: *The Human Condition* 106, 111, 115n33, 116n49; *The Origins of Totalitarianism* 75–76, 80, 88, 89n9, 98, 113n13, 124, 126–127, 136nn29–31, 136n36, 137n38

Aristotle 25n38, 105–106, 114n31, 115n32

Atlas Network 21; Anthony Fisher 63, 71n34, 108; headquarters 62

austerity vii, 5–7, 12, 29, 35, 45, 53–54, 55; effects on the working class 64; London riots 2011 57; origins of the term 56; reviving neoliberalism 61; rising household debt 66–67; solidarity 68–69; unmaking of the working class 67–68

Austin, John 75, 85

authoritarian populism 35–36, 49n29

Bang: A History of Britain in the 1980s (Graham Stewart) 66, 72n48, 91nn41–42

Baran, Paul 100

Baroness Warsi 132

Battle of Beachy Head 1690 56

BBC 13, 50n42, 59, 108–109; Panorama documentary on Labour anti-Semitism 13, 122

Benn Act 79–80, 90n21

Beveridge Report 68

Bevin, Ernest 122, 135nn21–22

Biden, Joe vii, 19, 94, 141

Big Bang Reforms 1986 39, 41, 44–46, 66

Blair, Tony 10, 12, 30, 44, 49n23, 58, 91n42, 117, 119

Blatcherite 10–11

Blunkett, David 119

Bolsanaro, Jair 17, 96, 111, 116n48

Bow Group 63

Brexit: Leave 5, 8, 13, 14–17, 40, 53, 59, 75, 78, 87, 95; no deal vi, ixn1, 1, 79; Remain 5, 8–9, 13, 15, 78, 87, 108, 113n12, 142

British Leyland 43

Brittan, Leon 41–42, 51n46, 63

Brixton 1981 riots 36, 58, 91n44

Brown, Gordon 44

Bullingdon Club 15, 61

Butskellite consensus 10

Callaghan, James 37, 85

Cambridge Analytica 5

Cameron, David 8, 30, 41, 48n12, 53–54, 57, 60–61, 72n36, 78, 112n5, 118; Munich Security Conference Speech 119, 132

Chou, Mark 22n12, 93, 112n1

Clegg, Nick 8

Cole, G.D.H. *see* English pluralists

conservatives 9–11, 13, 15–17, 34, 63–64, 67, 94; denial of Islamophobia 132–133, 138n51; Islamophobia120–121; problems with BBC 108; 'selling politics as if it was soap powder' 100

146 Index

Corbyn, Jeremy 4, 6, 9–10, 12–14, 16, 25n41, 75, 89n5, 94, 97; anti-Semitism 120–123, 135n15
coronavirus pandemic vi–vii, 2, 12, 22, 55, 68, 70n12, 94–95, 111, 126–127, 140, 143n11
Cox, Jo 80, 95, 112n8, 118, 134n4
Cummings, Dominic 2, 6, 19, 22n6, 80, 108–109, 115n39, 134

de Gaulle, Charles 38
de Silva, Lula 110
Dewey, John 101
Dhesi, Tanmanjeet Singh 119
Disraeli, Benjamin 34
Dreyfus Affair 89n5, 124

English pluralists 75–77, 78, 84–86, 88; G.D.H. Cole 82–84; George Unwin 75, 78, 90n16; Harold Laski 75, 89nn6–7
Equality and Human Rights Commission (EHRC) 14, 122, 133
Erdogan, Recep Tayyip 17–18, 26n53, 96–97
European Economic Community (EEC) 27, 38, 78
European Exchange Rate Mechanism (ERM) 46
European Monetary Union (EMU) 46
European Union (EU) vi–vii, 1–3, 5–6, 8, 13, 16, 21–22, 142–143; AstraZeneca vaccine 140–141; Brexit referendum 93; deal 139; environment and safety regulations 81–82; EU as neighbour 38–39; EU as supranational entity 125; Maastricht Treaty 1992 27; Norway not a member of EU 40; sovereignty 77–78; think tanks and hostility 63, 108; 'take back control' from 74, 78–80; trade deal 47; UKIP as force against EU 132–133; 'We send £350 million to the EU' 28, 95, 118
Euroscepticism 10, 13

Falklands War 40–42, 86, 128
Farage, Nigel ixn1, 11, 14, 19, 24nn30–31, 77, 79, 94, 112n5, 141–142
Fetzer, Thiemo 53, 69n1
Fisher, Anthony see Atlas Network
Foot, Michael 12, 78, 135n17
Fordist 35–36, 42–43, 49n31
Friedman, Milton 28–29, 37, 104–105

Gandhi, Rajiv 42
German ordoliberalism 104, 107, 142–143

'Get Brexit Done' 15, 20–21, 61, 63, 80–81, 88, 96
globalization 5, 8, 69nn4–5, 125; characteristics of 54; discontent against 16
Grass, Gunter 94, 112n6

Hall, Stuart 24n27, 28, 35, 47n6
Hammond, Philip 10, 62
Harman, Harriet 119, 135n12
Hayek, Friedrich 28–29, 38, 62, 104; market as signaling mechanism 106–107
Healey, Denis 37, 85, 100, 114n19
Heath, Edward 32, 38, 85
Heseltine, Michael: No Stone Unturned 54; Westland affair 41–42, 51n46
Hobbes, Thomas 76
House of Commons 1, 4, 10, 31, 79–81, 90n19, 90n21, 100, 115n36, 119
House of Lords 42, 85
Howe, Geoffrey 31, 44; resignation speech 46–47, 48n18, 52n60, 63

International Holocaust Remembrance Alliance (IHRA) 123
Islamophobia vii, 6, 17, 62, 89n5, 97, 124; anti-Semitism and Islamophobia 120; Boris Johnson 117–119; Brexit and Islamophobia 132; denial of 132–134; European Islamophobia Report 2018 127, 130–131, 132; macro levels of 128–132

Javid, Sajid 6, 23nn17–18
Johnson, Boris vi–vii, 1–2, 3, 6–7, 10–11, 13, 15–16, 19, 21, 30, 47, 60–62, 74–75, 77, 79, 81, 88, 94, 97, 108; Islamophobia 117–119, 121, 125, 132–133, 139, 141–142
Juncker, Jean Claude 1

Keynes, John Maynard 104
Keynesian 36–37, 43, 55, 62, 99, 103–105, 111
Kinnock, Neil 86

Labour Party 10–15, 33–34, 37, 94, 119, 140; 1979 defeat 100; accusations of anti-Semitism 120–123; Taff Vale 85
Laski, Harold see English pluralists
liberal-democracy vii, 4, 17, 129–130
liberal-democrats 8–10, 54
London riots 2011 57–60
Lord Reith 109, 116n42

Maastricht Treaty 27, 46
Macdonald, Ramsay 54, 69n3

Macmillan, Harold 37, 46, 86–87; 'our people have never had it so good' 65, 72n43
Maitland, F.W. 76, 89n10
Making of the English Working Class, The (E.P. Thompson) 31, 48n16, 49n22, 115n36
Malthouse compromise 57, 70n18
Marx, Karl 25n44, 78, 90n14, 96
Masters of the Universe: Hayek, Friedman and the Birth of Neoliberal Politics (Daniel Stedman Jones) 50n36, 62, 71nn32–34, 104, 114n22, 114n28, 115n37
May, Theresa vi–vii, 1, 5, 7, 13, 57; 2017 election 17, 121; EU deal 21; hostile environment on immigration 60, 118, 134n5; 'mend the roof when the sun was shining' 64, 72n36; refusal to accept definition of Islamophobia 132
Methodism 30–33, 37, 48n16
Miliband, David 12, 24n34, 121
Miliband, Ed 11–12; bacon sandwich photograph 121, 135n16; 'out Farage-Farage' 11, 24n29, 112n5
miners' strike 1984 85–87
Mirowski, Philip *(Never Let A Serious Crisis Go to Waste: How Neoliberalism Survived the Financial Meltdown)* 49n21, 56, 64, 70n15, 72nn37–39, 106, 115nn34–35, 116n41
Modi, Narendra 3, 96, 111
monetarism 30–31, 36–37
Mont Pelerin society 104, 106–107
Moro, Sergio 110–111, 116n48
Murdoch, Rupert 96, 121
multiculturalism: David Cameron's Munich Speech 119, 134n11; failure 117; Islamophobia 129, 136n28; New Labour Ministers 120

National Union of Miners (NUM) 32
nation-state vii, 17, 28, 77, 82; anti-Semitism 124–125, 136n29, 137n38; Brexit 125–127; New Racism 127–128; terrorism 130
New Labour 10–12, 24n34, 44, 49n21, 49n29, 119, 135nn12–13
NHS 3, 28, 68, 95, 108, 118
Nissan 40, 43, 52n54
North-sea oil 40, 50n42, 51n44
Norway 40, 50n42, 51n44, 129

Occupy Wall Street 69n2, 70nn16–17, 110, 116n46
O'Grady, Frances *see* Trade Union Congress

one-nation conservatism 11, 65, 86; Thatcherism as break from 34–35, 68
OPEC 103
Operation Car Wash 110, 116n48
Operation Yellowhammer 2, 22n5, 59–60, 71n23, 79, 90n22
Orban, Viktor 17, 96, 130
Orgreave, Battle of 86–87, 91n44
Osborne, George 12, 29, 35, 55, 61, 67, 70n11
Overton window 11–12, 24n35

Patel, Priti 6–7, 23n19, 24n20, 65
Parkinson, Cecil 44
Peace, David *(GB 84)* 86–87, 91n39, 92n45
Pinochet, Augusto 86, 91n42
populism vii, 4, 17–20, 24n30, 26n52, 34, 49n29, 61, 108
Powell, Enoch 37, 50n37, 78
public goods 53, 100–101, 108

Rees-Mogg, Jacob 6, 15, 19, 23n15
Robinson, Tommy 132
Roussef, Dilma 110, 116n48
Runnymede Trust 120

Saatchi and Saatchi 101, 114n19
Sandburg, Carl *(I am the People)* 98
Saramago Jose *(The Stone Raft)* 7, 24n21
Scargill, Arthur 32, 85–86
Schmitt, Carl *see* sovereignty
Schumpeter, Joseph *(Capitalism, Socialism and Democracy)* 96, 99, 112n9, 114n17
Scottish National Party (SNP) 77
Scruton, Roger 132
Sherman, Alfred 29
Skivers and Strivers 35, 49n26, 67, 73n52
Soames, Nicholas 10
solidarity: austerity and solidarity 55; London riots 59; working class 67–68, 73n57, 78
sovereignty vii, 5, 13, 16–17; Austinian conception 14, 74–75; Brexit and sovereignty 77–78; Carl Schmitt 87–88, 92n46; English Pluralism 84–85; G.D.H. Cole 82–84, 91n31; Geoffrey Howe on sovereignty 47; 'Let's take back control' 25n49; Miners' Strike 86; Partha Chatterjee 113n14, 114n26, 125, 142; severe versus soft sovereignty 75–77
Spiked (Brendan O'Neill) 59, 71n25, 133
Starmer, Keir 10–11, 13–14, 24n32, 25n39, 122; patriotism 140

148 Index

Straw, Jack 119, 135n12
Sun, The 12, 88n4, 96, 113n12, 121, 134n4
Sunak, Rishi 6–7
Swinson, Jo 8–9, 13, 16

Taff Vale Case 85, 91n36
'Take back control' 14, 16–17, 25n49, 74–75, 78, 82; as road to totalitarianism 88
Thatcher, Margaret 10–11; attitude towards neighbours and Europe 38–39; break from one-nation conservatism 34–35; end of prime ministership 46–47; events of 1986 44–45; influence of personality 29–30; Monetarism 36–38; Monetarism and Methodism 30–34; myopic short termism 39–40
There Ain't no Black in the Union Jack (Paul Gilroy) 137nn39–41
Think tank: Centre for Policy Studies 29; hard Brexit 21, 67, 71n34, 115n37; influence in the US and UK 62–63; intellectuals 107–108; Islamophobia denial 133
Tory 'wets' 31–32
Toxteth 36, 58
Trade Union Congress (TUC) 66
Trump, Donald vi, 3, 8; Brexiteers aligned with Trump 141; elitism19; rhetoric 95–96

'Turning Turk' 118
Twain, Mark 112

UKIP (United Kingdom Independence Party) 11, 14, 53, 94, 112n5; Islamophobia 132
Unwin George *see* English Pluralists
Uses of Literacy: Aspects of Working Class Life, The (Richard Hoggart) 66, 72n47, 73nn53–54, 90n15

Varadkar, Leo 21
Varoufakis, Yanis 15, 25n44
V for Vendetta vi
Von der Leyen, Ursula 139, 143n12

Warburg, Siegmund 44–45
Welby, Justin 141
Westland helicopters affair 41–43, 51n46, 51nn49–50, 51n53, 54
When the Lights Went Out: Britain in the 1970s (Andy Beckett) 47n8, 91n38
Wilson, Harold 32, 85
Windrush scandal 60, 71n27, 118
winter of discontent 1978 39, 85

Yom Kippur War 103

Zionism 120, 123
Zizek, Slavoj 58, 70n21

Ingram Content Group UK Ltd.
Milton Keynes UK
UKHW022116040523
421267UK00020B/239